'We live in times when education can be seen only as a means to material ends, especially financial reward. We can't deny that this is important – most of us must work and be paid to survive. But education can do so much more: it can change the way we view the world, how we relate to it and what we value. The European Convention on Human Rights (Article 14) provides its rights and freedoms without discrimination on any grounds, including race, colour or national or social origin. That we live in a world where this needs to be said may give pause for thought but, given that it must, what can education do to support it? First, Dr Hughes does us a real service in providing a very well-founded understanding of prejudice. But he goes further, and takes it beyond inert knowledge into cogent classroom practice aimed at countering prejudice, changing pernicious beliefs and developing values which pay more than lip-service to this fundamental human right. This is a book for all teachers and those who train them.'

—Professor Doug Newton, Durham University, UK

'Conrad Hughes' work is an original and profound contribution to academic literature in the field of education. He investigates a problem that is at once age-old and extremely contemporary: How to transform inequality and discrimination and by which intellectual, educational and pedagogical means. Hughes challenges us to see diversity as a richness and not a problem for educational institutions. Hughes' response to the dilemma of prejudice is subtle and innovative. He argues that individuals have the right to their differences and that equal rights are vital in contemporary society. Hughes reminds us that the painful heritage of slavery and colonisation cannot be brushed aside in modern society and that civil rights have not yet been attained. This book opens new theoretical and practical perspectives for critically-minded educators working in multicultural contexts.'

—Professor Abdeljalil Akkari, University of Geneva, Switzerland

UNDERSTANDING PREJUDICE AND EDUCATION

What is prejudice in the twenty-first century and how can education help to reduce it?

This original text discusses prejudice in detail, offering a clear analysis of research and theory on prejudice and prejudice reduction, drawn from findings in social psychology, critical thinking and education. Presenting the underlying principle that prejudice can be reduced through the development of four core attributes – empathy, understanding, cognitive flexibility and metacognitive thought – the book offers effective educational strategies for preparing young people for life.

Chapters explore a range of examples of classroom practice and provide a thorough engagement with the minefield of prejudice, set against challenging sociological, ideological, political and cultural questions. An integrative framework is included that can be adapted and adopted in schools, synthesising findings and emphasising the need for individuals and groups to work against preconceived beliefs and emotional reactions to situations, offering contra-intuitive, rational and affective responses.

Understanding Prejudice and Education is essential reading for all those engaged in relevant undergraduate, Master's level and postgraduate courses in education, social psychology and cultural studies, as well as teachers and school leaders interested in developing strategies to reduce prejudice in their schools.

Conrad Hughes is Director of La Grande Boissière, the International School of Geneva, Switzerland. He has published and worked with UNESCO, the United World Colleges and the International Baccalaureate.

UNDERSTANDING PREJUDICE AND EDUCATION

The challenge for future generations

Conrad Hughes

Routledge
Taylor & Francis Group

LONDON AND NEW YORK

First published 2017
by Routledge
2 Park Square, Milton Park, Abingdon, Oxon OX14 4RN

and by Routledge
711 Third Avenue, New York, NY 10017

Routledge is an imprint of the Taylor & Francis Group, an informa business

British Library Cataloguing in Publication Data
A catalogue record for this book is available from the British Library

Library of Congress Cataloging-in-Publication Data
Names: Hughes, Conrad, author.
Title: Understanding prejudice and education : the challenge for future
    generations / Conrad Hughes.
Description: Abingdon, Oxon ; New York, NY : Routledge is an imprint of
    the Taylor & Francis Group, an Informa Business, [2016]
Identifiers: LCCN 2016012534 | ISBN 9781138928596 (hardback) |
    ISBN 9781138928602 (pbk.) | ISBN 9781315681672 (ebook)
Subjects: LCSH: Multicultural education. | Prejudices—Study and teaching.
Classification: LCC LC1099 .H85 2016 | DDC 370.117—dc23
LC record available at https://lccn.loc.gov/2016012534

ISBN: 978-1-138-92859-6 (hbk)
ISBN: 978-1-138-92860-2 (pbk)
ISBN: 978-1-315-68167-2 (ebk)

Typeset in Bembo
by Apex CoVantage, LLC

*This book is dedicated to Estelle Guimbang A. Baroung, Héloïse
Assiah Jeanne and Melchior Alexander. Thank you for your
patience and support.*

CONTENTS

PREFACE

While, on the one hand, social psychology has investigated the issue of prejudice in detail from its own epistemological framework and the literature on critical thinking has developed various taxonomies and frameworks on the other, they both essentially point in similar directions: individuals and groups need to work against preconceived beliefs and emotional responses to situations that actually require contra-intuitive, rational and affective responses. This entails understanding and quelling cognitive biases, fallacies, group think, hasty generalisations and conclusions, selfishness, passive acceptance of propaganda and instinctual group identity preservation.

The time has come to bring the threads of social psychology and critical thinking together within the realm of education. The big question is: how can education help reduce prejudice? The answer to this question draws on research findings in social psychology, critical thinking and education.

This book can be used by students of education, psychology, cultural studies, sociology and philosophy as it synthesises the last 60 years of research from these fields on the specific themes of prejudice reduction and the potential or known role education has to play in this. By education I focus on school, or so-called K–12 education, but frequently relate to university education too.

The book can also be used by teachers and school leaders interested in developing strategies to reduce prejudice in their schools. Finally, the book is for anyone interested in the construct of prejudice and how education can reduce it.

1

INTRODUCTION

Situating prejudice and education

Introduction

Prejudice and education are inextricably linked as they both touch on the most fundamental attribute of human behaviour: learning to live together. A good education will teach a person to judge other people with some degree of intellectual, moral and social retinue whereas one could argue that an education would have failed were it to leave us with people who generalise about others easily, judge others harshly on little but assumptions and dislike individuals or entire groups of people without even knowing them. To behave this way would imply that lessons of good judgement and understanding have been futile, lost or never taught.

It seems even more crucial today than before to educate for less prejudice as social tensions rise, world demographics swell and violent words and actions become increasingly widespread. In an increasingly uncertain global environment, an analysis of what prejudice is, what works to reduce it and how this might be done through educational strategies is prescient. This chapter discusses these questions by summarising topical, historical and theoretical positions, facts and trends so as to give the reader an overview of the relationship between education and prejudice.

The purposes of an education

What is an education for? This is a question that has plagued philosophers and educators for at least two and a half thousand years. There are constants that have run through systems and cultures since the earliest known educational philosophies that come to us from Socrates and Confucius: on the one hand, education has always been about the transmission of knowledge; on the other hand, the inculcation of values. A third area, between the two, that educational systems have always aimed to

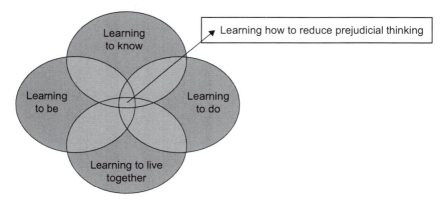

FIGURE 1.1 Learning to reduce prejudicial thinking: at the core of the four pillars of education

develop, is what we could call skills or competences. These three areas only mean something when put into the context of a fourth area: what it means to actually live them out and apply them in the real world. These four areas of learning were made clear in the 1996 UNESCO Delors report, which described the overarching purposes of education as 'learning to know, to do, to be, and to live together' (Delors et al., 1996). In other words, learners should appropriate knowledge, learn how to apply knowledge, to self-regulate and behave in society.

What is prejudice?

Prejudice lies at the intersection of all four pillars of learning in that it draws on them for its development and reduction. The etymological root of the word prejudice is the Latin praejudicium, meaning 'precedent' (Allport, 1954, p. 6), but in a modern sense the term more accurately denotes a priori, unwarranted and usually negative judgement of a person due to his or her group membership: it is a 'unified, stable, and consistent tendency to respond in a negative way toward members of a particular ethnic group' (Aboud, 1988, p. 6).

Prejudice comes about because of the mind's necessary categorisation of experience into information through language, thus simplifying and labelling phenomena to make them more easily manageable. This can lead to stereotyping and over-simplification, especially when dealing with human beings and the social categories we might use to define them (gender, ethnic origin, creed, nationality, class, political beliefs). Stereotyping becomes prejudice when it is hardened into a stable, judgemental and negative belief about individuals based on perceived properties of the group to which they belong.

Pettigrew and Meertens (1995) have suggested that one can distinguish between 'subtle' and 'blatant' prejudice; the former being more insidious, carefully justified and therefore less easily detectable than the latter.

Prejudice and learning to know

At a cognitive level, therefore, prejudice comes about when there are problems with learning to know: it is a cognitive bias that stems from over-generalisation (Allport, 1954, pp. 7–9). Some studies suggest that the prejudiced person has lower cognitive ability and overgeneralises in cognitively challenging situations such as ambiguity (Dhont & Hodson, 2014). Concepts associated with this over-generalisation include the 'illusory correlation' (perceiving unfounded or untrue relationships between groups and behaviours) and the 'ultimate attribution error' (mistakenly attributing negative traits to entire groups) (Pettigrew, 1971). Devine (1989) outlined a two-step model of cognitive processing whereby initial stereotype formation needs to be tempered with a conscious, cognitive effort. As such, reducing prejudice requires cognitive functioning that resists 'the law of least effort' (Allport, 1954, p. 391).

Prejudice and learning to be

As concerns learning to be, prejudice is linked to a lack of careful self-reflection as it tends to be self-gratifying in its function (Allport, 1954, p. 12; Fein & Spencer, 1997); it is a 'will to misunderstand' (Xu, 2001, p. 281) that one uses to protect a 'deep-seated system of emotions' (Thouless, 1930, p. 146). Prejudice frequently masks fear and/or anger, often with the self and as such masks 'beliefs held on irrational grounds' (Thouless, 1930, p. 150). Fiske et al. (2002) have suggested that stereotyping tends to be predicated by strong emotional states ranging from pity and sympathy to contempt, disgust, anger and resentment (p. 881). Therefore, reducing prejudice implies a degree of self-regulation and self-criticism.

Prejudice, learning to live together and learning to do

Prejudice is a strong, hasty over-generalisation of an individual or group that tends to be negative in character. This means that the social interactions that follow tend to make learning to live together difficult because relationships are predicated by mistrust. In its most well-documented forms (racism, sexism, xenophobia, homophobia, snobbery and bigotry), prejudice implies deficient models of social interaction based on feelings of antipathy that stand in the way of constructive dialogue, collaboration or common goals.

Prejudice can affect knowing to do since it is an active, virulent over-generalisation that implies action. This is one of the points that differentiates prejudice from stereotyping since stereotypes are merely representational – they are 'pictures in the head' (Lippman, 1922) of individuals or societal fabric. According to Fiske et al.'s stereotype content model (2002, reviewed in 2008 by Cuddy et al.), stereotypes tend to be articulated along a warmth–competence axis, meaning that groups tend to be essentialised in terms of a number of combinations as either warm (friendly, close) or competent (clever, high-performing). Prejudice, on the other hand, is not just a cold thought but an emotionally driven attitude that can lead to acts of discrimination and violence.

Allport suggested a scale of prejudice that goes from 'antilocution' through 'avoidance' and 'discrimination' to 'physical attack' and finally 'extermination' (1954). This would suggest that reducing prejudice means reducing strong feelings of antipathy to outgroups and/or members of those groups before these thoughts translate into actions. Dovidio et al. (1996) point out that empirical research suggests that this is only moderately true.

Why is reducing prejudice so important?

This book argues that efforts to reduce prejudice are of huge import to the fundamental enterprise of education. Prejudicial thinking spans the four pillars of education as does aiming to reduce it.

In the table below I have listed, under the four pillars of learning, facets for each that display less and more prejudiced mindsets. A good education will take learners from more to less prejudiced mindsets as this will develop higher levels of cognitive, affective and social competence.

The role of education is to take human beings from states of ignorance, intuitive and unfounded understanding and unskilled ability to higher levels of knowing, thinking and doing. This is why Socrates said that 'knowledge is virtue': knowledge brings with it a moral conscience that predicates how we behave. In theory, a good education should temper prejudiced thinking as it should teach learners to think twice, to suspend judgement, to keep an open mind, to better understand others

TABLE 1.1 Prejudice and the Delors report

More prejudiced mindset	Less prejudiced mindset
Knowing selectively	*Learning to know*
Poor understanding of context: 'will to misunderstand'	Domain, cultural, historical and propositional knowledge and deep, conceptual understanding of systems, contexts and facts
Over-generalisation and lack of nuance of theory	Knowledge of theory
Knowledge is put to negative practice	Practical knowledge
Inability to critically self-examine	Metacognition (knowing how we know and learning how we learn)
A priori judgement, rationalisation of negative, emotions, little reflexivity	Critical thinking (reasoning, inference-making, judgement, hypothesis testing, reflective thought)
Narrow transfer in the form of judgement of the individual in terms of the group and the group in terms of the individual	Transfer of knowledge
Fixed, narrow thinking, inability to imagine the world otherwise	Imagination, divergent thinking, creative thinking
Selective memory, refusal to accept disconfirmation	Short and long term memory functioning: information storage and retrieval

More prejudiced mindset	Less prejudiced mindset
Over-generalisation	Synthesising
Learning to do with prejudice	*Learning to do*
Prejudicial and sometimes unethical behaviour	Ethics: doing the right thing
Tends to blame outgroup rather than look for solutions	Problem finding and problem solving
Inflexibility	Adaptation
Learning to be (and to stay) prejudiced	*Learning to be*
Aggressive, obsessive, defensive thought	Mindfulness
Resilience in the name of prejudice	Resilience (particularly to remain open-minded and accepting of others)
Motivation for prejudice	Motivation (to dispel prejudiced inclinations and to suspend judgement)
Lack of interest in outgroup beyond erected stereotype	Curiosity in other people
Lack of wisdom since prejudice leads to conflict	Wisdom (understanding the value of respect and understanding across frontiers)
Faith in a prejudiced set of beliefs and lack of faith in other people	Faith in other people's potential
Unfair, unbalanced judgement	Balance: temperance
Lack of control of strong emotions and intuitive reasoning	Discipline
Negative emotions which can lead to violence	Health (striving for productive, healthy relationships)
Lack of care for victim of prejudice	Responsibility
Frustration, anxiety, anger	Happiness
Feeling of dispossession, potential leadership in scapegoating and othering	Positive, inclusive leadership
Low self-esteem disguised by outwardly directed anger	Self-confidence
Lack of sensitivity	Emotional intelligence
Learning to live apart	*Learning to live together*
Selfish or exclusively in-group sense of community and service	Community and service
Conception of 'civil' as exclusive and conditional	Civic education
Closed-mindedness	Open-mindedness
Difficulty or inability to listen to the views of targeted outgroup members or counter-claims	Communication and social skills (interpersonal intelligence, the art of listening)
Disrespect	Respect
Meanness	Kindness
Intolerance	Tolerance
Antipathy	Empathy
Desire for conflict or separateness	Conflict-resolution
Lack of trust	Trust-building
Catastrophism	Sustainability
Disrespect for others	Appreciation of others

and the self and to act in constructive, civil ways for the betterment of humanity – we come back to the four pillars of the UNESCO Delors report (1996).

However, it is clear that the different educational systems around the world have only been partially successful in doing this, depending of course on how one measures success and how one measures prejudice. Tawil and Cougoureux (2013) point out that while the UNESCO Delors report has generated much theoretical follow-through and interest through various conferences, statements and white papers, practical application has not been tangible. This is mainly because schools are primarily concerned with fuelling market-driven levels of social productivity that are less focused on social competence and more on performativity (see Cuéllar Reyes, 2006) and also because the social goals of the Delors report are seen as too overwhelming and Utopian for schools to tackle (see Sancho Gil, 2001).

Trying to measure prejudice

Prejudice is a subtle construct that is difficult to measure. This is due to two fundamental reasons. First, one needs to define exactly where prejudice starts in the spectrum of human attitudes, behaviours and beliefs. This in itself is almost impossible. When exactly does a statement veer from substantiated generalisation into prejudice? Who is to say that someone is moderately, strongly or extremely prejudiced and how? Which moral and sociological standpoint does one use to judge another as prejudiced? For some an extremist group might be said to vehicle prejudiced statements (Decker et al., 2010) but for members of that group this allegation might well be rejected. Prejudice is inextricably linked to interaction and context: it needs to be redefined in each set of circumstances that surrounds and, in essence, defines it. Fiske, Cuddy and Glick (2007) have shown how contextual factors influence stereotype formation in extremely significant and dynamic ways: people erect stereotypes according to levels of competition, power and status and these need to be re-evaluated in each specific set of circumstances. This is an epistemological chestnut, meaning a problem of measurement that will not go away.

Developing metrics for prejudice is exceedingly difficult – there is no quantitative way of evaluating what is essentially a fluid, interconnected, culturally specified perspective of the world. Therefore, one cannot extract scores on prejudice tests and draw them up in a Gaussian curve to allow for statistical analysis of range and distribution without nagging questions about the criteria for measurement scales in the first place, and these threaten the validity of the study throughout. This is not to say that metrics have not been developed to report on degrees of prejudice. Hundreds of studies spanning nearly 100 years have attempted to do this and many of them will be discussed throughout this book.

The second reason why prejudice is so difficult to measure, another threat to the validity of any experimental or quasi-experimental study of prejudice, is the so-called Hawthorne effect. This means that when subjects are interviewed about their views on other groups, they will tend to play up to the dominant cultural paradigm of the day that suggests conformity to a certain set of declared values.

In other words, asking someone what he or she thinks about gays, immigrants or racial groups other than his/her own will not yield a genuine response but more one crafted in the light of the interviewer's background. After all, who wants to be seen as prejudiced and would be happy to share prejudiced views openly? One way around this is to study attitudes, behaviours and statements without informing the subject what the purpose of the study is. This is highly problematic from an ethical standpoint as it amounts to lying to people involved in a study and measuring something of which they are not aware. Much of the quasi-experimental work in psychology in the aftermath of World War II was done this way, such as: the 1954 Robbers Cave experiment by Muzafer Sherif (Sherif et al., 1961; Sherif, 1966), in which 22 boys were split into two groups without knowing of the existence of the other group and left to build solidarity within each group before being brought into competitive contact with one another; the Milgram experiments (1960–63, see Milgram, 1963), which involved study participants believing that they were administering electric shocks to subjects when in reality they were not; and Zimbardo's Stanford Prison experiment (Zimbardo, 1971) whereby participants played prisoner and guards in simulated prison conditions and engaged in sadistic, unethical behaviour to the point that the study had to be abandoned. Since then ethics boards in universities and research laboratories have made this type of study difficult if not impossible to carry out.

Levy Paluck and Green (2009, p. 360) summarise a research review on what works in prejudice reduction with six critical points, including the following:

1 Notwithstanding the enormous literature on prejudice, psychologists are a long way from demonstrating the most effective ways to reduce prejudice. Due to weaknesses in the internal and external validity of existing research, the literature does not reveal whether, when, and why interventions reduce prejudice in the world.
2 Entire genres of prejudice-reduction interventions, including diversity training, educational programs, and sensitivity training in health and law enforcement professions, have never been evaluated with experimental methods.
3 Nonexperimental research in the field has yielded information about prejudice-reduction program implementation, but it cannot answer the question of what works to reduce prejudice in these real-world settings.
4 Laboratory experiments test a wide range of prejudice-reduction theories and mechanisms with precision. However, researchers should remain skeptical of recommendations based upon environments, interventions, participants, and theories created in laboratory settings until they are supported by research of the same degree of rigor outside of the laboratory.

So reporting on what works well in prejudice reduction is a complex enterprise that must take into account the inherent weaknesses that exist in the related research design. However, enough has been said and done to synthesise the research and consider it critically – we are by no means in a position to say nothing at all about prejudice reduction. Furthermore, much research in education on learning, higher-order thinking and critical thinking, can be related to prejudice reduction.

Prejudice in the world today

In the light of these substantial problems of measurement, what can be said about the state and degree of prejudiced thinking in the world today? One might argue that it is simply not possible to make any statement about whether there is more or less prejudice in the world today than there was in the past. Besides, the concept of the world has expanded dramatically in the past 40 years to incorporate many more people, contexts, fields and systems, so trying to compare beliefs and attitudes today with those in the interwar period, for example, is a flawed exercise at the very outset. Here are some examples that have attracted attention in recent times. Of course, in earlier times, at least some may not have been a cause for discrimination, and the list may have contained other instances long since forgotten:

- In 1992, the American Psychological Association reported that 'prejudice and discrimination' were leading causes of violence among American youth (Civil Rights, 2016).
- The 2007 Federal Bureau of Investigation Hate Crime Statistics Act Report claimed that approximately 51 per cent of reported hate crimes were race-based (18.4 per cent linked to religion, 16.6 per cent to sexual orientation and 13.2 per cent to ethnicity). These statistics included a steady increase in hate acts against Hispanics from 2003 to 2007 (Civil Rights, 2016).
- Between 2004 and 2012, the US Department of Justice recorded over 220,000 cases of hate crime every year (Office of Justice, 2014).
- The UK Home Office reported that 'in 2013/14, there were 44,480 hate crimes recorded by the police, an increase of five per cent compared with 2012/13, of which 37,484 (84%) were race hate crimes' (Home Office, 2014).
- Bond, DiCandia and McKinnon (1988) found that psychiatric ward workers believed black patients to be more violent than whites despite evidence showing no such trend.
- A 2011 Gallup poll claimed that '66% of Jewish Americans and 60% of Muslim Americans say that Americans in general are prejudiced toward Muslim Americans'. (Gallup, 2011).
- The 1995 study 'Race and Gender Discrimination in Bargaining for a New Car' (Ayres & Siegelman, 1995) showed that car dealers discriminated against females and blacks by asking them to pay more for cars: 'black males were asked to pay $1,100 more than white males, black females $410 more, and white females $92 more' (p. 307).
- Greenberg and Pyszczynski (1985) and Henderson-King and Nisbett (1996) found, in separate studies, that blacks were rated lower than whites in similar circumstances because of commonly held stereotypes. Stone et al. (1997)

detected stereotypical beliefs about blacks and whites concerning athletic ability.

- In 2012, half of the 1,414 hate-crimes reported in Canada were motivated by race or ethnicity (Statistics Canada, 2014).
- Surveys conducted between 2001 and 2008 by the University of Western Sydney of 12,512 Australians showed that over 17 per cent of respondents had experienced racism with over 23 per cent claiming that they had been treated less respectfully because of their ethnic origin (Western Sydney University, 2016).
- Hebl et al. (2002) found subtle homophobic discriminatory practice among potential employers for confederate community jobs.
- The Canadian organisation 'Under the Same Sun' reports on hundreds of killings and mutilation of Albinos in Africa (UTSS, 2016).
- A survey run in 2013 showed particularly high levels of ethnic prejudice in Korea: 'Although the country is rich, well-educated, peaceful and ethnically homogenous – all trends that appear to coincide with racial tolerance – more than one in three South Koreans said they do not want a neighbor of a different race. This may have to do with Korea's particular view of its own racial-national identity as unique – studied by scholars such as B.R. Myers – and with the influx of Southeast Asian neighbors and the nation's long-held tensions with Japan' (Washington Post, 2013).
- The 2008/2009 'Group-focused Enmity in Europe' research project surveyed over 8,000 Europeans to find that '41 percent of all European respondents agree somewhat or strongly that they would not send their child to a school where a majority of the pupils are immigrants' (Zick, Küpper & Hövermann, 2011, p. 116) and 'one third of all European respondents believe there to be a natural hierarchy of white and black' (p. 59).
- In February 2015, the Commissioner for Human Rights of the Council of Europe published a report stating that discrimination and hate speech were on the rise in France (Muižnieks, 2015).
- Since the late 1990s, French public debates have seen a rise in xenophobic rhetoric: 'xenophobic attitudes and opinions increased across French society for the first time in nearly two decades. And the main factor fuelling that rising wariness of "the other" appears to be the growing ease with which French public figures – including politicians – feel they can stigmatize foreigners and minorities in ways that until recently had been considered the unacceptable reserve of the extreme-right' (Crumley, 2011).
- NatCen's British Social Attitudes (BSA) survey released a report in 2013 suggesting that self-reported racial prejudice had risen over 5 per cent since 2000. The highest levels of self-reported racial prejudice were found among uneducated and/or blue-collar survey respondents and interwar generations. This would suggest that in the UK, as concerns racial prejudice, more educated and recently born populations are less prone to racial prejudice (NatCen, 2013).

- The website and activist movement 'Black Lives Matter' argues that black people still live under the yoke of oppression in the United States and are victims of wide-scale prejudice, including police brutality, despite the tenure of a black president (Black Lives Matter, 2016).
- Wide-scale race protests shook numerous North American Universities, particularly the campuses of Yale and Missouri. Students argued that campuses were still largely white and largely racist (Libresco, 2015).
- The 2015 so-called 'Rhodes Must Fall' movement in South Africa, whereby statues of the colonial figure Cecil John Rhodes were dismantled across the country, argued that post-Apartheid South African universities are still very much dominated by patriarchal, Eurocentric syllabi and white professors, keeping blacks in a state of ideological and economic subordination (Fairbanks, 2015).
- A critical re-edition of Adolph Hitler's *Mein Kampf* (1924) was published in Germany in 2016 and was so popular that it sold out immediately. The publishers had intended to release 4,000 copies but found pre-publication orders for over 15,000 (Addady, 2016).

These figures and statistics might seem surprising on the one hand since there has never been as much mobility, cross-continental travel and contact between people of different origins in human history. Intuitively, one might assume that increased contact would lead to less prejudice as people are able to strip away stereotypical beliefs in the light of real, lived experiences that should allow for more considered positions. However, globalisation has clearly brought tension with it, possibly due to planetary demographic, social and economic challenges. Increases in immigration also bring an increase in competition and therefore a feeling of threat, one of the common conditions for stereotype formation (see Cottrell & Neuberg, 2005). Immigration is not the only reason why prejudiced sentiments seem not to have waned: racial and social divide in countries such as South Africa, Brazil and the United States has not necessarily decreased in the last decades and if anything has become exacerbated over time. For an analysis of racism in the new South Africa, see Malala (2015). Concerning racial prejudice in particular, Forbes points out: 'there has never been so much contact between people of different races, religions, and nationalities as there is today. Yet never before, it seems, has there been so much hatred and violence associated with ethnic differences' (Forbes, 2004, p. 83).

While there is little statistical evidence that cases of prejudice or hate crime have increased in recent times, many high-profile events in the media have fuelled the impression that prejudice is on the rise world-wide. An added level of complexity to the situation is the world wide web, highlighting many case studies and opinions, including those that denounce institutionalised discrimination but also those that broadcast extremist and intolerant views in blogs, comments threads and videos, which contribute to the creation of a specific representation of a prejudiced world.

One might argue that much of the political tension in the world today is in some way connected to prejudice. Consider the following events that all suggest an increase in prejudice:

- A steady breakdown in Western/Muslim relationships that has been exacerbated by the Israeli–Palestine conflict, Gulf Wars, 9/11 bombings, terrorist attacks such as those in Madrid (2004), London (2005), Beslan (2009), Nairobi (2014), Ottawa (2014), Paris (January and November 2015) and Tunis (2015) not to mention repeated attacks in Iraq, Cameroon, Syria and Yemen.
- The radicalisation of fundamentalist discourses and practices in Nigeria, Pakistan, Syria, Yemen and Afghanistan, often with instances of strong anti-Christian and anti-female rhetoric and policy.
- The extraordinary surge in immigration in Europe has been identified as the largest since the Second World War: 'Europe will record in 2015 an unprecedented number of asylum seekers and refugees with up to one million asylum applications; an estimated 350,000 to 450,000 people could be granted refugee or similar status, more than in any previous European refugee crisis since World War II' (OECD, 2015).
- Stiff immigration laws, the popularisation of xenophobic ideas in Europe with a rise of extremist right-wing political ideology in France, Austria, Poland, Denmark, Greece and Switzerland including anti-Gypsy legislation in France.
- Strong cases of homophobic discourses and practices have been recorded in Uganda and Zimbabwe.
- Wide-scale abortion of female foetuses in certain states of India suggesting strongly ingrained misogyny. Census of India statistics suggest that the abortion of female foetuses has risen dramatically in that country: 'In 1961, for every 1,000 boys under the age of seven, there were 976 girls. Today, the figure has dropped to a dismal 914 girls' (Pandey, 2011). This practice is predicated on the superior value males are given over females in traditional Indian society.
- According to the World Organisation Against Torture, marital customs that objectify or discriminate against women (for example, making it impossible for them to leave their husbands) are still rife in Afghanistan, India, Yemen, Tunisia, the Democratic Republic of Congo and Iraq:

> Women are frequently treated as property, they are sold into marriage, into trafficking, into sexual slavery. Violence against women frequently takes the form of sexual violence. Victims of such violence are often accused of promiscuity and held responsible for their fate, while infertile women are rejected by husbands, families and communities. In many countries, married women may not refuse to have sexual relations with their husbands, and often have no say in whether they use contraception [. . .] Ensuring that women have full autonomy over their bodies is the first crucial step towards achieving substantive equality between women and men. Personal issues – such as when, how

and with whom they choose to have sex, and when, how and with whom they choose to have children – are at the heart of living a life in dignity.

(Pillay, 2012)

• According to Zainab Bangura, Senior UN official, the radical Islamic State pamphlets circulated in Iraq, Jordan and Turkey with child sex slave prices. Captured children are thus treated as commodities (Yoon, 2015).

Even in instances where symbols of reconciliation have purportedly ushered in an enlightened state of affairs where there is less prejudice (the United States under Barack Obama, post-Apartheid South Africa, the overthrowing of numerous dictatorships in the Middle East in the so-called Arab Spring, gay rights legislation including the right to marriage and adoption in many Western countries, supposedly greater awareness of Aboriginal rights in Australia), cases of discrimination and hate crimes continue.

Pettigrew (2008) has pointed out that prejudice follows different configurations according to the culture in question; in Latin America he argues that social class is a divider whereas in Europe the question of citizenship has been strongly divisive. Europe's history has been marked and continues to be marked by prejudice: 'Prejudice, discrimination, anti-immigrant political parties, and violence have erupted throughout Europe for many years' (Pettigrew, 2008).

So prejudice is a deeply anchored phenomenon, it has existed in societies across the globe historically and could even been seen as on the rise: the last seven years (counting back from January 2015) have seen a steady decrease in peace and increase in war (Institute of Economics and Peace, 2015; Harrison & Wolf, 2011) and while one might not be able to systematically place prejudice at the centre of violence, war, inequity and persecution, it clearly has a part to play in the process. After all, genocide, slavery and persecution all rely on deeply prejudiced beliefs about groups.

If the goal of an education is anchored in the 1996 Delors report (learning to know, to be, to do and to live together), it would be difficult to claim that the last decades of education have been successful. If education can reduce prejudice, then it has a considerable distance to go before we see any evidence of this, even empirical non-scientific evidence.

Why are people prejudiced? A short historical overview of theories of prejudice

A central question that lies at the heart of the matter is why people are prejudiced. Without some understanding of the reasons, motivations, processes, catalysts and causes that trigger prejudice, it would be difficult to develop strategies for its reduction.

There is no simple answer to the question. Dozens of theories have been developed over time to suggest that prejudice has its roots in cognitive or social domains but no one theory can be considered entirely adequate. Furthermore, while one might run experiments to find evidence of a given theory, seeking evidence to falsify it is often not possible, this being a generic problem with the social sciences.

The overwhelming emphasis in historical narratives of humanity up until the twentieth century has not been on tolerance, equality or the understanding of others but more one of difference (tribalism, Empire building, nationalism, war, slavery and colonisation). Ancient Greek society, very much like Egypt, was turned resolutely against the 'barbarians' and 'savages' of other backgrounds; only male non-slave citizens of Athens enjoyed rights (Cartwright, 2013). Beliefs in race and original separateness of races (polygenics) are rife in ancient European philosophy, ranging from: Hippocrates (circa 500 BC), Posidonius (135–51 BC) and Vitruvius (70–25 BC), who placed white- and black-skinned people in a distinct hierarchy, to Enlightenment thinkers who, despite their beliefs in human rights and humanism, produced extremely racist writings on blacks, notable examples being those of Voltaire (1733, 1769), Hume (1753) and Kant (1764). Misogyny also has a long history, at least in the Western world, stemming from Ancient Roman laws disallowing women power or suffrage (Frier & McGinn, 2004, pp. 31–32) to the *Malleus Maleficarum* (Kramer & Sprenger, 1487/2010), systematically associating women with witchcraft. Many examples can be given from these areas and of discourses, acts and beliefs of an anti-Semitic, homophobic and xenophobic nature. Against this backdrop, however, there are examples of efforts to counter prejudice, even before the notion of prejudice as we understand it today had been fully formulated and conceptualised.

Some ancient texts such as the 'Indian Edicts of Asoka' (Sen, 1997) or the so-called Cyrus Cylinder have been argued as being the earliest texts emphasising tolerance. It should be noted that the Roman Empire, particularly during the silver age of the Antonines, was tolerant of different languages and cultures provided that they subscribed to fundamental tenets of Roman identity and that subjects paid taxes. Marcus Aurelius's Pax Romana extended the notion of the Roman citizen to make it extremely inclusive. Heterogeneity can be seen in the profiles of many of the Emperors: Septimius Severus and Caracalla were North African, Heliogabalus Middle Eastern, Trajan and Hadrian were Spanish, Pertinax was the son of a freedman as was the Dalmation Emperor Diocletian. Furthermore, many women were extremely powerful in the Roman Empire such as Julia Domna, Xenobia or Agrippina the Elder.

Early Islam involved philosophies of tolerance: Muhammad preached for the rights of ethnic minorities (Lewis & Churchill, 2008) and the Charter of Medina in 622 instituted rights for minority religions.

The early fifteenth century 'Age of Discovery' or exploration of the so-called new world did not go uncriticised, Michel de Montaigne's essay 'Of Cannibals' (1580) suggests that divisions between civilised and savage communities are constructs: 'each man calls barbarism whatever is not his own practice; for indeed it seems we have no other test of truth and reason than the example and pattern of the opinions and customs of the country we live in (Frame, 1948, p. 152).

Francis Bacon's development of what is commonly called the scientific method in his *Novum Organum* (1620/2015) was premised on his recognition of prejudice as a threat to the scientific mindedness: 'early modern philosophy, which distanced itself both from the Renaissance and scholasticism, defined "ingenium" as the fundamental *agens* in order to produce a rational methodology, which abolishes eidola and prejudices' (Burwick & Klein, 1996, p. 30). Here is one of the earliest suggestions for a remedy to prejudice (prejudice in the broadest literal sense of intuitive, unchallenged assumption): Bacon suggests that a systematic inductive, often counter-intuitive method must be developed in order to overcome lazy thinking. One might extend this to the twentieth century with Karl Popper's theory of falsification:

> It is easy to obtain confirmations, or verifications, for nearly every theory – if we look for confirmations. Confirmations should count only if they are the result of risky predictions. [. . .] A theory which is not refutable by any conceivable event is non-scientific. Irrefutability is not a virtue of a theory (as people often think) but a vice. Every genuine test of a theory is an attempt to falsify it, or refute it.
>
> *(Popper, 1963, p. 36)*

The Enlightenment ushered in numerous voices for tolerance, moderation and human rights as developed by philosophers who all preached against dogmatism such as Rousseau, Mill, Locke and Voltaire. In his 1755 essay 'Tolerance', and by giving historical examples from Europe, China, Persia and Japan, Voltaire wrote: 'the whole of our continent shows us that we must neither preach nor practise intolerance' (Voltaire, 1755 [1912]). Swift's satirical 'A Modest Proposal' (1729) mocked anti-Irish sentiment in England while De Tocqueville, in relating to early American Democracy, recognised the fundamental importance of learning to live together, as he spoke of 'the reciprocal influence of men upon one another' (cited in Battistoni, 1985, p. 117), a theme that would be later emphasised by Dewey in his insistence on participative citizenry in democratic society. We note here one element of the complexity of prejudice: despite Allport's assertion that people tend to be prejudiced in general across a range of domains (1954, p. 68), examples from history show us how individuals preaching in favour of open-mindedness or tolerance often held, simultaneously, bigoted views (the examples here being Voltaire's position on Africans).

More pronounced voices against prejudice in the social sense (discrimination and attacks on human rights) were broadcast by abolitionists, Quakers and moral philosophers. In response to the transatlantic slave trade, The Quaker teacher and abolitionist Anthony Benezet wrote in the 1750s:

> I am bold to assert, that the notion entertained by some, that the blacks are inferior in their capacities, is a vulgar prejudice, founded on the pride of ignorance of their lordly masters, who have kept their slaves at such a distance, as to be unable to form a right judgment of them.
>
> *(The Abolition project, 2016)*

During the nineteenth century, scientific racism and neo-Darwinian theories, such as eugenics, were popular and became influential doctrines that persisted well into the twentieth century; popular examples include theories on white supremacy by Gobineau (1856) and Galton (1883). With the transatlantic slave trade at its highest point and slavery as a powerful economic institution in the Deep South of the United States, literature openly broadcasting racist ideology such as Twain's *Adventures of Huckleberry Finn* (1884) and *The Adventures of Tom Sawyer* (1876) was highly popular. In Europe, authors such as Dostoevsky and the composer Wagner were openly anti-Semitic whereas influential philosophers such as Nietzsche, Hegel and Maurrass endorsed a hierarchical model of society built on a master–slave dynamic, underpinning an iniquitous ideology of human organisation. These theories were expounded against a backdrop of violent conquest and separation: the pogroms of the Russian Empire, colonisation and the transatlantic slave trade.

However, at the same time, we should not believe that voices against prejudice, discrimination or stereotypes were non-existent: the nineteenth century saw the birth of the Suffragettes, voices against racism such as the British Quaker Catherine Impey (1847–1923) who founded the first anti-racist journal in Britain or the American journalist Ida B. Wells-Barnett (1862–1931) who protested against lynch laws by publishing photographs of lynching. For a historical overview of some of the strongest abolitionist ideas before and during the American Civil War and how these led to the pragmatist philosophical movement, see Menand (2001).

It was only with the growth of psychology as a recognised field of study that prejudice in the modern sense was first understood. Milner (1975) suggests that the first real recognition of prejudice was during the First World War, where soldiers of mixed backgrounds were exposed to a similar fate and the early Black Civil rights movement in the United States prompted the increased community of psychologists to investigate beyond the predominance of scientific racism that prevailed as a belief system (Garth, 1925). The social psychologist Floyd Allport is attributed as spearheading this change in perspective (Milner, 1975). This first movement, therefore, was essentially to identify and locate prejudice.

Duckitt (1992) describes the next two decades (1930s and 1940s) as a 'paradigm' whereby prejudice was seen as 'an expression of unconscious psychological defences diverting inner conflicts and hostilities, often originating from externally induced frustrations and deprivations, against innocent outgroups and minorities' (p. 1186). Freudian and Jungian theories of scapegoating and expiation were used to explain prejudicial attitudes, particularly group acts such as lynching.

These early theories of prejudice were relatively simplistic: while they attempted to explain some aspects of the emotional side of prejudice, they did not account for more sophisticated, cool-headed forms of prejudice built on rationally defended belief systems such as statistical evidence of group behaviour (the percentage of immigrants or people of a certain ethnic background involved in types of crime for instance) or historico-cultural narratives such as the curse of

Caiphus to justify anti-Semitism, the creation of Eve from Adam's rib used to promote discourses of male dominance, the sons of Ham argument against African civilisations and the star of the east (as a metaphor for Satan) used to argue for anti-Eastern discourses.

The Holocaust created a wave of psychoanalytical theories on personality disorder, now seeing prejudice not only as an emotional response but, in extreme cases, as a psychological dysfunction. The research of Rokeach (1960) on dogmatism and Adorno et al. (1950) on the authoritarian personality, along with Allport's (1954) seminal insights into the prejudiced personality, pointed to the complex traits that make up the so-called prejudiced personality. Allport saw different forms of prejudice as linked to each other in a broad, prejudiced personality: 'people who reject one out-group will tend to reject other out-groups. If a person is anti-Jewish, he is likely to be anti-Catholic, anti-Negro, anti any out-group' (1954, p. 68). Furthermore, Allport grouped characteristics of the prejudiced personality (insecurity, fear, rigidity, poor self-knowledge – what he called 'ego weaknesses') under the following seven traits:

> emotional ambivalence (complex and volatile relationships with parents and self); moralism and rigid conventionalism; dichotomising (oversimplified black and white thinking about groups); need for definiteness, structure, order; externalisation (an understanding of behaviour in terms of external forces and not inner processes); institutionalisation (a desire to belong to strong, monolithic institutions) [and] authoritarianism (discipline, strong leadership).
>
> *(Duckitt in Dovidio et al., 2005, p. 396)*

For Allport, therefore, the prejudiced personality can be opposed to a tolerant personality built on liberal values, open-mindedness and a high tolerance for ambiguity. The prejudiced person is seen as someone who is suffering from an unbalanced set of psycho-emotional and social states and shows limited cognitive potential since he or she relies on over-simplification. While much of what Allport said about prejudice in the 1950s holds today and is respected, I would argue that it is not altogether helpful to over-pathologise prejudice at an individual level since this strips the phenomenon of some of its more complex socially created elements such as language, media, historical narratives and the plethora of representations of human difference that are embedded in inherited symbols that in themselves bear the seed of prejudice. Examples can be found in the English language with terms such as 'blackmail', 'Mankind', 'white lie', 'half-wit', 'queer' and so on (even if one might argue that these terms are less and less politically correct and are being rephrased). Allport's prejudiced personality gives us clues but by no means evidence for the type of education that might be designed to lessen prejudice.

The wave of prejudice theory generation in the late 1940s to 1950s was the most incisive in social psychology, marked by well-known experiments such as the 1939 Clark doll experiment (Clark & Clark, 1947), in which people were asked to comment on racially typified dolls, and Muzafer Sherif's Robbers Cave experiment in 1954 (Sherif et al., 1961; Sherif, 1966), where subjects were grouped in a fairly hostile environment and gradually lapsed into aggressive interaction (an example of Sherif's Realistic Conflict Theory), this suggesting not only a prejudiced personality, but group prejudice. Allport (1954) is still considered the definitive voice on prejudice and prejudice reduction, but the theory that prejudice comes out of a personality type can be challenged by more recent theories on socio-cultural influences and cognitive psychology.

Duckitt (1992) refers to the 1960s and 1970s as a period in theories of prejudice that focused less on personality structure than social conformity. Countries with legally institutionalised or culturally normalised prejudiced values, such as Apartheid South Africa (towards Blacks), Israel (towards Palestinians), Australia (towards Aborigines), Afghanistan (towards women) and India (towards outcasts or 'Harijans') will pressure people, either consciously or subliminally into conforming to and/or internalising those values. Institutionalised anti-Communist or anti-Western beliefs throughout the Cold War and post 9/11 rhetoric on terrorists or Westerners are examples of how prejudiced beliefs can be created, exacerbated and directed in times of war.

There are also far more subtle forms of institutionalised prejudice that run through most educational and nationalist narratives as the antithetical shadows of a stable, decent society. These include commonly held and media-reinforced positions and assumptions held about deviants (drug users, criminals, mentally unstable people, 'drop outs'), outsiders (immigrants, tourists, foreigners) and members of religious communities (sects, non-Western religions, Voodoo, Animism). Institutionalised prejudice is part of a continuum of stereotypes that are essential to the structure of society, at least in the conventional Western sense with class-defined roles (working class, upper class, poor, wealthy) and a host of professions that bring stereotypes with them about status (sex worker, politician, lawyer, policeman, etc).

While this analysis of prejudice recognises the importance of societal forces in shaping it, hereby suggesting that an education for less prejudice needs to involve critical reflection on norms and institutions, it neglects the personal emotional battles that are often at the core of prejudice and the highly personalised belief structure that inevitably varies across individuals in any given society or institution. Furthermore, the fact that stereotypes are generated culturally does not mean that all members of that culture should necessarily endorse them or internalise them to the point of holding prejudiced beliefs.

The 1980s to the present can be considered as the most recent wave in prejudice theory with an emphasis on cognitive psychology and, more recently, neuroscience. With this evolution in the schools of psychology that analyse and seek to understand prejudice, the emphasis is on the innate, linguistically, cognitively and biologically pre-conditioned dispositions within meaning, information and the human mind that, in a sense, make us all prejudiced. Pettigrew (1971) looked at prejudice in terms of cognitive biases, Gaertner (Frey & Gaertner, 1986) in terms of perceptual exaggerations, while Greenwald and Banaji (1995) have put forward research on a universal implicit association bias whereby humans tend to make associations that are more or less prejudiced with 'others'.

This set of cognitive and neuroscientific theories, like previous ones, is not enough in and of itself to explain the phenomenon of prejudice as it does not take into account hardened cases of prejudice built upon resentment, frustration and sentiments of insecurity rather than mere biological architecture. Nor does it take into account collective acts of prejudice built on historical events.

Allport (1954) pointed out the fact that theories on prejudice development tend to focus on one or two elements but do not offer a global appreciation of the problem that takes numerous variables into account simultaneously, they 'call attention to [. . .] one important causal factor, without implying that no other factors are operating' (Allport, 1954, p. 207). This early point remains pertinent and is helpful to keep in mind when searching for educational responses to prejudice.

An overview of the main theories on prejudice development helps us better visualise the manner in which it has evolved as a concept (Table 1.2).

Throughout this study, different theories of prejudice will be evoked and described in more detail as we discuss how to best reduce it.

TABLE 1.2 An overview of the main theories on prejudice development

Theory	Main advocates
Superior race theory (scientific racism): an underlying theory behind anti-Semitism, nineteenth-century slavery and colonisation, eugenics.	Crawfurd (1866), Hunt (1865), Gobineau (1856), Galton (1883)
Frustration–aggression theories: (projection, frustration, scapegoating) used to explain collective acts of discrimination such as lynching and the Holocaust.	Projection (Ackerman & Jahoda, 1951), frustration (MacCrone, 1937), scapegoating (Veltford & Lee, 1943), displacement of hostility or 'emotional maladjustment' (Dollard et al., 1939; Hovland & Sears, 1940)
Personality analysis: drawing from psychoanalytical theories to explain individual traits through personality types.	The authoritarian personality (Adorno et al., 1950), dogmatism (Rokeach, 1960), the nature of prejudice (Allport, 1954), the tolerant personality (Martin & Westie, 1959), mimesis of parental behaviour (Bandura, 1997; Kinder & Sears, 1981)
Sociocultural theories: emphasising the sociological dynamics of prejudice whereby cultural, social and institutional norms create climates of prejudice.	Institutionalised, normative prejudice (Ashmore & Del Boca, 1981; Carmichael & Hamilton, 1967), social pressure (DeFriese & Ford, 1969; Ewens & Ehrlich, 1972; Fendrich, 1967; Hamblin, 1962), socialisation (Proshansky, 1966; Westie, 1964), conformity (Pettigrew, 1958, 1959; Westie, 1964)

Theory	Main advocates
Social psychology: with an emphasis on the perception of in-and out-groups (endogenous and exogenous perceptions), behaviour and values.	Realistic Conflict Theory (Sherif et al., 1961; Vivian, Brown & Hewstone, 1995), social identity theory (Tajfel & Turner, 1979), symbolic racism (McConahay & Hough, 1976; Frey & Gaertner, 1986), minimal intergroup paradigm (Tajfel, 1970), intergroup bias (Ashmore & Del Boca, 1981), relative deprivation theory (Runciman, 1966), in-group favouritism (Dion, 1979; Condor & Brown, 1988), belief congruence theory (Rokeach, 1960)
Cognitive psychology: explaining how cognitive biases trigger prejudicial thinking.	Illusory correlations and fundamental attribution error (Pettigrew, 1979), 'just world' belief (Lerner, 1980), developmental theories (Frenkel-Brunswick, 1948; Radke & Sutherland, 1949; Remy et al., 1975; Aboud, 1988; Aboud & Amato, 2001; Cushner, 2008), implicit association (Greenwald & Banaji, 1995)

How do we reduce prejudice?

As early as the 1950s, hypotheses have been aimed at reducing prejudice. In many ways, these are as empirical, tentative and easily falsifiable as theories generated to explain why prejudice exists. However, one can cite comparative studies that support the efficacy or lack thereof of these strategies to reduce prejudice. The theory that has been shown to work the most, in so far as any study in reducing prejudice can be evaluated with enough reliability and validity to say that it does work, is Allport's contact hypothesis (1954):

> Prejudice (unless deeply rooted in the character structure of the individual) may be reduced by equal status contact between majority and minority groups in the pursuit of common goals. The effect is greatly enhanced if this contact is sanctioned by institutional supports (i.e., by law, custom or local atmosphere), and provided it is of a sort that leads to the perception of common interests and common humanity between members of the two groups.
>
> *(p. 281)*

Pettigrew and Tropp (2000) reviewed 203 studies in 25 different countries and found that for the pool of 90,000 participants, 94 per cent of cases showed a reduction of prejudice with increased contact. One of the better known expressions of this strategy in a classroom setting is the so-called 'jigsaw classroom' (Aronson & Patnoe, 1997) whereby students teach each other in small rotating groups. Contact hypothesis relies on a climate of mutual respect and superordinate values. If people of different backgrounds are thrown together without direction and goals, there is little evidence that prejudice will be reduced. Chapter 6 is dedicated to contact hypothesis and will go into greater detail on the subject.

Other strategies that can be considered include intercultural education with an emphasis on intercultural and postcolonial approaches to the teaching of history (see Chapters 2 and 7), dialogic learning environments allowing for intergroup dialogue, teaching values as suggested in Kohlberg's (1976; 1981) framework of moral education, conflict resolution and group work (these are treated essentially in Chapters 4 and 5 on metacognition and empathy).

The better-known hypotheses on how prejudice can be reduced have been synthesised by Stephan (in Dovidio et al., 2010) and can be outlined in Table 1.3.

None of these strategies is mutually exclusive: each one interlinks with another on certain commonalities such as the ideas of working together, discussion and learning about other people. Indeed, it is an epistemological challenge to cleanly categorise both theories on the development of prejudice and strategies to reduce it given the interrelatedness of the various constituents at work.

TABLE 1.3 Established hypotheses on how prejudice can be reduced

Hypothesis	Researchers	Educational expression
Contact hypothesis	Allport, 1954	Jigsaw classroom (Aronson, & Patnoe, 1997)
Intercultural education	Allport, 1954; Banks, 1973, 2012; Katz, 1975; Stephan, 1985, 1987, 1989	Group discussion, role-play, simulation games, postcolonial history syllabi
Diversity training programmes	Allport, 1954; Landis & Brislin, 1983; Tansik & Driskell, 1977	Lectures, readings, role-play, simulation
Intergroup dialogues	Allport, 1954; Gurin, Nagda & Lopez, 2004; Gurin et al., 1999; Nagda & Zuniga, 2003	Transparent focus group discussions
Group work	Aronson et al., 1978; Aronson & Bridgeman, 1979; Blaney et al., 1977; DeVries, Edwards & Slavin, 1978; Johnson & Johnson, 1992; Weigel, Wiser & Cook, 1975	Cooperative learning groups with group-related assessment criteria
Conflict resolution	Carruthers et al., 1996; Johnson & Johnson, 1996; Lam, 1989; Deutsch & Coleman, 2012	Mediation, negotiation, third-party consultation
Moral education	Kohlberg, 1976, 1981; Watson & Ecken, 2003; Oser, 1986;	Values-based educational discourse
Stereotype inhibition	Devine, 1989	Stimulating metacognitive awareness
Reflective judgement model	King & Kitchener, 1994	

Links with education

While these theories of prejudice reduction have been tested on university students, in experiments, quasi-experiments and through focus groups and fieldwork, there have been few systematic efforts to apply this research in schools to curriculum design with the aim to sequence learning objectives, classroom projects, assessments and tasks in such a way that an educational experience consciously and purposefully addresses the issue of prejudice and equips students with the means to reduce it within themselves and others.

Although there is some evidence that specific elements of research on prejudice reduction are used in classroom settings (for example: the jigsaw classroom (Aronson & Patnoe, 1997); contact hypothesis (Allport, 1954); blue eyes/brown eyes experiment (Elliott, 1968; see Chapter 5 of this book); cultural exchanges; service learning) and some educational systems place an emphasis on pedagogy related directly or indirectly to prejudice reduction (for example, international education, philosophy for children, inquiry based learning), I would argue that given the centrality of prejudice as an educational theme, the time has come for the research and theory to be integrated into curriculum design more systematically. Furthermore, for a prejudice-reducing education to have any global impact, practice should take place across different geographical settings. Until now, most of the known efforts to reduce prejudice through education have been focused in North America and, to a lesser extent, Australia and Great Britain.

An essential area that I would argue has been neglected in the researched approaches to prejudice reduction; one that runs through all of them but given its centrality requires stand-alone analysis, is self-reflection. Most of the strategies used from Allport to the present focus on people working together or looking out to other groups or individuals. However, these externalising actions will only be successful at an intrapersonal level if there is self-doubt, self-criticism and self-knowledge. Indeed, a group working together requires individual concessions, the ability to listen to others, empathy, suspension of belief and conviction and hard work on one's own profile. Chapter 4 of this book on metacognition suggests that this field of education is a potentially powerful tool for the reduction of prejudice as it pushes the learner back into him or herself to ensure inner development and self-control.

The goals of this book

This book aims to examine the notion of prejudice and how it may be reduced through educational interventions in six core areas: first, through four levels of intrapersonal and interpersonal development, namely understanding the other, critical thinking, metacognition and empathy; and second, through two institutional approaches, namely Allport's (1954) contact hypothesis and the tenets of international education.

These approaches will be substantiated with reference to research and theory in the fields of social psychology, cognitive psychology, education, critical thinking and philosophy. The fundamental purpose is to leave the reader with a developmental framework that brings these six areas together in a coherent, workable fashion for implementation.

Figure 1.2 is a diagrammatic representation of this framework, as follows: the bold lines represent the four main lines of personal development that should be nurtured if the individual (placed at the centre of the diagram as subject) is to reduce his or her levels of prejudicial thinking, feeling and acting. The reason why the arrows point outward is that these changes must come from within. The four bold lines correspond to the four chapters of the book that discuss reducing prejudice in the individual (Chapters 2, 3, 4 and 5).

The two institutional approaches that the book advises as strategies to reduce prejudice are represented by the seven phrases around the circumference of the circle (the study of world literature, service learning, additional language learning,

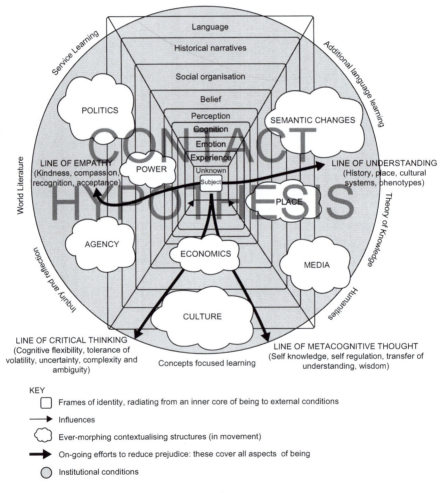

FIGURE 1.2   Approaches to reducing prejudice

theory of knowledge, humanities, concepts-focused learning, inquiry and reflection) and the phrase 'contact hypothesis' that spans the area of the circle. These two institutional strategies correspond to the chapters of the book that deal with the conditions necessary for prejudice reduction (Chapters 6 and 7).

The large circle represents the various environmental factors that influence the field of prejudice. These factors are made up of rectangles, which represent frames of identity that radiate outward from the individual. As they do this, the rectangles represent factors that are less personal and subjective and more shared by society. The clouds represent contextually defined sites of meaning that are shaped by political and social change. The circle and its contents are factors that need to be negotiated in the battle against prejudice; they influence both personal and institutional approaches.

Conclusion

If some of the fundamental goals of an education are to equip learners with the knowledge, attitudes and competences needed to make the right moral and social choices in life, to think clearly and to know how to live together, then reducing prejudice must feature as an essential part of education.

However, such a goal is ambitious at best for three main reasons:

1   Historically and geographically, the concept of prejudice has not remained stable and trying to give an all-encompassing definition of prejudice is difficult. This means that reducing prejudice is extremely complex since there is no overriding consensus of what it is we are trying to reduce. This is less the case for relatively stable constructs in education such as knowledge of mathematics, the sciences and languages.
2   There is evidence of high levels of prejudicial thinking, discrimination and hate crimes throughout the world. It is difficult to say whether the current educational provision that learners are receiving is affecting prejudice and there is much informal argumentation based on statistics and events in the media that would suggest quite the opposite.
3   Since Allport's work, numerous strategies for reducing prejudice have been elaborated and they will be explored in detail throughout this study. However, the empirical studies carried out to measure the effectiveness of these strategies all suffer from flaws in research method and design, all of them face considerable threats to validity and reliability and no one strategy in isolation can be said to reduce prejudice.

So the issues in the way of dealing with prejudice are profound but so too is the depth of study in social psychology and the knowledge that this has left us with. It is by wedding social psychology and education and by synthesising the numerous studies that have been conducted and looking at their potential to reduce prejudice in an educational setting that one will be best equipped to take on the challenge of reducing prejudice for future generations.

References

Aboud, F.E. (1988). *Children and prejudice*. Oxford: Basil Blackwell.

Aboud, F.E., & Amato, M. (2001). Developmental and socialization influences on intergroup bias. In G.J.O. Fletcher and M.S. Clark (Eds), *Handbook of social psychology: Interpersonal processes* (pp. 65–85). Oxford: Blackwell.

Ackerman, N., & Jahoda, M. (1951). Anti-Semitism and emotional disorder. *Science & Society*, 15(1), pp. 74–77.

Addady, M. (2016). 'Mein Kampf is the Hottest Book in Germany'. Fortune. Online. Available at: http://fortune.com/2016/01/11/hitler-mein-kampf/ (accessed 8 April 2016).

Adorno, T.W., Frenkel-Brunswik, E., Levinson, D.J., & Sanford, R.N. (1950). *The authoritarian personality*. New York: Harper and Row.

Allport, G. (1954). *The nature of prejudice*. Cambridge, MA: Addison-Wesley.

Aronson, E., & Bridgeman, D. (1979). Jigsaw groups and the desegregated classroom: In pursuit of common goals. *Personality and Social Psychology Bulletin*, 5, 438–446.

Aronson, E., & Patnoe, S. (1997). *The jigsaw classroom* (2nd edn). New York, NY: Longman.

Aronson, E., Blaney, N., Stephan, C., Sikes, J., & Snapp, M. (1978). *The jigsaw classroom*. Beverly Hills, CA: Sage.

Ashmore, R.D., & Del Boca, F.K. (1981). Conceptual approaches to stereotypes and stereotyping. In D.L. Hamilton (Ed.), *Cognitive processes in stereotyping and intergroup behavior* (pp. 1–35). Hillsdale, NJ: Lawrence Erlbaum Associates.

Ayres, I., & Siegelman, P. (1995). Race and gender discrimination in bargaining for a new car. *The American Economic Review*, 85(3), 304–321.

Bacon, F. (1620/2015) *Novum organum*. Germany: Jazzybee Verlag.

Bandura, A. (1997). Self-efficacy: Toward a unifying theory of behaviour change. *Psychological Review*, 84, 191–215.

Banks, J.A. (1973). *Teaching strategies for the social studies: Inquiry, valuing, and decision making*. Reading, MA: Addison-Wesley.

Banks, J.A. (2012). *Encyclopedia of Diversity in Education* (4 volumes). Thousand Oaks, CA: Sage Publications.

Battistoni R. (1985). *Public schooling and the education of democratic citizens*. Jackson, MS: University Press of Mississippi.

Black Lives Matter. (2016). Online. Available at: http://blacklivesmatter.com/ (accessed 8 April 2016).

Blaney, N., Stephan, C., Rosenfield, D., Aronson, E., & Sikes, J. (1977). Interdependence in the classroom: A field study. *Journal of Educational Psychology*, 69, 121–128.

Bond, C.F., Jr., DiCandia, C.D., & MacKinnon, J.R. (1988). Responses to violence in a psychiatric setting: the role of patients' race. *Personality and Social Psychology Bulletin*, 14, 448–458. doi: 10.1177/ 0146167288143003

Burwick, F., & Klein, J. (1996). *The Romantic imagination: literature and art in England and Germany*. Amsterdam: Rodopi.

Carmichael, S., & Hamilton, C.V. (1967). *Black Power: The politics of liberation in America*. New York, NY: Vintage.

Carruthers, W.L., Sweeney, B., Kmitta, D., & Harris, G. (1996). Conflict resolution: An examination of the research literatures and a model for program evaluation. *The School Counselor*, 44, 5–18.

Cartwright, M. (2013). *Greek society*. Ancient history encyclopaedia. Online. Available at: www.ancient.eu/article/483/ (accessed 27 April 2016).

Civil Rights. (2016). Online. Available at: www.civilrights.org/publications/hatecrimes/nature-and-magnitude.html (accessed 8 April 2016).

Clark, K.B., & Clark, M.P. (1947). Racial identification and preference among Negro children. In T.M. Newcomb and E.L. Hartley (Eds), *Readings in social psychology* (pp. 169–178). New York, NY: Holt, Rinehart & Winston.

Condor, S., & Brown, R. (1988). Psychological processes in intergroup conflict. In W. Stroebe, A.W. Kruglanski, D. Bar-Tal and M. Hewstone (Eds), *The social psychology of intergroup conflict: Theory, research, and applications* (pp. 3–26). Berlin: Springer-Verlag.

Cottrell, C.A., & Neuberg, S.L. (2005). Different emotional reactions to different groups: A sociofunctional threat-based approach to 'prejudice'. *Journal of Personality and Social Psychology*, 88, 770–789.

Crawfurd, J. (1866). On the physical and mental characteristics of European and Asian races of man. *Transactions of the Ethnological Society of London*, 5, 58–81.

Crumley, B. (2011). France: Hate crimes on the decline, xenophobia on the rise. *Time Magazine*. Online. Available at: http://world.time.com/2011/04/12/france-hate-crimes-on-the-decline-xenophobia-on-the-rise/ (accessed 25 April 2016).

Cuddy, A.J.C., Fiske, S.T., & Glick, P. (2008). Warmth and competence as universal dimensions of social perception: The stereotype content model and the BIAS Map. *Advances in Experimental Social Psychology*, 40, 61–149.

Cuéllar Reyes, F. (2006). *Globalizacion-Educacion-Posmoderninan: Análisis del Informe a la UNESCO de la Comisión Internacional sobre la Educación para el Siglo XXI. Materiales Para Estudios del Futuro (Vol. II).* Universidad Nacional Autonoma de Mexico.

Cushner, K. (2008). International socialization of young people: Obstacles and opportunities. *International Journal of Intercultural Relations*, 32, 164–173.

Decker, O., Weibmann, M., Kiess, J. & Brahler, E. (2010). *Die mitte i der krise: Rechtsextreme einstellungen in Deutschland*. Berlin: Friedrich-Ebert-Stiftung.

DeFriese, G., & Ford, W.S. (1969). Verbal attitudes, overt acts, and the influence of social constraints in interracial behavior. *Social Problems*, 16, 493–504.

Delors, J. et al. (1996). *Learning: The Treasure within*. Paris: UNESCO.

Deutsch, M., & Coleman, P.T. (2012). *Psychological components of sustainable peace*. New York, NY: Springer.

Devine, P.G. (1989). Stereotypes and prejudice: Their automatic and controlled components. *Journal of Personality and Social Psychology*, 56(1), 5–18.

DeVries, D.L., Edwards, K.J., & Slavin, R.E. (1978). Biracial learning teams and race relations in the classroom: Four field experiments on Teams-Games-Tournaments. *Journal of Educational Psychology*, 70, 356–362.

Dhont, K., & Hodson, D. (2014). Does lower cognitive ability predict greater prejudice? *Current Directions in Psychological Science*, 23, 454–459. doi: 10.1177/0963721414549750

Dion, K.L. (1979). Intergroup conflict and intragroup cohesiveness. In W.G. Austin and S. Worchel (Eds), *The social psychology of intergroup relations* (pp. 211–224). Belmont, CA: Brooks/Cole.

Dollard, J., Doob, L.W., Miller, N.E., Mowrer, O.H., & Sears, R.R. (1939). *Frustration and aggression*. New Haven, CT: Yale University Press.

Dovidio, J.F., Brigham, J.C., Johnson, B.T., & Gaertner, S.L. (1996). Stereotyping, prejudice, and discrimination: Another look. In C.N. Macrae, C. Stangor and M. Hewstone (Eds), *Stereotypes and stereotyping* (pp. 276–319). New York, NY: Guilford Press.

Dovidio, J.F., Glick, P., & Rudman, L. (2005). *On the nature of prejudice: Fifty years after Allport*. Malden, MA: Wiley-Blackwell.

Dovidio, J.F., Hewstone, M., & Esses, V.M. (Eds). (2010). *The Sage handbook of prejudice, stereotyping and discrimination*. London: Sage.

Duckitt, J. (1992). Psychology and prejudice: A historical analysis and integrative framework. *American Psychologist*, 47, 1182–1193.

Elliott, J. (1968). 'Blue eyes/brown eyes' exercise. Online. Available at: www.janeelliott.com (accessed 9 April 2016).

Ewens, W.L., & Ehrlich, H.J. (1972). Reference-other support and ethnic attitudes as predictors of intergroup behavior. *The Sociological Quarterly*, 13, 348–360.

Fairbanks, E. (2015). Why South African students have turned on their parents' generation. *The Guardian*. Online. Available at: www.theguardian.com/news/2015/nov/18/why-south-african-students-have-turned-on-their-parents-generation (accessed 8 April 2016).

Fein, S. & Spencer, S.J. (1997). Prejudice as self-image maintenance: Affirming the self through derogating others. *Journal of Personality and Social Psychology*, 73, 31–44.

Fendrich, J.M. (1967). Perceived reference group support: Racial attitudes and overt behavior. *American Sociological Review*, 32, 960–969.

Fiske, S.T., Cuddy, A.J.C., & Glick, P. (2007). Universal dimensions of social perception: Warmth and competence. *Trends in Cognitive Science*, 11, 77–83.

Fiske, S., Cuddy, A.J.C., Glick, P. & Xu, J. (2002). A model of (often mixed) stereotype content: Competence and warmth respectively follow from perceived status and competition. *Journal of Personality and Social Psychology*, 82(6), 878–902.

Forbes, H.D. (2004). Ethnic conflict and the contact hypothesis. In Y.T. Lee, C. McAuley, F. Moghaddam and S. Worchel (Eds), *The psychology of ethnic and cultural conflict* (pp. 69–88). Westport, CT: Praeger.

Frame, D.M. (Ed.). (1948). *The complete essays of Montaigne*. Palo Alto CA: Stanford University Press.

Frenkel-Brunswick, E. (1948). A study in prejudice in children. *Human Relations*, 1, 295–306.

Frey, D.L., & Gaertner, S.L. (1986). Helping and the avoidance of inappropriate interracial behaviour: A strategy that perpetuates a nonprejudiced self-image. *Journal of Personality and Social Psychology*, 50, 1083–1090.

Frier, B.W. & McGinn, T.A.J. (2004). *A casebook on Roman family law*. Oxford: Oxford University Press, American Philological Association.

Gallup. (2011). Online. Available at: www.gallup.com/poll/157082/islamophobia-under standing-anti-muslim-sentiment-west.aspx (accessed 8 April 2016).

Galton, F. (1883). *Inquiries into human faculty and its development*. London: Macmillan.

Garth, T.R. (1925). A review of racial psychology. *Psychological Bulletin*, 22, 343–364.

Gobineau (Compte de), A. (1856). *The moral and intellectual diversity of races* (H. Hotz., Trans.). Philadelphia, PA: Lippincott.

Greenberg, J., & Pyszczynski, T. (1985). The effects of an overheard ethnic slur on the evaluations of the target: How to spread a social disease. *Journal of Experimental Social Psychology*, 21(1), 61–72.

Greenwald, A.G., & Banaji, M.R. (1995). Implicit social cognition: Attitudes, self-esteem, and stereotypes. *Psychological Review*, 102, 4–27.

Gurin, P., Nagda, R., & Lopez, G. (2004). The benefits of diversity in education for democratic citizenship. *Journal of Social Issues*, 60, 17–34.

Gurin, P., Peng, T., Lopez, G., & Nagda, B.R. (1999). Context, identity, and intergroup relations. In D. Prentice and D. Miller (Eds), *Cultural divides: The social psychology of intergroup contact* (pp. 133–170). New York: Russell Sage Foundation.

Hamblin, R.L. (1962). The dynamics of racial discrimination. *Social Problems*, 7, 102–121.

Harrison, M., & Wolf, N. (2011). The frequency of wars. *The Economic History Review*, 65(3), 1055–1076.

Hebl, M.R., Foster, J., Mannix, L.M., & Dovidio, J.F. (2002). Formal and interpersonal discrimination: A field study understanding of applicant bias. *Personality and Social Psychological Bulletin*, 28, 815–825.

Henderson-King, E.I. & Nisbett, R.E. (1996). Anti-black prejudice as a function of exposure to the negative behavior of a single black person. *Journal of Personality and Social Psychology*, 71(4), 654–664.

Home Office. (2014). Online. Available at: https://www.gov.uk/government/uploads/system/uploads/attachment_data/file/364198/hosb0214.pdf (accessed 25 April 2016).

Hovland, C., & Sears, R.R. (1940). Minor studies in aggression VI: Correlation of lynching with economic indices. *Journal of Psychology*, 9, 301–310.

Hume, D. (1753). *Of national characters. Essays, moral, political and literary*. Library of Economic and Liberty. www.econlib.org/lib

Hunt, J. (1865). On the Negro's place in nature. *The Anthropological Review*, 3, 53–54.

Institute of Economics and Peace. (2015). Online. Available at: www.visionofhumanity.org/#/page/news/1121 (accessed 8 April 2016).

Johnson, D.W., & Johnson, R. (1992). Positive interdependence: Key to effective cooperation. In R. Hertz-Lazarowitz and N. Miller (Eds), *Interaction in cooperative groups: The theoretical anatomy of group learning*. New York, NY: Cambridge University Press.

Johnson, D.W., & Johnson, R.T. (1996). Conflict resolution and peer mediation programs in elementary and secondary schools: A review of the research. *Review of Educational Research*, 66, 459–506.

Kant. E. (1764). *Observations on the feeling of the beautiful and sublime and other writings* (P. Frierson & P. Guyer, Trans. and Ed.). Cambridge: Cambridge University Press.

Katz, M. (1975). *Class, bureaucracy, and schools: The illusion of educational change in America*. New York: Praeger Publishers.

Kinder, D.R., & Sears, D.O. (1981). Prejudice and politics: Symbolic racism versus racial threats to the good life. *Journal of Personality and Social Psychology*, 40, 414–431.

King, P.M., & Kitchener, K.S. (1994). *Developing reflective judgment: Understanding and promoting intellectual growth and critical thinking in adolescents and adults*. San Francisco, CA: Jossey-Bass.

Kohlberg L. (1976). Moral stages, moralization: The cognitive developmental approach. In Lickona T. (Ed). *Moral development and behavior*. New York, NY: Holt, Rinehart & Winston.

Kohlberg, L. (1981). *Essays on moral development*. New York, NY: Harper and Row.

Kramer, H. & Sprenger, J. (1487/2010). *The Malleus Maleficarum*. Digireads.com.

Lam, J. (1989). *The impact of conflict resolution programmes on schools: A review and synthesis of the evidence* (2nd edn). Amherst MA: National Association for Mediation in Education.

Landis, D., & Brislin, R.W. (1983). *Handbook of intercultural training* (vols 1–3). Elmsford, NY: Pergamon.

Lerner, M.J. (1980). *The belief in a just world: A fundamental delusion*. New York, NY: Plenum Press.

Levy Paluck, E., & Green, D.P. (2009). Prejudice reduction: What works? A review and assessment of research and practice. *Annual Review of Psychology*, 60, 339–367. doi: 10.1146/annurev.psych.60.110707.163607

Lewis, B., & Churchill, B.E. (2008). *Islam: The Religion and the People*. Indianapolis, IN: Wharton Press.

Libresco, L. (2015). *FiveThirtyEight*. Online. Available at: http://fivethirtyeight.com/features/here-are-the-demands-from-students-protesting-racism-at-51-colleges/ (accessed 8 April 2016).

Lippman, M. (1922). *Public opinion*. New York, NY: Harcourt Brace.

MacCrone, I. (1937). *Race attitudes in South Africa*. London: Oxford University Press.

McConahay, J.B., & Hough, J.C., Jr. (1976). Symbolic racism. *Journal of Social Issues*, 32, 23–45.

Malala, J. (2015). *We have now begun our descent: How to stop South Africa losing its way*. Johannesburg: Jonathan Ball.

Martin, J.G., & Westie, F.R. (1959). The tolerant personality. *American Sociological Review*, 24, 521–528.

Menand, L. (2001). *The metaphysical club*. New York, NY: Farrar, Strauss and Giroux.

Milgram, S. (1963). Behavioral study of obedience. *Journal of Abnormal and Social Psychology*, 67(4), 371–378.

Milner, D. (1975). *Children and race*. Thousand Oaks, CA: SAGE.

Muižnieks, N. (2015). *Rapport du commissaire aux droits de l'homme du conseil de l'Europe*. Online. Available at: https://wcd.coe.int/ViewDoc.jsp?Ref=CommDH(2015)1&Language=lanFrench (accessed 8 April 2016).

Nagda, B.A. & Zuniga, X. (2003). Fostering meaningful racial engagement through intergroup dialogues. *Group Processes and Intergroup Relations*, 6, 111–128.

NatCen. (2013). Online. Available at: www.natcen.ac.uk/media/338779/selfreported-racial-prejudice-datafinal.pdf (accessed 8 April 2016).

OECD. (2015). Online. Available at: www.oecd.org/migration/Is-this-refugee-crisis-different.pdf (accessed 8 April 2016).

Office of Justice. (2014). Online. Available at: www.bjs.gov/content/pub/pdf/hcv0412st.pdf (accessed 8 April 2016).

Oser, F.K. (1986). Moral education and values education: A discourse perspective. In M.C. Wittrock (Ed.), Handbook of research on teaching (3rd edn) (pp. 917–931). New York, NY: Macmillan.

Pandey, G. (2011). Where are India's millions of missing girls? BBC. Online. Available at: www.bbc.com/news/world-south-asia-13264301 (accessed 8 April 2016).

Pettigrew, T.F. (1958). Personality and socio-cultural factors in intergroup attitudes: A cross-national comparison. *Journal of Conflict Resolution*, 2, 29–42.

Pettigrew, T.F. (1959). Regional differences in anti-Negro prejudice. *Journal of Abnormal and Social Psychology*, 59, 28–36.

Pettigrew, T.F. (1971). *Racially separate or together?* New York, NY: McGraw Hill.

Pettigrew, T.F. (1979). The ultimate attribution error: Extending Allport's cognitive analysis of prejudice. *Personality & Social Psychology Bulletin*, 5, 461–476.

Pettigrew, T.F. (2008). Intergroup prejudice: its causes and cures. Online. Available at: http://pepsic.bvsalud.org/scielo.php?pid=S0258–64442008000100006&script=sci_arttext (accessed 8 April 2016).

Pettigrew, T.F. & Meertens, R.W. (1995). Subtle and blatant prejudice in western Europe. *European Journal of Social Psychology*, 25, 57–75. doi: 10.1002/ejsp.2420250106

Pettigrew, T.F., & Tropp, L.R. (2000). Does intergroup contact reduce prejudice? Recent meta-analytic findings. In S. Oskamp (Ed.), *Reducing prejudice and discrimination: Social psychological perspectives* (pp. 93–114). Mahwah, NJ: Erlbaum.

Pillay, N. (2012). Valuing women as autonomous beings: Women's sexual reproductive health rights. United Nations Human Rights Office of the High Commissioner. Online. Available at: www.chr.up.ac.za/images/files/news/news_2012/Navi%20Pillay%20Lecture%2015%20May%202012.pdf (accessed 8 April 2016).

Popper, K. (1963). *Conjectures and refutations: the growth of scientific knowledge*. New York, NY: Routledge.

Proshansky, H.M. (1966). The development of intergroup attitudes. In L.W. Hoffman and M.L. Hoffman (Eds), *Review of child development research* (pp. 311–371). New York, NY: Russell Sage Foundation.

Radke, M., & Sutherland, J. (1949). Children's concepts and attitudes about minority and majority American groups. *Journal of Educational Psychology*, 40, 449–468.

Remy, R.C., Nathan, J.A., Becker, J.M., & Torney, J.V. (1975). International learning and international education in a global age. Bulletin 47, *National Council for the Social Studies*, 39–40.

Rokeach, M. (1960). *The open and closed mind: Investigations into the nature of belief systems and personality systems*. New York, NY: Basic Books.

Runciman, G. (1966). *Relative deprivation and social justice: A study of attitudes to social inequality in twentieth-century Britain*. Berkeley, CA: University of California Press.

Sancho Gil, J.M. (2001). Hacia una vision compleja de la sociedad de la informacion y sus implicaciones para la educacion, In F. Blazquez Entonado. (Ed.), *Sociedad de la informacion y educación* (pp. 140–158). Mérida, Junta de Extremadura, Consejeria de Educacion; Ciencia y tecnologie.

Sen, P. (1997). Asoka: The Great Emperor-Rabrindranath Tagore. In H.B. Chowdhury (Ed.), *Asoka 2300 – Jagajjyoti: Asoka* (Commemoration Volume) (pp. 9–10). Calcutta: Bauddha Dharmankur Sabha.

Sherif, M., Harvey, O.J., White, B.J., Hood, W.R., & Sherif, C.W. (1961). *Intergroup conflict and cooperation: The Robbers Cave experiment (Vol. 10)*. Norman, OK: University Book Exchange.

Sherif, M. (1966). *Group conflict and co-operation: Their social psychology*. London: Routledge.

Statistics Canada. (2014). Online. Available at: www.statcan.gc.ca/pub/85–002-x/2014001/article/14028-eng.htm#a1 (accessed 8 April 2016).

Stephan, W.G. (1985). Intergroup relations. In G. Lindzey and E. Aronson (Eds), *Handbook of Social Psychology* (3rd edn), vol. 2 (pp. 599–658). New York, NY: Random House.

Stephan, W.G. (1987). The contact hypothesis in intergroup relations. In C. Hendrick (Ed.), *Review of personality and social psychology: Group processes and intergroup relations* (vol. 9) (pp. 13–40). Newbury Park, CA: Sage.

Stephan, W.G. (1989). A cognitive approach to stereotyping. In D. Bartal, C.F. Graumann, A.W. Kruglanski, & W. Stroebe (Eds), *Stereotyping and Prejudice: Changing conceptions* (pp. 37–58). Berlin: Springer.

Stone, J., Perry, Z.W., & Darley, J.M. (1997). 'White men can't jump': Evidence for the perceptual confirmation of racial stereotypes following a basketball game. *Basic and Applied Social Psychology*, 19, 291–306.

Swift, J. (1729). A modest proposal. In M. H Abrams (Ed.), *The Norton anthology of English literature* (pp. 2174–2180). New York, NY: Norton.

Tajfel, H. (1970). Experiments in intergroup discrimination. *Scientific American* (November), 96–102.

Tajfel, H., & Turner, J.C. (1979). An integrative theory of intergroup conflict: The social identity theory of intergroup behaviour. In W.G. Austin and S. Worchel (Eds), *The social psychology of intergroup relations* (pp. 33–47). Monterey, CA: Brooks/Cole.

Tansik, D.A., & Driskell, J.D. (1977). Temporal persistence of attitudes induced through required training. *Group and Organization Studies*, 2, 310–323.

Tawil, S. & Cougoureux, M. (2013). Revisiting learning: Revisiting the treasure within. UNESCO occasional paper. UNESCO: Paris.

The Abolition project. (2016). Online. Available at: http://abolition.e2bn.org/people_27.html (accessed 9 April 2016).

Thouless, R. (1930). *Straight and crooked thinking*. London: Pan Books.

Twain, M. (1876). *The adventures of Tom Sawyer*. London: Chatto & Windus.

Twain, M. (1884). *Adventures of Huckleberry Finn*. London: Chatto & Windus.

UTSS (Under the Same Sun). (2016). Online. Available at: www.underthesamesun.com (accessed 25 April 2016).

Veltford, H., & Lee, G.F. (1943). The cocoanut grove fire: A study in scapegoating. *Journal of Abnormal and Social Psychology*, 38, 138–154.

Vivian, J., Brown, R., & Hewstone, M. (1995). Changing attitudes through intergroup contact: The effects of group membership salience. Unpublished manuscript. Wales: Universities of Kent and Cardiff.

Voltaire. (1733, 1755, 1769) In J. McCabe (Trans.) (1912). *Toleration and other essays by Voltaire*. New York, NY: G.P. Putnam's Sons. Online. Available at: http://oll.libertyfund.org/titles/349#Voltaire_0029_81 (accessed 3 January 2015).

Washington Post. (2013). Online. Available at: www.washingtonpost.com/blogs/worldviews/wp/2013/05/15/a-fascinating-map-of-the-worlds-most-and-least-racially-tolerant-countries/ (accessed 8 April 2016).

Watson, M., & Ecken, L. (2003). *Learning to trust*. San Francisco, CA: Jossey-Bass.

Weigel, R.H., Wiser, P.L., & Cook, S.W. (1975). The impact of cooperative learning experiences on crossethnic relations and helping. *Journal of Social Issues*, 31, 219–244.

Western Sydney University. (2016). Online. Available at: www.uws.edu.au/ssap/ssap/research/challenging_racism (accessed 8 April 2016).

Westie, F. (1964). Race and ethnic relations. In R. Faris (Ed.), *Handbook of modern sociology*, (pp. 576–618). Chicago, IL: Rand McNally.

Xu, S. (2001). Critical pedagogy and intercultural communication: Creating discourses of diversity, equality, common goals and rational-moral motivation. *Journal of Intercultural Studies*, 22, 279–293.

Yoon, S. (2015). Islamic State circulates sex slave price list. Bloomberg. Online. Available at: www.bloomberg.com/news/articles/2015–08–03/sex-slaves-sold-by-islamic-state-the-younger-the-better (accessed 8 April 2016).

Zick, A., Küpper, B., Hövermann, A. (2011). *Intolerance, prejudice and discrimination: A European report*. Berlin: Friedrich-Ebert-Stiftung. Online. Available at: http://library.fes.de/pdf-files/do/07908–20110311.pdf (accessed 8 April 2016).

Zimbardo, P.G. (1971). The power and pathology of imprisonment. Congressional Record. (Serial No. 15, October 25, 1971). Hearings before Subcommittee No. 3, of the Committee on the Judiciary, House of Representatives, 92nd Congress, First Session on Corrections, Part II, Prisons, Prison Reform and Prisoners' Rights: California. Washington, DC: U.S. Government Printing Office. Online. Available at: www.prisonexp.org/pdf/congress.pdf (accessed 8 April 2016).

PART I
Reducing prejudice in the individual

2

UNDERSTANDING BEYOND THE OTHER

Bridges across prejudice

Introduction

At the core of prejudice is the idea that people do not possess the individual traits that allow them to escape their group identity, making them predictable in their actions and words and, therefore, easy to categorise and judge. If prejudice is the negative over-generalisation of people and groups leading to hasty judgement, it stands to reason that education should attempt to give learners tools to better understand their interlocutors so that they can temper such over-generalisations and refrain from such hasty judgements.

This chapter focusses on five core differences between human beings that educational institutions need to grapple with if we are to reduce prejudice. They are history, culture, race, gender (including sexuality) and handicaps (the focus will be on special educational needs as this is the main playing field for prejudices around handicaps in schools). Other differences could be treated too, such as class, religion, physicality and age but the goal of the chapter is not to outline educational strategies for each and every conceivable facet of socially exacerbated prejudice but more to offer insights into a few that can be considered and generalised to other domains. Furthermore, other faces of prejudice such as those mentioned above are treated in other chapters of this book.

The central purpose of this chapter is the overriding idea that socially, human beings, when prone to prejudicial thinking, tend to define people's differences not as accidental or inconsequential variations of a common human likeness but, on the contrary, as fundamental, using this as a reason to distance themselves from the other person to a maximum. This process of maximising another person's differences and rendering the person not only an outsider, but in extreme cases, a negative of the self, can be referred to as 'Othering'.

The Other can be described as a social construct; 'the unknown interlocutor who is reduced to fit preconceived internal references and prejudices' (Hughes,

2009, p. 132). The term was developed by post-structuralist French philosophers such as Althusser (1971) and Lacan (1977) working off Levinas (1947) and de Beauvoir (1949) (who famously stated in her work *Le Deuxième Sexe* that 'one is not born a woman, but becomes one'). Postcolonial philosophers such as JanMohamed (1985) and Said (1993) have used the term to describe the process whereby the coloniser uses the colonised as the 'recipient of the negative elements of the self that [are projected] onto him' (JanMohamed, 1985, p. 86).

Some attribute the initial coinage of the concept to Hegel who saw it as a vital, seemingly unavoidable process in the master–slave dialectic that drives human interactions. Kojève's well-known reference to this idea explains it:

> To be human, man must act not for the sake of subjugating a thing, but for the sake of subjugating another Desire (for the thing). The man who desires a thing humanly acts not so much to possess the thing as to make another recognize his right [. . .] to that thing, to make another recognize him as the owner of the thing. And he does this – in the final analysis – in order to make the other recognize his superiority over the other.
>
> *(Kojève, 1980, p. 40)*

This suggests that prejudice is an expression of a power struggle, that at the heart of it we have the desire for power more than simple dislike of another person or group. Furthermore, the implications of this for prejudice in schools are profound. In order to understand other people, learners have to understand the socially prescribed dynamics of relationships that tease out notions of identity, power and meaning. This chapter argues that understanding beyond the Other is taking a much bolder step than simply celebrating difference; it requires the learner to go through a complex process of recognising difference, appreciating it, then relativizing it according to the context that creates that difference in the first place and, finally, at the highest level of reflexive thought, deconstructing difference as a social edifice.

As such, the passage is one in increasing cognitive complexity and can be seen as age-appropriate: learners start with knowing more about other people, then they are brought to understand and appreciate those differences before – as they become older and more mentally flexible – conceptualising them within the frameworks of social organisation and power-relations.

Why it is important to understand other people's history and culture

Understanding happens at different levels. At a group level, this means understanding a people's history, culture, language and geography. Such an endeavour is highly problematic because there are innumerable cultures, 196 countries in the world, and no education system or individual would be capable of processing so much information.

This much said, education can use literature, history, the arts and languages to work towards such a goal. If learners can discover more about the rich cultural heritage of the world and engage in learning experiences that give them more understanding of world history, there is a higher chance that they will be less prone to oversimplify or overgeneralise other individuals or groups out of ignorance since there will be a higher likelihood of them knowing about and understanding others' cultural backgrounds.

Furthermore, there is an argument that certain episodes in history are particularly salient as they explain the socio-political landscape of a globalised world economy. These episodes include the world wars and the Cold War, the Holocaust, the transatlantic slave trade, colonialism, decolonisation, the Civil Rights movement, The Israeli–Arab conflict, Gulf wars and 9/11. At the same time, learners should be given opportunities to learn about regional and local history.

Understanding at the individual level involves a different process and, in a sense, an undoing of the appreciation learners will have of history and culture. In order to accept other people as individuals and not merely members of a group, education should develop a resistance to classify people too quickly within their supposed social categories. For this, learners need to become familiar with some of the fundaments of social psychology, sociology and cultural anthropology.

Therefore, education for understanding the Other can be considered in two movements: on the one hand, learning about the history and culture of other people and, on the other, accepting that individuals may transcend those self-same social categories and should not be reduced to them.

National history

If history is the study of the past then the salient question to ask is 'Whose past?'. On the one hand, national examination boards will place an emphasis on national history so that learners know about their own country's traditions. As such, one assumes that a person educated in the United States will know something about American independence, the Civil War and civil rights, a French educated person will know something about the lineage of French kings from Clovis to Louis Phillipe I, the French Revolution and De Gaulle whereas a Chinese-educated person will know about the Han dynasty, Mao's cultural revolution and so on.

However, the study of one's own history is by no means a simple process as it entails an ideological positioning that might entail prejudice formation. Textbook research shows how national history narratives can shape stereotypical and prejudicial thinking (Ben-Yehuda, 1995; Blackburn, 1985; Domnitz, 1971; Funkenstein, 1989; Kammen, 1991; Koulouri, 2001; Philippou, 2012; Pingel, 1999, 2000; Stewart, 1950). The best known examples of this can be found in Nazi textbooks where anti-Semitic rhetoric was normalised and institutionalised. Less obvious examples can be found in more recent publications such as the 1990 *A History of the United States since 1861* in which the authors Boorstin and Kelley state: 'a reason for going into Vietnam was to protect our reputation. We wanted other free countries to believe that we could stand by them if they were attacked by Communists' (quoted in Brighouse 2003, p. 529).

Within national historical narratives, events may be portrayed in a more or less problematized light but are more typically at best over-simplified portrayals of events; at worst, propagandist endorsements of existing power structures built on one-sided, sometimes untrue versions of the past. For example, in France, article 4, paragraph 4 of the 23 February 2005 law on colonialism asked that teachers teach the 'positive values' of colonialism, a system clearly built on prejudicial values whereas in Canada, between the 1940s and 1950s, history textbooks celebrated Canada as a country that was opposed to slavery and did not allow it (Brown, 1958, p. 480; Chafe & Lower, 1948, p. 309) when in fact it did (Walker, 1997, pp. 124–126).

Montgomery points out that

> History textbooks present as rational, normal and entirely unproblematic the position that defense of the civil society constituting the nation has warranted in the past, and will warrant in the future, the spilling of blood as an essential obligation of citizenship. War is often cast in these nationalist narratives as an unfortunate duty, obligating 'all citizens' of the nation to step forward to bring justice to 'all humankind' in conflicts reduced to such binary oppositions as 'good versus evil' or 'war versus peace'.
>
> *(Montgomery, 2006, pp. 20–21)*

Clearly, the study of national history has an important role to play in the exacerbation or reduction of prejudicial thinking. Teachers hoping to develop a tolerance for ambiguity when looking at the past and an acceptance of the ideological nature of history writing should engage in the study of history with a critical mind, placing students before artefacts that present events from more than one viewpoint.

However, this is by no means straightforward; it implies a high level of analytical and evaluative thought that might not be easily available to all types of learner. Indeed, detecting bias, inferences, vested interests and various tropes of persuasion and manipulation in written and visual texts requires a cognitively demanding approach. Furthermore, teachers attempting to give their students the apparatus to critically examine history might not be appreciated by parents or districts for sowing the seeds of rebellious thoughts and dissent.

The sensitive areas of a history education are those that describe injustices by representatives of nation states. The slave trade for American history textbooks, colonisation for French, British, Portuguese and Spanish textbooks, the Holocaust for German, Dutch, French and Italian history textbooks, the Armenian genocide for Turkish history textbooks, the history of native Americans in American textbooks to mention a few, all pose deep historiographical problems about truth, representation and values. The majority of these themes are treated in a simplistic and sometimes distinctly under-represented manner.

For an education that reduces prejudice to be successful, such events need to be treated not only openly and factually but through critically minded discussion, discernment and higher order awareness of the effects that power and culture have on the act of narrating the past. At an affective level, students should be brought to consider historical narratives with empathy and human understanding.

Where this is particularly difficult is when historical events that entail prejudice are either recent (for example, Apartheid South Africa, the Rwandan genocide, human rights violations under Eastern bloc, Asian, African or Latin American dictators) or ongoing (for example, the Israeli–Palestinian situation, human rights violations in China and the United States, the treatment of the Roma in France, homosexuals in Zimbabwe and women under the Taliban). Even more problematic are events that are not fully accepted or recognised within national ideological frameworks such as the plight of untouchables in the Indian caste system or the Aborigines in Australia.

Indeed, the study of recent history and history in the making is a debate that should be dramatized in classrooms through critical accounts of the news, structured debates about current affairs and the encouragement of student and teacher expression of opinion and belief as concerns topical themes. In a sense, for the study of history to target prejudice reduction, schools need to take risks and go down some of the slippery paths of politics, religion and ideology. This is not an easy thing to do and something that most schools will avoid.

However, as Socrates said, 'the unexamined life is not worth living' – a critical account of nationhood is essential if learners are to draw a balanced, informed account of the socioeconomic, political and organisational structure of modern society. The schools of critical pedagogy (Paulo Freire, Peter McLaren, Michael Apple and the Frankfurt School), using some of the historiographical lenses of Marxist philosophers such as Michel Foucault, Franz Fanon, Ngugi WaThiongo and Louis Althusser, should be activated in the study of national history if we are to hope for students to come out of that learning experienced with a sense of the complexity of history writing. It is this necessarily complex and difficult problematizing of events that can lead to a more nuanced and less prejudiced account of the past and, therefore, the future.

International history

If understanding one's own history is a vital step towards reducing prejudicial thinking, then the understanding of other people's history is a similarly important step. This is for the simple reason that much prejudicial thinking, which consists of prejudgement and over-generalisation, is borne out of ignorance, in particular, ignorance of history.

For example, if one looks at statistics on salaries earned and high positions held in the business world throughout the globe, particularly in Western countries, one will see that men and whites tend to earn more and hold higher positions than women and blacks (*The Economist*, 2015; Shin, 2015). Someone who takes this information at face value, and has no understanding of the historical reasons for such inequity, might draw the conclusion that men and whites are somehow superior to women and blacks. However, if one has studied slavery, colonisation and women's rights historically, particularly the themes of access to education and discrimination, an altogether different conclusion will be drawn: unequal levels of success in today's world are very much the result of historical social and economic injustice and inequality.

Studying another person's history opens the mind to some of the codes that underscore beliefs, language, customs and behaviours. Hence, for a non-Westerner to understand deeply and appreciate well the centrality of democracy in Western narratives, he/she needs to have reflected upon models of citizenship in Athens, political organisation in the Roman Republic, the breakaway from the Church and monarchy. For a non-Muslim or non-Jew to appreciate the significance of the Mecca for Muslims or the Shabbat for Jews, some understanding of the five pillars of Islam, the Surats of the Koran and the life of Muhammad or the Tora and the Old Testament will be required.

How can one grasp the meaning of Chinese politics without some understanding of the historical significance of the near 5,000-year-old Han dynasty and the idea that China is not so much a nation state but a civilisation state? To understand the fact that many colonists were welcomed into African tribal communities and given land is linked to the ancient custom of hospitality such as the Senegalese tradition of 'Teranga', a Wolof word meaning hospitality – the handing over of the land was not necessarily out of naiveté but an ancient custom.

The study of international history was part of the educational philosophy of international-mindedness as practised at the International School of Geneva in the early part of the twentieth century. From those early days, the idea of teaching the humanities was to educate students beyond frontiers and for them to reflect upon humanity in an inclusive, international manner. National history was taught roughly from the age of 12 after international history so that students' first encounter with history would be one that focused on trends and patterns across the globe.

Learning about other people's history requires a substantial effort, just as adjusting to different cultural paradigms, as Allport points out,

> with plenty of people at hand to choose from, why create for ourselves the trouble of adjusting to new languages, new foods, new cultures, or to people of a different educational level? It requires less effort to deal with people who have similar presuppositions.
>
> *(Allport, 1954, p. 17)*

If the effort to learn another person's history is considerable then even more arduous is the need to then problematise that history lesson and realise that it may or may not apply to all members of the group in question. Indeed, an idea of another person's group's history can lead to hasty generalisations built not on empirical evidence but simplified lessons taught in the history classroom. Allport gives an example:

> In a certain Guatemalan community there is fierce hatred of the Jews. No resident has ever seen a Jew. How did the Jew-is-to-be-hated category grow up? In the first place, the community was strongly Catholic. Teachers had told the residents that the Jews were Christ-killers. It also so happened that in the

local culture was an old pagan myth about a devil who killed a god. Thus two powerfully emotional ideas converged and created a hostile prejudgment of Jews.

(Allport, 1954, p. 22)

Indeed, a number of stereotypical assumptions are made on the basis of basic, undeveloped notions of international history (for example, linking all Germans with the Holocaust or assuming that all French and British people dislike one another, latching onto idiomatic but incorrect myths of history such as those that tell us Christopher Columbus 'discovered' America or, as students learnt during apartheid South Africa, that when Jan van Riebeeck arrived at the Cape Colony, it was unpopulated).

If international history is taught badly or, worse, with a deliberately propagandistic mission to misrepresent fact, it could lead to a string of clichés that students could use to fuel prejudicial and stereotypical views of other nationals and ethnicities. Prejudice tends to operate off a 'kernel of truth', meaning that there is some element of a prejudiced belief or statement that is true, albeit usually peripheral, specific to a subset or grossly undeveloped. A smattering of international history could give students shreds of truth that would be used as kernels to build up unhelpful generalisations.

Therefore, just as the teaching of national history requires some distancing and critical thought, schools teaching international curricula need to approach the way other people are represented in careful, mindful ways that ensure students do not clutch onto simplistic essentialising facets of other people's pasts and use them to vehicle prejudiced thoughts. This involves the more sophisticated act of historiographic reasoning, something that should be done through the analysis of national history too. 'History is a pack of lies' Voltaire once said; the teacher's job is to show students the deeper meaning of this disturbing statement.

We see how reducing prejudice through the study of history takes us to a high level of critical thinking that must problematise not only the field of one's own history but the histories of other people. At this point, we could consider the concept of another person and how education can respond to this.

At the heart of prejudicial thinking is 'Otherness' – the maximising of another person's differences to support a polarising discourse and mindset that creates oversimplified notions of self and other. Three core elements of identity that will be considered here are culture, race and gender as these are frequently the subject of prejudiced thinking. For each of these aspects of identity, we will see how education can allow learners to appreciate but also deconstruct them.

Culture

Education is vital to the preservation of culture (UNESCO, 2006, p. 13) since it involves the transmission of cultural artefacts such as language, history, belief systems and social practices. The passing down of skills and knowledge of a group makes education a vehicle for the construction of cultural identity: one learns the history, beliefs and ways of one's national and/or cultural group through an educative process, be it institutionalised or informal.

It is for this reason that religious education, national history, literature and language programmes are developed in schools, to give learners access to the traditions, codes and meaning-making instances that define their cultures.

One should not only learn about one's own culture through education but about that of others. By learning about other people's culture, individuals and groups can better understand situations, behaviours and social phenomena. Understanding other people's culture is a skill that is increasingly demanded in a globalised, culturally diverse economy.

Since individual and group behaviour is predicated by some level of culture, the better the understanding of the culture, the more in-tune and appreciative the interlocutor will be of that behaviour. This is very much the premise of ethnography, the belief that human behaviours need to be interpreted through the rites and customs that contextualise them. 'The final goal [Malinowski stated in discussing peoples of the Western Pacific] is to grasp the native's point of view, his relation to life, to realise his vision of his world' (Malinowski, 1922, p. 25).

Hence, learners should be afforded opportunities that enable them to see the world through the cultural gaze of others. This mind-opening experience allows individuals to relativize their own perspectives, to understand the role that culture has in shaping those perspectives but also to empathise with other people and gain some understanding of what it means to appreciate the world from their perspectives.

Understanding culture has the potential to reduce prejudicial thinking because it lessens the barriers of 'otherness' that are prevalent in situations where people do not know each other well as individuals or groups: 'Understanding a people's culture exposes their normalness without reducing their particularity. . . . It renders them accessible: setting them in the frame of their own banalities, it dissolves their opacity' (Geertz, 1973, p. 14).

To appreciate the cultural practices of a group, one should have some understanding of the way that these practices have developed and the deep significance they have within that culture. Often, when these cultural practices are not understood, prejudiced assumptions are made. For example, if one does not have some appreciation of the value of respect for elders and ancestry in typical African culture (Makinwa-Adebusoye, 2001, p. 5), one will struggle to understand approaches to the future and notions of societal development, especially when compared with more positivist technocratic Western models of progress. Previous French president Nicolas Sarkozy said, in his 2007 Dakar speech, that 'the tragedy of Africa is that the African has never really entered into history. . . . They have never really launched themselves into the future' (quoted in McGreal, 2007). His own minister of Sports, the Senegalese-born Yama Rade riposted that 'I think that not only has the African man made his mark on history, but he was even the first to do so, because I know about the culture' (RFI, 2010).

Sarkozy's statement about Africa is an example of a judgemental and unappreciative approach to difference. Although the social anthropologist Ulf Hannerz points out that the anthropological interest 'is a search for contrasts rather than uniformity', this is not so much to judge other cultures as to take interest in them, 'to become acquainted with more cultures is to turn into an aficionado, to view them as art works (Hannerz, 1990, p. 239).

Education for less prejudice, like the premise of social or cultural anthropology, 'entails a certain metacultural position. There is, first of all, a willingness to engage with the Other, an intellectual and ethic stance of openness toward divergent cultural experiences' (Hannerz, 1992, p. 252).

Therefore, an education for less prejudice must take the complex, cognitively challenging route of deconstructing the idea of culture itself.

Definitions of culture

Culture is a particularly nebulous and highly problematic term. One might start with static definitions that are predicated by the notion that humans operate within set communicative configurations that are described as sets: 'the whole set of signs by which the members of a given society recognize . . . one another, while distinguishing them from people not belonging to that society' or 'the set of distinctive spiritual, material, intellectual and emotional features of a society or social group . . . (encompassing) in addition to art and literature, lifestyles, ways of living together, value systems, traditions and beliefs' (UNESCO, 2006, p. 12).

A more subtle, less static definition of the construct of culture reminds us that it is not merely a set but a system, implying dynamic relations: 'a system of inherited conceptions expressed in symbolic forms by means of which men communicate, perpetuate, and develop their knowledge about and attitudes toward life' (Geertz, 1973, p. 89).

At a more contemporary and problematized level still, we have the notion that culture itself is fluid whereas individuals and groups move through culture and define themselves in continually evolving ways: 'Cultures are made of continuities and changes' (Appiah, 2012, p. 1178).

Indeed, as soon as one starts grouping people into cultures such as Western, Islamic or Eastern, a highly unstable, contextually limited definition is used that does not necessarily hold across different viewpoints or users and is, therefore, highly unreliable.

Ideas about culture are perspectival in that they change according to the person defining them. Gillespie, Howarth and Cornish (2012) point out how simplistically defined cultural groups are actually much more complex than their appellation implies. This is especially the case when one considers that each group means something different to the person observing it. For example, the idea of Indian culture will have a quite different meaning for Indians, non-Indian tourists and different groups within what we might call Indian culture (wealthy, poor, male, female, Hindu, Christian, Muslim, etc).

So culture, as a defining term, is both ambiguous and paradoxical and therefore intrinsically difficult to conceptualise. Educational practices must enhance sufficient higher-order thinking for students to embrace such complex configurations of meaning purposefully, without creating confusion. Students need to be educated to identify the enunciator of any discourse about culture and problematize that source of information. This is a similar design to that which urges students to interrogate historical sources critically.

Definitions of culture are also historical (Gillespie et al., 2012]): symbolic arte-facts of culture tend to become outdated quickly, especially in the twenty-first century in which many traditions are being lost and human diversity is increasingly drawn into a homogeneous 'third culture'. Some of the superficial signifiers of culture such as food, fashion and folklore have a certain shelf-life and need to be revisited to accurately depict what could be called cultural practice. For example, to associate French culture with the beret is not something that resonates in current dress codes in France but is an image inherited from the nineteenth and early twen-tieth centuries. A similar point could be made with the English bowler hat. Defini-tions of culture are disrupted by the movement of people between them (Gillespie et al., 2012) since individuals can easily have more than one cultural reference point and can convert from one cultural site to another through naturalisation, religious conversion, immigration, marriage or merely personal choice. Definitions of cultural groups are also 're-constitutive of the phenomena they seek to describe' (Gillespie et al., 2012), meaning that they respond to the clichés and stereotypes that are used to depict them in a type of self-fulfilling prophecy. As such, if someone is made to believe that his or her culture is defined by a certain set of symbols and practices, (s)he may well incorporate and perform these incidents to create a sense of belonging and identity.

So to define someone by his or her culture is highly problematic. The learner educated away from prejudice should be given the intellectual arms necessary to relativise any over-deterministic categorisation of the individual or group through cultural references by recognising and understanding the tenuous nature of culture as a site of meaning.

Furthermore, some would argue that the notion of culture itself is a Western construct and does not sufficiently explain other ontological frameworks that describe the human condition:

> the assumption that at some level all forms of cultural diversity may be under-stood on the basis of a particular universal concept, whether it be "human being", "class" or "race", can be both very dangerous and very limiting in trying to understand the ways in which cultural practices construct their own systems of meaning and social organisation.
>
> *(Bhabha, 1990, p. 209)*

To reduce cultural prejudice is not only to question the notion of culture itself but also to be prepared to release someone from any restrictive definition one might have of that interlocutor and allow them the space to belong to that culture but also to belong somewhere else. The relationship between nationality and culture is not straightforward as each coalesces and spills over the other: 'nation-state driven conceptualisation of culture and cultural identity cannot avoid reducing culture to a set of standardised commonalities which fails to capture the dynamics of the discursive construction of national identities' (Angouri, 2010, p. 209).

Similarly, conflations are often made between religion and culture when describing groups: a classic case being that of the confusion between Arab and Muslim. In 2015, the mayor of Beziers (France), Robert Ménard, claimed to have used the lists of pupils' names to determine how many were Muslim, to which Abdallah Zekri, Head of the National Observatory against Islamophobia pointed out that 'you can be called Mohammed without being a practising Muslim' (Agence France-Presse, 2015) just as you can be called John without being a Christian. Another common conflation is between skin colour and continental identity: a classic case being that which assumes Africans are all black.

So to deal with the slippery signifier of culture is to engage the mind in a challenging set of overlapping categories that are generalised, brought together and cast asunder historically and from various perspectives. People move in and out of cultures and cultures themselves evolve. The twenty-first century poses particularly complex challenges to learners trying to define other people's identities and reference points so the teaching of culture as a heterogeneous, polyvalent living tissue is necessary.

This leaves educators with a major challenge since it is clearly difficult to find consensus over what exactly the word 'culture' actually means and to whom and how one might operationalise the construct in the classroom. Teachers need to make a shift from simplistic comfort zones of what constitutes culture (Kumashiro, 2004; Motha, 2006) with standard stereotypic examples of cultural groups, to a more discursive practice where they are co-learners alongside students, constantly discovering and rediscovering the universe and discourse of culture.

Race

A common expression of prejudice, more polemical and less subtle than cultural discrimination, is racism. In the 1982 *Declaration on Race and Racial Prejudice*, UNESCO defines racism as including 'racist ideologies, prejudiced attitudes, discriminatory behaviour, structural arrangements and institutionalized practices resulting in racial inequality as well as the fallacious notion that discriminatory relations between groups are morally and scientifically justifiable' (UNESCO, 1982, 2.2). In an earlier text (1951, 1), UNESCO made a statement to deconstruct the biological notion of race, pointing out that 'scientists are generally agreed that all men living today belong to a single species, homo sapiens, and are derived from a common stock'. While biological definitions of race, popular during the nineteenth and early twentieth centuries, are today largely considered invalid, this mainly being because of the increasingly understood genetic interrelatedness of human phenotypes, race should still be understood as a marker in many societies to separate, control and hierarchise human beings (Epstein & Gist, 2015; Hall, 1996; Darder & Torres, 2004). Furthermore, Williams and Eberhardt (2008) found that people subscribing to a biological definition of race were more prone to stereotypic depictions of Black Americans whereas those who were more inclined to see race as a social construct were less inclined to fall prey to such stereotypes.

Race is 'a complex system of ideas and practices regarding how some visible characteristics of human bodies such as skin color, facial features, and hair texture relate to people's character, intellectual capacity, and patterns of behaviour' (Markus & Moya, 2010, p. 22). Some would like to see the entire concept disbanded. For example, in 2013, French president François Hollande passed a bill to remove the word 'race' from all legislation and said that 'there is no place for race in the republic' (*The Telegraph*, 2013).

However, whether wishing to distance statements on race from early biological definitions should lead to a colour blind approach can be debated. According to the literature on racial literacy, schools should not hide away from the topic or try to gloss over it with uncritical accounts of interculturality and anti-racist thinking that discard the idea of race altogether. This is because such discourses do not grapple with the essence of the problem and may lead to politically correct situations that avoid the reality of race as a society-structuring discourse:

> liberal discourses of multiculturalism, equality and tolerance such as those prevalent in the Canadian context of multicultural diversity lull us into complacency that we have moved away from these dark pasts, but have we genuinely moved to more critically aware spaces, or have we merely languaged our way out of the shadows of the past while remaining subject to its discourses and common-sense notions?
>
> *(Lee, 2015, p. 81)*

Indeed, it would be naive to assume that by occulting the word 'race', one can do away with racism. A more critical viewpoint would suggest that, on the contrary, by avoiding the notion of race, we allow it to flourish as it becomes another elephant in the classroom:

> Scholars argue that [colour blind racial ideology] has supplanted old-fashioned racism as an acceptable expression of modern racial intolerance (Bonilla-Silva, 2001). Individuals who ignore racial differences and minimize racism consciously or unconsciously perpetuate racism by justifying the racial status quo in the United States (Bonilla-Silva, 2001; Carr, 1997).
>
> *(Lewis, Neville & Spanierman, 2012, p. 122)*

The question of race is, therefore, one that should be brought out into the open in educational systems seeking to reduce prejudicial thinking: students should be taught 'racial literacy' (Guinier, 2004) since race is 'the prevailing narrative in the lives of racial minority individuals and groups' (Skerrett, 2011, p. 314) and is used 'to position difference and power relations in the process of identification' (Fergus, 2009, p. 345).

According to Epstein and Gist (2015), racial literacy is achieved through the following educational pathways:

1   Educational experiences need to disrupt 'the common narrative structured around themes of increasing progress and greater equality in order to explicate the "foundational, indeed constitutional" (Guinier, 2004, 98) role that racism has played in the development of the nation' (Epstein & Gist, 2015, p. 43). This means making visible 'the complex ways in which racism has operated historically and today'.

2   Educators need to consider using 'culturally relevant pedagogy' (p. 42) which entails popular culture but also works from students' own references rather than anticipating these references and possibly falling into the trap of essentialising assumed identities with chosen stereotypical artefacts (such as using rap with black students based on the assumption that this is culturally relevant to them).

3   Addressing race directly.

4   Creating safe, discussion-inducing environments so that experiences of racism can be discussed and shared (Tatum, 1992).

Others suggest that by educational institutions openly embracing racial diversity, positive steps can be taken. Research by Engberg and Hurtado (e.g. 2004; Engberg & Hurtado, 2011) has shown that attitudes to race and social justice are enhanced by diversity experiences in university campuses. To investigate further the effects of campus diversity, see Lewis, Neville and Spanierman (2012), p. 121.

Race is a polemical subject that has more currency in university circles than in schools. This is because parental pressure for safe subjects is less predominant in universities and because critical race theory is not a field that has been associated traditionally with K–12 education but more with graduate and post-graduate level political theory.

Teachers wishing to treat the question run the risk of entering a minefield since aiming for tolerance, acceptance, respect and appreciation of diversity might force them to label students racially and frankly identify different races – which in itself is a highly problematic, unscientific enterprise and can create justified upset. On the other hand, playing down the concept of race and pretending it does not exist will not equip students to deal with the matter in their adult lives and runs the risks of allowing it to predominate in surreptitious forms such as disguised playground and institutionalised racism.

The research suggests that educational institutions should not be afraid to discuss the subject openly and to allow it to feature prominently in educational discourse and institutional consciousness. What is essential is for students to understand that race is a complex, socially constructed idea that has been used politically, economically and historically to advance various forms of capitalism: it is not about labelling students black and white but explaining that concepts of whiteness and blackness have been ideological drivers in the past and continue to be in the present. Furthermore, educational discourse on race, if it is to be sincere and critical, cannot shy away from uncomfortable questions related to slavery and colonisation but also current affairs such as blackness in the United States, the status of non-Europeans in Europe, Aborigines in Australia or racial division in modern South Africa. It is by embracing these subjects head on and discussing them that a forum for exchange and understanding can be established.

Given the sensitive nature of the subject and the cognitive demands required for meaningful engagement, critical discussions on race could not realistically be expected to take place before the equivalent of upper secondary school or high school (16+ years). At the level of institutional organisation, schools wishing to send out a message of respect for diversity should aim for ethnically diverse staffing including management positions so that students of different origins can believe that success is possible for them too.

Gender

Like most stereotypes, concepts and symbols of gender roles are produced, distributed and exacerbated by out-of-school factors such as the family, the workplace and mass media. The latter as a vehicle of gender stereotypes is particularly important (Craig, 1992) in an age of saturated information load and wide-scale, easily accessible popular iconography. Jordan (1995) reports on how carefully designed classroom learning experiences meant to reduce gender stereotypes can be easily disrupted by the stereotype and, potentially, prejudice-induced games children bring into the playground.

The archetypal representations of the male and female in traditional Western fairy tales, myths, and also many modern iconographic depictions through film, the pop industry and advertising, delineate some of the assumptions and prejudices people might have about either sex. In these stereotypic depictions, men are seen as outgoing, conquering and controlling heroes in the line of Odysseus while women tend to incarnate passive, patient and servile personalities such as Penelope. Where women are strong they become freakish witches such as Medea, Clytemnestra or Lady Macbeth. These archetypes were coined as the animus (male principle) and anima (female principle) by Jung (1964).

Unlike racial, homophobic or overtly sexist insults that are usually fairly straightforward to detect and act upon since they stand out from what is considered in most social organisations as acceptable behaviour and speech, schools looking to diminish gender prejudice are faced with subtle, well-anchored practices and beliefs that have been normalised by society to an extent that to unearth them and question them can be deeply unsettling. For example, to ask students to critique family models with a working father and house mother might be asking them to question their own parents' relationship, identity and familial organisation. Islamic culture's clear demarcation of men and women is another area that is challenging to discuss with students in the light of prejudice and discrimination.

Schools and universities must have the courage to discuss gender stereotypes and prejudice against women – as well as men – openly and reflectively. Indeed, the facts that men still earn more than women (US Labor Force statistics, 2015), that there is an overwhelmingly predominant population of males in political leadership and that women suffer from strong acts of prejudice and discrimination in many countries in the world ('global prevalence figures indicate that 35% of women worldwide have experienced either intimate partner violence or non-partner sexual violence in their lifetime' (World Health Organization, 2014) need to be analysed critically, at a demanding cognitive level.

Schools exacerbating gender prejudice

To do this comprehensively, schools should reflect carefully on the ways they themselves operate since studies have shown how schools institutionalise gender separation in, at first glance, imperceptible ways, such as through the spatial distribution of playground activities where, Prendergast (1996) has shown for British working class schools, the control of the playground by predominantly male games including football has marginalised girls and invaded their space.

A well-known area of gender imbalance is subject enrolment in upper secondary school. The 2013 Institute of Physics report (UK), using the UK National Pupil Database's statistics from 2010 to 2013, states that 'English, biology and psychology have a balance towards "girls" and physics, mathematics and economics towards "boys"' (Institute of Physics, 2013). Numerous studies have shown that in schools girls tend to have lower self-esteem than boys in general (Niederle and Vesterlund, 2007; Streitmatter, 2002; Pomerantz, Altermatt & Saxon, 2002), particularly in mathematics and sciences, believing that they are naturally weak in these areas (Kurtz-Costes et al., 2008).

Exactly why this should be is not entirely clear. Some studies in neuroscience suggest that boys tend to excel in spatial and logical-mathematical intelligences whereas girls tend to have more developed verbal and emotional intelligences (Kimura, 2000). This might explain gradual patterning in studies in schools over time (Killgore & Yurgelun-Todd, 2004; Lenroot et al., 2007). However, there is also the likelihood that girls are made to believe that mathematics and physics are not for them through a repertoire of subconscious apparatuses within the school such as teacher genders and attitudes, university guidance counselling and societal role models (there are, for example, few well known female mathematicians, physicists or economists). The issue of girls' patterned subject enrolment may also be to do with conformity (Cooley, 2006; Sacerdote, 2001) and in this sense becomes a self-fulfilling prophecy or vicious cycle.

The 2013 Institute of Physics report recommends that 'schools should reflect on their own statistics and put in place whole-school measures to counter gender stereotyping' and that 'primary schools should reflect on the gender messages they may be giving to pupils, which may unwittingly reinforce gender stereotypes, and work to remove them' (Institute of Physics, 2013).

Van de gaer et al. (2004) found in their study of 4,000 students in upper second-ary schools in Belgium that girls performed better in mathematics in single-sex schools than in co-educational schools whereas boys performed better in languages in co-educational schools than in single-sex schools.

However, although single-sex education may improve performances of each gender group in respective domains, it will not necessarily build a tolerant outlook on members of the opposite gender. Thorne's work (1992) on gender arrangements in elementary schools points out that teachers tend to exacerbate gender stereo-types through segregation. This practice is socialised by students who remain, for the large part, segregated in playtime activities, reinforcing patterns of gender divi-sion, and will often ostracise those that cross over symbolic lines of identity. Wood (1984) found that sexist language among boys was less frequent when they kept company with mixed-gender groups.

Hence we are faced with a similar paradox to that concerning racism: if girls have been the victims of discrimination then equity can be achieved through sepa-ratist implementation of learning conditions. However, separating girls and boys runs the risk of polarising groups and fuelling prejudiced mindsets. On the other hand, if differences between girls and boys are minimised and mixed grouping is encouraged – as would be the case with a racially desegregated 'colour blind' school – iniquities may well continue since the playing ground has not been lev-elled although prejudiced attitudes might be lessened. It seems, therefore, to be a trade-off between empowerment of victims of discrimination with the potential for prejudice versus less prejudice but without affirmative action. One hopes there is a middle ground.

Educating for gender differences in the twenty-first century

How different are males and females and to what extent are differences constructed? Despite obvious physical differences that come from sexual identity, a large part of gender identity is constructed. Diamond points out that 'one's sexual identity is prenatally organized as a function of the genetic-endocrine forces and emerges (is activated) with development. One's gender identity, recognition of how he or she is viewed in society, develops with post-natal experiences' (Diamond, 2005, p. 127).

Clichés about female characteristics usually involve 'empathy, intuitiveness, adaptability, awareness of growth as a process rather than as goal-ended, inventive-ness, protective feeling toward others, and a capacity to respond emotionally as well as rationally' (Alpert, 1974, p. 92). Stereotypic male characteristics involve logical thinking, competitiveness, domination and goal-orientation. These generalisations, whether true or not, have had an important effect on the collective psyche of many societies. For example,

> at the end of the 60s [. . .] there was a minor panic in the United States about schools' destroying 'boy culture' and denying boys their 'reading rights'

because of the prevalence of women teachers and the 'feminine, frilly content' of elementary education.

(Connell, 1996, p. 207)

However, Connell points out that gender roles are historically and culturally constructed:

> There is no one pattern of masculinity that is found everywhere. Different cultures and different periods of history, construct masculinity differently. Some cultures makes heroes of soldiers, and regard violence as the ultimate test of masculinity; other look at soldiering with disdain and regard violence as contemptible. Some cultures regard homosexual sex as incompatible with true masculinity; other think that no-one can be a real man without having had homosexual relations.

> *(p. 208)*

Tulviste et al. (2010) describe a 2004 meta-analysis by Leaper and Smith: 'children's language use showed that girls were more talkative and used more affiliative speech (e.g., praise, agreement, acknowledgement, responsiveness) than boys, whereas boys used more assertive speech (e.g., directives, negative speech, giving and requesting information)' (p. 319). They went on to conduct a qualitative study of Swedish, Finnish and Estonian pre-school children and found that gender-correlated patterns of directive or non-directive speech (associated with gender) were primarily a result of cultural differences.

In the twenty-first century, especially in the West, ideas of gender are being reviewed substantially with polymorphous, androgynous, homo and bi-sexual identities being recognised more and more. Extreme views from militant feminists in the 1960s and 1970s suggested that we should do away with gender roles altogether. The idea that one is free to define oneself has been celebrated by some such as Koedt, Levine and Rapone, who state that 'the most basic right of an individual is to create the terms of its own definition' (1973, p. 370) and bemoaned by others, such as Finkielkraut (2015), who describes the free reign of individualism as a decadent deconstruction of traditional roles and values, leading to the disintegration of the family.

Gender equality laws passed in France between 2012 and 2014 led to reforms in the educational system that were designed to teach gender equality. This led to false rumours that were circulated by parents using social media claiming that children were going to be taught that they were 'not born a girl or a boy, as God intended, but choose to become one' (Samuel, 2014). This is an example of the prejudicial views that predominate in many countries about sexual categories and the fear that educational initiatives might reverse gender roles in the family structure.

The fear that some parents might have of bisexuality, homosexuality or androgyny and the resultant prejudices that will arise from such positions is unlikely to be addressed in schools in the near future as the topic is still considered too taboo for most households. This is not to say that the conventional heterosexual models of identity that are projected into young people by schools are true representations of adult behaviours. Gebhard and Johnson's (1979) carefully reviewed study of the 1948 Kinsey report on 'Sexual Behaviour in the Human Male' (reviewed because the original study was heavily criticised for not being randomised) found that 36.4 per cent of men in the US had engaged in homosexual activities (Gebhard & Johnson, 1979).

Addressing gender-related stereotypes through education can be considered institutionally, through equitable gender representation of roles of power and authority (for example, heads of department, principal positions and other management positions) to send out the message to boys and girls that success in social organisations is not the reserve of one group alone. Schools should aim to strike a balance in subject enrolment patterns whenever possible so as to move away from the clichés of female primary school teachers, male physics teachers and so on.

It would appear that a co-educational environment is more prone to reduce prejudicial views of the opposite gender than single-sex education but if this is done, schools must be sensitive to the insidious presence of sexism that is likely to be reproduced in breaktime activities and other forms of informal interaction. Kitzinger (2001) points out that 'heterosexism [. . .] is one of the ways in which strict adherence to gender role stereotypes is enforced, and gender oppression maintained' (p. 277). Silverschanz et al. (2007) conducted research using 3,128 students from north-western universities in the United States and found that 'approximately 40% reported experiences of heterosexist harassment' in the course of a year (p. 179).

Therefore, a sensitive approach that takes note of the surreptitious codes upon which sexist prejudice is formulated beyond the classroom within the tissue of school culture is needed to sustain a meaningful approach.

Special needs

Another human category that is frequently othered in society is the handicapped person. Hodkinson, referring to fieldwork he conducted in 2007 in the UK, reports 'I was dismayed to observe that, when questioned, a majority of mainstream children had no conception of what inclusive education was and, more worryingly, they held extremely negative views of disability and disabled people' (Hodkinson, 2010, p. 63).

Schools can make a difference by educating learners to view such individuals in a more critical and sociological way so as to deconstruct the way they are represented and treated in mainstream, so called 'normal', society. Dunne describes the ways that many schools deal with Special Educational Needs (SEN) students as 'a powerful othering framework' (Dunne, 2009, p. 49) mainly because of diagnosis and tracking.

The medical discourse is particularly powerful and creates strong prejudices when it comes to SEN students for two essential reasons: first, medical diagnoses carry a legitimisation with them that is anchored in the social authority of the medical field (see Foucault, 1963, for the power of the clinic); second, because medical diagnoses create an identity-constraining and deterministic labelling effect that is difficult to shrug off (see Molloy & Vasil, 2002, p. 661).

The medical approach pathologises difference and exacerbates the divide between those who consider themselves 'normal' and individuals with special learning needs. Goodley takes this idea far by stating that 'the "difference" of people with learning difficulties, understood as being located in some biological deficit, individualizes their very humanity: ripping them out of a social context, placing them within the realms of pathological curiosity' (2000, p. 35).

A critique of schools' approaches to SEN that is that they tend to shift the onus of difficulty accessing the curriculum onto the student without questioning their own practices:

> Children with behavioural, social and emotional issues are segregated and contained in Pupil Referral Units and consequently marginalised. They are labelled as deviants without any critical interrogation of the 'within school' factors (inappropriate curriculum or assessment processes that label them as failures) or external factors (inappropriate parenting or lack of cultural capital) that may have contributed to their 'undesirable' behaviours.
>
> *(Glazzard, 2013, p. 184)*

Glazzard's critique is at the heart of deconstructing otherness as it relies on a postmodern approach to truth and knowledge in the vein of Michel Foucault whereby edifices of normality are no longer seen as absolute or intrinsic but socially constructed through discourses of power and tradition. This implies that education should provide learners with the means to look beyond individual differences into the contexts that decree those individuals to be different.

Educating for less prejudice towards handicapped individuals can be done through the experience of artistic works that shift the perspective from a conventional discourse, with the handicapped individual as object, to one where the reader sees the world through the eyes of a marginalised person and therefore empathises, understands and relates to that point of view while recognising some of the horrors of 'normality'. Two classic novels that do this very effectively are J.D. Salinger's *The Catcher in the Rye* (1951) and Ken Kesey's *One Flew Over the Cuckoo's Nest* (1962).

Researchers in the UK have argued that, institutionally, for schools to be genuinely inclusive so that students with special learning needs feel fully integrated and valued in the fabric of school life, the entire concept of success needs to be revisited (Audit Commission, 2002; Cole, 2005; Lunt & Norwich, 1999; Black-Hawkins, Florian & Rouse, 2007; Lloyd, 2008). As long as schools are trying on the one hand to admit students of varying cognitive profiles but at the same time are competing with one another by comparing achievement on high-stakes performance assessments, they will be polarising the student body and further othering students with special learning needs whose strengths might not be valued through examinations.

The question of assessments is a fundamental one that goes beyond schools into the economic system that drives so many societal values. Glazzard states that 'inclusion cannot be entangled with neo-liberal values that focus on competition and education for the purpose of economic productivity' (2013, p. 103). In order for students with special educational needs to escape ostracism, prejudice and discrimination, schools will have to ensure that 'the teaching and learning, achievement, attitudes and well-being of every person matter' (Ofsted, 2000).

One way of doing this is to ensure that schools design assessments of character-related constructs such as wisdom, decision-making, resilience, open-mindedness and kindness. If these aspects of humanity are celebrated more emphatically in schools and regarded with the same importance as academic knowledge and technical skill, students with special learning needs will be better appreciated by other students and will feel more empowered. The International School of Geneva is an example of a school with an integrated special needs programme, allowing for frequent, non-competitive contact between students with and without learning needs in a context where the affective domain is celebrated and modelled (Ecolint, 2016).

Another way of celebrating difference is by making salient heterogeneous models of intelligence such as Howard Gardner's multiple intelligences (Gardner, 2004), which look beyond so-called 'natural intelligence' or mathematical, logical or verbal intelligence alone towards less socially recognised areas such as kinaesthetic, interpersonal or intrapersonal intelligence. By celebrating these domains and designing classroom assessment that allow them to be operationalised, a more inclusive and less prejudice-prone learning environment will be induced.

A school model to deconstruct otherness

Figure 2.1 represents three levels of knowing beyond the Other that can be considered developmentally. At level 1, appropriate for young children (up until a consolidation of Piaget's pre-operational stage, so age 7), experiences should focus on diversity and an appreciation of diversity. Schools should be wary not to turn this into an educational philosophy that insists on difference and forces individuals into identities that they might not wish to appropriate but rather to focus on engineering environments that allow for an equitable exchange of cultural, ethnic, gender-related and profile-related experiences. Care should be taken to offer a physical educational programme that does not polarise groups and play on gender stereotypes (skipping and tic tac toe for girls, football and basketball for boys) but allows for single-sex learning environments (swimming, gymnastics, martial arts).

At stage 2, leading to abstract thought and a capacity to deal with complex philosophical and epistemic notions (so up to age 11), students should be exposed to international history so as to open their minds to the different legacies and narratives that make up the rich tissue of humanity. This can include some effort to move away from ethnocentric or gender biased accounts of history in order to appreciate diversity further.

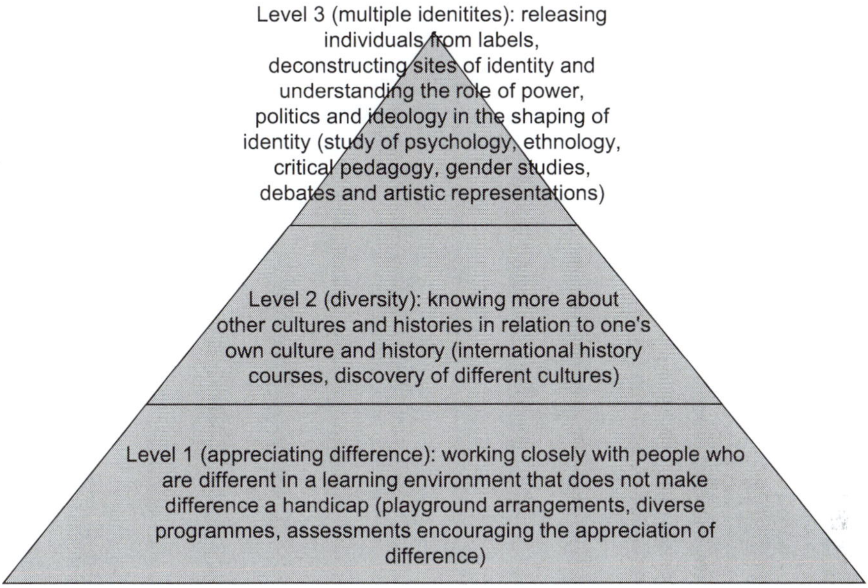

Level 3 (multiple idenitites): releasing individuals from labels, deconstructing sites of identity and understanding the role of power, politics and ideology in the shaping of identity (study of psychology, ethnology, critical pedagogy, gender studies, debates and artistic representations)

Level 2 (diversity): knowing more about other cultures and histories in relation to one's own culture and history (international history courses, discovery of different cultures)

Level 1 (appreciating difference): working closely with people who are different in a learning environment that does not make difference a handicap (playground arrangements, diverse programmes, assessments encouraging the appreciation of difference)

FIGURE 2.1 Understanding beyond the Other

At stage 3, where learners are at the abstract level of thinking and are consolidating their understanding of systems, concepts and counter-intuitive notions (so, from a traditional Piagetian stance, after 11, but more realistically, closer to age 16), students should be exposed to an educational experience that affords them an understanding of the role of racism, sexism and powerful discourses of normality in the writing of history and the institutionalisation of power.

Conclusion

The enterprise of educating beyond otherness is a fragile one since it involves striking a balance between a critical approach to human differences and a temptation to render differences obsolete and strive for a whitewashed third culture. Diversity enriches our lives (variety is the spice of life) and the aim is not to erase it but to know it. One thought to cling on to in the light of these suggestions is what it means to belong to a group in the twenty-first century. New technologies and the world-wide distribution of cultural artefacts threaten diversity. Levi-Strauss foresaw a disintegration of the richness of culture many years ago:

> It is only through difference that progress can be made. What threatens us right now is probably what we may call over-communication – that is, the tendency to know exactly in one point of the world what is going on in all other parts of the world. In order for a culture to be really itself and to produce something, the culture and its members must be convinced of their

originality and even, to some extent, of their superiority over the others; it is only under conditions of under-communication that it can produce anything. We are now threatened with the prospect of our being only consumers, able to consume anything from any point in the world and from any culture, but of losing all originality.

(Levi-Strauss, 1979, p. 7)

A good education is one that reduces prejudicial thinking but at the same time, we need to remember that educational institutions have a duty not to disintegrate the structure of cultural, ethnic or gender difference to the point when humanity becomes engulfed in a type of monochromatic, formless third culture without relief. A danger of internationalism is that it deprives humanity of the differences that make humanity so interesting and passionate.

This chapter has shown how for questions of culture and history, if an education is to reduce prejudice by reducing otherness, learners should be knowledgeable of different historical narratives and cultural practices to avoid prejudicial thinking borne out of ignorance and stereotypes. This is something that should be done from an early age to ensure that the two million minutes spent in school are used to cover a variety of national and cultural expressions of humanity and not just national history and local culture since time is needed to cover a multiplicity of different histories. This much said, the pillars of self-knowledge that constitute national history are critical as they create a vantage point from whence other histories and cultures can be viewed. The extent to which a learner's own history and culture is evoked in school exclusively, aggressively and monotonically or, on the contrary, relativistically, inclusively and with some critical distance, will affect the way learners go on to learn about others.

Differences in gender and learning needs can be lessened by more inclusive approaches to curriculum, by 'replacing confrontational disciplinary systems, restructuring physical education to emphasise participation rather than competitive selection, and restructuring the gender-divided curriculum' (Connell, 1996, p. 226). Schools should be mindful of the way that students socialise in free time. They can make a difference by scaffolding learning environments that are not exclusivist, gender-biased or inaccessible to students with special needs. The idea of allowing gender boundaries to be crossed and so-called 'borderwork' to lessen gender stereotype reproduction and male-dominated social organisation, especially among young learners, should be considered (see, for example, the work of Thorne, 1992). This might include a variety of games on offer for students at break time other than only traditionally male-centred games such as football, classroom activities that put the emphasis less on talking and dominating group work and more on listening, supporting other people and collaborating. Teachers should not assume that quiet students are not making an effort or that low performance on an assessment is necessarily the student's fault as it could also be due to biased assessment and task design.

Cultural, gender and learning need diversity should be celebrated in schools in inclusive ways; not through labelling and explicit separatist provision but by ensuring that schools are open to the voice of different types of learners and are allowing them to have a say in their own education by bringing their diversity to the table. So knowing another person beyond otherness does not only mean studying differences, but celebrating them and allowing them to influence school policy. As Danforth points out, 'research and practice have effectively defined individual lives under the pathology heading without addressing the politics of knowledge, without allowing for significant personal meanings of those categorized persons (the persons we serve) to be valued as knowledge' (Danforth, 1995, p. 138).

If knowledge and integration are the first steps towards understanding the Other, then the more challenging but necessary steps are those that take us beyond those definitions, allowing for individualism, freedom from labels and an ongoing becoming of human potential. Learners must understand that 'no one today is purely one thing. Labels like Indian, or woman, or Muslim, or American are not more than starting-points, which if followed into actual experience for only a moment are quickly left behind' (Said, 1993, p. 336).

To leave sites of identity behind, steps must be taken to embed in educational systems fundamental concepts of ethnology, sociology, psychology and anthropology. This is an ambitious project that requires a high level of instruction and reflection, possibly only at the senior years of schooling and at university level. Some of the key notions that must be imparted to students include:

1   The relative deprivation of identity: 'Identity is always a structured representation which only achieves its positive through the narrow eye of the negative' (Hall, 1996, p. 21).
2   Gender as a site of political strife: 'Man establishes his "Manhood" in direct proportion to his ability to have his ego override woman's, and derives his strength and self-esteem through this process' (Koedt, Levine & Rapone, 1973, p. 380)
3   Race as a social construction that has been used for the distribution of power in modern human history.
4   That special needs and, more broadly, handicaps are not merely biological realities and pathologies but socially constructed representations that serve to prop up the liturgy of convention and so-called normality.
5   That essentialised notions of 'Others' are embedded in and created by language: 'language objectifies the world, transforming the *panta rhei* of experience into a cohesive order. In the establishment of this order language realizes a world, in the double sense of apprehending and producing it' (Berger & Luckman, 1966, p. 173).

This can be achieved only through 'radical reform of the school in terms of curriculum, assessment pedagogy and grouping of pupils' (Mittler, 2000, p. 10). Every teacher should consider him or herself as a critically minded person, a cultural studies teacher and a participant in a critical dialogue about history, culture and identity. Furthermore, it seems difficult to imagine such a level of conscious-raising educational practice without awareness of and, perhaps, a striving for social justice: 'social justice demands deconstructing those realities in order to disclose the multiple ways schools and their leadership reproduce marginalizing and inequitable treatment of individuals because their identities are outside the celebrated dominant culture' (Marshall & Oliva, 2010, p. 22).

Competence assessments, records of meaning-making such as portfolios or response journals, should feature in this project, students should engage in pertinent, reflective dialogue, debates and artistic productions to dramatise their understanding of identity and culture. Furthermore, salient works of literature, film and art can be used to trigger reflection and debate along these lines. The humanities, languages and arts might seem like obvious areas to develop understanding beyond the Other, but it can be done in mathematics with approaches to non-Western traditions, physical education through a wider, less Western and male-dominated repertoire of activities for students and the sciences, where students can be brought to reflect upon the application of science in non-positivist ways, drawing on indigenous knowledge systems, themes of sustainability and bioethics. Students can also be introduced to the history of scientific paradigms in a sociological sense so that they view scientific progress not as truth or givens but a socially constructed dialectic (Kuhn, 1962).

For students to understand the Other beyond otherness, they will have to learn about other people, unlearn the fatalism and stereotypes that lie behind such systems of representation and re-learn what it means to be another person. As Alvin Toffler said,

> the new education must teach the individual how to classify and reclassify information, how to evaluate its veracity, how to change categories when necessary, how to move from the concrete to the abstract and back, how to look at problems from a new direction — how to teach himself.
>
> *(Toffler, 1970, p. 367)*

References

Agence France-Presse. (2015). French mayor attacked for counting schoolchildren with 'Muslim names'. Online. Available at: www.theguardian.com/world/2015/may/05/french-mayor-attacked-for-counting-schoolchildren-with-muslim-names (accessed 26 April 2016).

Allport, G. (1954). *The nature of prejudice*. Cambridge, MA: Addison-Wesley.

Alpert, J. (1974). *MotherRight: A new feminist theory*. Pittsburgh, PA: Know Inc.

Althusser, L. (1971). *Lenin and philosophy and other essays*. (B. Brewster, Trans.). New York, NY: Monthly Review Press.

Angouri, J. (2010). 'If we know about culture it will be easier to work with one another': Developing skills for handling corporate meetings with multinational participation. *Language and Intercultural Communication*, 10(3), 206–224. doi: 10.1080/14708470903348549

Appiah, Kwame A. (2012). The case for contamination: Multiculturalism as the norm in contemporary Africa. In H. Lauer and K. Anyidoho (Eds), *Reclaiming the Human Sciences and Humanities Through African Perspectives*, Volume 2. Accra: Sub-Saharan Publishers.

Audit Commission (2002). *Special Educational Needs: A mainstream issue*. London: HMSO.

Ben-Yehuda, N. (1995). *The Masada myth: Collective memory and mythmaking in Israel*. Madison, WI: University of Wisconsin Press.

Berger, P., & Luckmann, T. (1966). *The social construction of reality*. Harmondsworth: Penguin.

Bhabha, H.K. (1990). The third space: Interview with Homi Bhabha. In J. Rutherford (Ed.), *Identity, community, culture, difference* (pp. 207–221). London: Lawrence and Wishart.

Blackburn, G.W. (1985). *Education in the Third Reich: A study of race and history in Nazi textbooks*. Albany, NY: State University of New York Press.

Black-Hawkins, K., Florian, L. & Rouse, M. (2007). *Achievement and inclusion in schools*. London: Routledge.

Bonilla-Silva, E. (2001). *White supremacy and racism in the post civil rights era*. Boulder, CO: Lynne Rienner.

Boorstin, D., & Kelley, B.M. (1990). *A history of the United States since 1861*. Needham, MA: Prentice Hall.

Brighouse, H. (2003). Should we teach patriotic history? In K. McDonough and W. Feinberg (Eds), *Education and citizenship in liberal-democratic societies* (pp. 157–175). Oxford: Oxford University Press.

Brown, G.W. (1958). *Building the Canadian nation* (revised ed.). Toronto: J.M. Dent.

Carr, L.G. (1997). *'Color-blind' racism*. Thousand Oaks, CA: Sage.

Chafe, J.W. & Lower, A.R.M. (1948). *Canada – a nation and how it came to be*. Toronto: Longmans, Green & Co.

Cole, B. (2005). Good faith and effort? Perspectives on educational inclusion. *Disability and Society*, 20(3), 331–344.

Connell, R.W. (1996). Teaching the boys: New research and gender strategies for schools. *Teachers College Record*, 98(2), 206–235.

Cooley, J. (2006). Desegregation and the achievement gap: Do diverse peers help? Unpublished manuscript, University of Wisconsin-Madison.

Craig, S. (Ed.) (1992). *Men, masculinity and the media*. Thousand Oaks, CA: Sage.

Danforth, S. (1995). Toward a critical theory approach to lives considered emotionally disturbed, *Behavioral Disorders*, 20, 136–143.

Darder, A., & Torres, R.D. (2004). *After race: Racism after multiculturalism*. New York, NY: NYU Press.

De Beauvoir, S. (1949). (1949) *Le Deuxième Sexe 1*. Paris: Gallimard.

Diamond, M. (2005). Sex and gender: same or different? In D. Inglis, J. Bone and R. Wilke (Eds), Critical concepts in the social sciences. Oxford: Routledge.

Domnitz, M. (1971). Prejudice in textbooks. *Patterns of Prejudice*, 5(3), 7–10.

Dunne, L. (2009). Discourses of inclusion: A critique. *Power and Education*, 1 (1), 42–56.

Ecolint. (2016). Online. Available at: www.ecolint.ch (accessed 27 April 2016).

Engberg, M.E. (2004). Improving intergroup relations in higher education: A critical examination of the influence of educational interventions on racial bias. *Review of Educational Research*, 74(4), 473–524.

Engberg, M.E. & Hurtado, S. (2011). Developing pluralistic skills and dispositions in college: Examining racial/ethnic group differences. *Journal of Higher Education*, 82(4), 416–443.

Epstein, T., & Gist, C. (2015). Teaching racial literacy in secondary humanities classrooms: Challenging adolescents' of color concepts of race and racism. *Race Ethnicity and Education*, 18(1), 40–60. doi: 10.1080/13613324.2013.792800

Fergus, E. (2009). Understanding Latino students' schooling experiences: The relevance of skin color among Mexican and Puerto Rican high school students. *Teachers College Record*, 111(2), 339–375.

Finkielkraut, A. (2015). *La seule exactitude*. Paris: Stock.

Foucault, M. (1963). *Naissance de la clinique. Une archeologie du regard medical.* Paris: Presses universités de France.

Funkenstein, A. (1989). Collective memory and historical consciousness. *History and Memory,* 7(1), 5–26.

Gardner, H. (2004). *Frames of mind: The theory of multiple intelligences* (Twentieth Anniversary Ed.). New York, NY: Basic Books.

Gebhard, P., & Johnson, A. (1979). *The Kinsey data: Marginal tabulations of the 1938–1963 interviews conducted by the Institute for Sex Research.* Bloomington, IN: Indiana University Press.

Geertz, C. (1973). *The interpretation of cultures.* New York, NY: Basic Books.

Gillespie, A. Howarth, C.S., & Cornish, F. (2012). Four problems for researchers using social categories. *Culture & Psychology,* 18, 391–402.

Glazzard, J. (2013). A critical interrogation of the contemporary discourses associated with inclusive education in England. *Journal of Research in Special Educational Needs,* 13(3), 182–188. doi: 10.1111/1471-3802.12018

Goodley, D. (2000). *Self-advocacy in the lives of people with learning difficulties.* Buckingham: Open University Press.

Guinier, L. (2004). From racial liberalism to racial literacy: Brown V. Board of Education and the interest-divergence dilemma. *Journal of American History* 91, 92–118.

Hall, S. (1996). Who needs identity? In S. Hall and P. du Gay (Eds), *Questions of Cultural Identity* (pp. 1–17). London: Sage.

Hannerz, U. (1990). Cosmopolitans and locals in world culture. In M. Featherstone (Ed.), *Global culture: Nationalism, globalisation and modernity* (pp. 237–251). London: Sage.

Hannerz, U. (1992). *Cultural complexity: Studies in the social organisation of meaning.* New York, NY: Columbia University Press.

Hodkinson, A. (2010). Inclusive and special education in the English educational system: Historical perspectives, recent developments and future challenges. *British Journal of Special Education,* 37(2), 61–67. doi: 10.1111/j.1467-8578.2010.00462.x

Hughes, C. (2009). International education and the International Baccalaureate Diploma Programme: A view from the perspective of postcolonial thought. *Journal of Research in International Education,* 8(2), 123–141.

Institute of Physics. (2013). Closing doors: Exploring gender and subject choice in schools. Online. Available at: www.iop.org/publications/iop/2013/closingdoors/ (accessed 26 April 2016).

JanMohamed, A. (1985). The economy of manichean allegory: The function of racial difference in colonialist literature. *Critical Inquiry,* 12, 59–87.

Jordan, E. (1995). Fighting boys and fantasy play: The construction of masculinity in the early years of school. *Gender and Education,* 7, 69–86.

Jung, C.G. (1964). *Man and his symbols.* New York, NY: Anchor Books, Doubleday.

Kammen, M. (1991). *Mystic chords of memory: The transformation of tradition in American culture.* New York, NY: Vintage Books.

Kesey, K. (1962/2005). *One flew over the cuckoo's nest.* London: Penguin.

Killgore, W.D.S. & Yurgelun-Todd, D.A. (2004). Sex related developmental differences in the lateralized activation of the prefrontal cortex and the amygdala during the perception of facial affect. *Perceptual and Motor Skills,* 99(2), 371–391.

Kimura, D. (2000). *Sex and cognition.* Cambridge MA: The MIT Press.

Kitzinger, C. (2001). Sexualities. In Rhoda K. Unger (Ed.), *Handbook of the psychology of women and gender* (pp. 272–285). New York, NY: Wiley.

Koedt, A, Levine, E. & Rapone, A. (Eds). (1973). Radical feminism. New York, NY: Quadrangle Books.

Kojève, A. (1980). *Introduction to the reading of Hegel*, Allan Bloom (Ed., J.H. Nichols Jr, Trans.). Ithaca, NY: Cornell University Press.

Koulouri, C. (2001). The tyranny of history. In C. Koulouri (Ed.), *Teaching the history of Southeastern Europe*. Thessaloniki: Center for Democracy and Reconciliation in Southeast Europe, Southeast European Joint History Project.

Kuhn, T. (1962). *The structure of scientific revolutions*. Chicago, IL: University of Chicago Press.

Kumashiro, K.K. (2004). *Against common sense: Teaching and learning toward social justice*. New York, NY: Routledge Falmer.

Kurtz-Costes, B., Rowley, S.J., Harris-Britt, A., & Woods, T.A. (2008). Gender stereotypes about mathematics and science and self-perceptions of ability in late childhood and early adolescence. *Merrill-Palmer Quarterly*, 54(3), 386–409.

Lacan, J. (1977). *Ecrits: A selection*. (A. Sheridan, Trans.). London: Tavistock.

Lee, E. (2015). Doing culture, doing race: everyday discourses of 'culture' and 'cultural difference' in the English as a second language classroom. *Journal of Multilingual and Multicultural Development*, 36(1), 80–93. doi: 10.1080/01434632.2014.892503

Lenroot, R.K., Gogtay, N., Greenstein, D.K., Wells, E.M., G.L., Wallace, G.L., Clasen, L.S., Blumenthal, J.D., Lerch, J., Zijdenbos, A.P., Evans, A.C., et al. (2007). Sexual dimorphism of brain developmental trajectories during childhood and adolescence. *Neuroimage*, 36(4), 1065–1073.

Levinas, E. (1947). *De l'existence à l'existant*. Paris: Vrin.

Levi-Strauss, C. (1979). *Myth and meaning*. New York, NY: Schocken.

Lewis, J.L., Neville, H.A., & Spanierman, L.B. (2012). Examining the influence of campus diversity experiences and color-blind racial ideology on students' social justice attitudes. *Journal of Student Affairs Research and Practice*, 49(2), 119–136.

Lloyd, C. (2008). Removing barriers to achievement: A strategy for inclusion or exclusion? *International Journal of Inclusive Education*, 12(2), 221–236.

Lunt, I., & Norwich, B. (1999). *Can effective schools be inclusive schools?* London: Institute of Education.

Makinwa-Adebusoye, P. (2001). Sociocultural factors affecting fertility in sub Saharan Africa. The Nigerian institute of social and economic research (NISER), Lagos.

Malinowski, B. (1922). *Argonauts of the Western Pacific*. New York, NY: E.P. Dutton.

Markus, H.R., & P.M.L. Moya. (Eds). (2010). *Doing race: 21 essays for the 21st century*. New York, NY: W.W. Norton and Company.

Marshall, C., & Oliva, M. (2010). Leadership for social justice: Making revolutions in education (2nd edn). Upper Saddle River, NJ: Pearson Education.

McGreal, C. (2007). Mbeki criticised for praising 'racist' Sarkozy. Online. Available at: www.theguardian.com/world/2007/aug/27/southafrica.france (accessed 26 April 2016).

Mittler, P. (2000). *Working towards inclusive education: Social contexts*. London: David Fulton.

Molloy, H., & Vasil, L. (2002). The social construction of Asperger Syndrome: The pathologising of difference? *Disability & Society*, 17(6), 659–669. doi: 10.1080/0968759 022000010434

Montgomery, K. (2006). Racialized hegemony and nationalist mythologies: Representations of war and peace in high school history textbooks, 1945–2005. *Journal of Peace Education*, 3(1), 19–37. doi: 10.1080/17400200500532094

Motha, S. (2006). Out of the Safety Zone. In A. Curtis and M. Romney (Eds), *Color, race, and English language teaching: Shades of meaning* (pp. 161–172). Mahwah, NJ: Lawrence Erlbaum Associates.

Niederle, M., & Vesterlund, L. (2007). Do women shy away from competition? Do men compete too much? *Quarterly Journal of Economics*, 122(3), 1067–1101.

Ofsted. (2000). *Evaluating educational inclusion: Guidance for inspectors and schools*. London: Ofsted.

Philippou, S. (2012). Official histories in Greek Cypriot geography and civics curricula. In Y. Papadakis and R. Bryant (Eds), *Cyprus and the politics of memory: History, community and conflict* (pp. 51–70). London: I.B. Tauris.

Pingel, F. (1999). *UNESCO guidebook on textbook research and textbook revision*. Hannover: Hahn/UNESCO/Georg Eckert Institute for International Textbook Research.

Pingel, F. (2000). *The European home: Representations of 21st century Europe in history textbooks*. Strasbourg: Council of Europe.

Pomerantz, E.M., Altermatt, E.R., & Saxon, J.L. (2002). Making the grade but feeling distressed: Gender differences in academic performance and internal distress. *Journal of Educational Psychology*, 94(2), 396.

Prendergast, S. (1996). Boys, bodies and pedagogy: Constructing emotions in school. Paper given at Gender, Body and Love Seminar, Centre for Women's research, University of Oslo.

RFI. (2010). Yade criticises Sarkozy's speech on Africa. Online. Available at: www.english.rfi.fr/france/20101029-yade-criticises-sarkozys-speech-africa (accessed 10 April 2016).

Sacerdote, B. (2001). Peer effects with random assignment: Results for Dartmouth roommates. *Quarterly Journal of Economics*, 116(2), 681–704.

Said, E. (1993). *Culture and imperialism*. New York, NY: Vintage Books.

Salinger, J.D. (1951/2010). *The catcher in the rye*. London: Penguin.

Samuel, H. (2014). French parents in panic over warning of lessons that 'boys can be girls'. The Telegraph. Online. Available at: www.telegraph.co.uk/news/worldnews/europe/france/10602928/French-parents-in-panic-over-warning-of-lessons-that-boys-can-be-girls.html. (accessed 16 April 2016).

Shin, L. (2015). The racial wealth gap: Why a typical white household has 16 times the wealth of a black one. Online. Available at: www.forbes.com/sites/laurashin/2015/03/26/the-racial-wealth-gap-why-a-typical-white-household-has-16-times-the-wealth-of-a-black-one/#1426bc9c6c5b (accessed 20 April 2016).

Silverschanz, P., Cortina, L.M., Konik, J., & Magley, V.J. (2007). Slurs, snubs, and queer jokes: Incidence and impact of heterosexist harassment in academia. *Sex Roles*, 58, 3–4, 179–191.

Skerrett, A. (2011). English teachers' racial literacy knowledge and practice. *Race Ethnicity and Education*, 14, 313–330.

Stewart, M.S. (1950). Prejudice in textbooks. Public Affairs pamphlet no. 160. New York: Public Affairs Committee.

Streitmatter, J. (2002). Perceptions of a single-sex class experience: Females and males see it differently. In A. Datnow and L. Hubbard (Eds), *Gender in policy and practice: Perspectives on single-sex and coeducational schooling* (pp. 212–226). London: Routledge.

Tatum, B.D. (1992). Talking about race, learning about racism: The application of racial identity development theory in the classroom. *Harvard Educational Review*, 62 (1), 1–24.

The Economist. (2015). Why politicians are asking the wrong questions about gender inequality. Online. Available at: www.economist.com/blogs/freeexchange/2015/11/women-workplace (accessed 21 April 2016).

The Telegraph. (2013). Francois Hollande to remove word 'race' from French constitution. Online. Available at: www.telegraph.co.uk/news/worldnews/francois-hollande/9843241/Francois-Hollande-to-remove-word-race-from-French-constitution.html (accessed 26 April 2016).

Thorne, B. (1992). Girls and boys together . . . but mostly apart: Gender arrangements in elementary schools. In J. Wrigley (Ed.), *Education and Gender Equality* (pp. 117–132). London: Falmer Press.

Toffler, A. (1970). *Future shock*. New York, NY: Random House.

Tulviste, T., Mizera, L., De Geer, B., & Tryggvason, M.T. (2010). Cultural, contextual, and gender differences in peer talk: A comparative study. *Scandinavian Journal of Psychology*, 51, 319–325.

UNESCO. (1951). Statement on race. Online. Available at: http://unesdoc.unesco.org/images/0017/001789/178908eb.pdf (accessed 25 April 2016).

UNESCO. (1982). Declaration on race and racial prejudice. 2.2. Online. Available at: www.unesco.org/education/information/nfsunesco/pdf/RACE_E.PDF (accessed 26 April 2016).

UNESCO (2006). UNESCO guidelines on intercultural education. Paris: UNESCO. Online. Available at: http://unesdoc.unesco.org/images/0014/001478/147878e.pdf (accessed 26 April 2016).

US Labor Force statistics. (2015). Online. Available at: www.bls.gov/cps/cpsaat39.htm (accessed 26 April 2016).

Van de gaer, E., Pustjens, E., Van Damme, E., & De Munter A. (2004). Effects of single-sex versus co-educational classes and schools on gender differences in progress in language and mathematics achievement. *British Journal of Sociology of Education*, 25, 307–322.

Walker, J.W.S.G. (1997). *Race, rights, and the law in the supreme court of Canada: Historical case studies*. Toronto, ON: The Osgoode Society for Canadian Legal History and Wilfred University Press.

Williams, M.J., & Eberhardt, J.L. (2008). Biological conceptions of race and the motivation to cross racial boundaries. *Journal of Personality and Social Psychology*, 94, 1033–1047.

Wood, J. (1984). Groping towards sexism: Boys' sex talk. In A. McRobbie and M. Nava (Eds), *Gender and generation* (pp. 54–84). London: Macmillan.

World Health Organization. (2014). Violence against women. Online. Available at: www.who.int/mediacentre/factsheets/fs239/en/ (accessed 26 April 2016).

3
CRITICAL THINKING AND PREJUDICE

Introduction

A strong element of prejudice is cognitive bias: the prejudiced person falls into a number of traps in thinking ranging from basic cognitive lacunae involving memory and perception to more complex errors in thinking such as overgeneralisation and subjective validation (this means seeing truths and connections where there may be none). However, critical thinking goes further than cognition alone: different theories point to a broad repertoire of attitudes, emotions and developmental patterns that can all be considered in the educational response to prejudice.

Few can debate the centrality of critical thinking in an education of quality: learners should be brought to appreciate situations with subtlety, intellectual honesty, rigour and the ability to question their own convictions. While critical thinking strategies in classrooms tend to be concentrated in stand-alone courses on critical thinking or attached to academic domains such as the humanities, my argument in this chapter is that critical thinking is a particularly useful tool to dismantle many of the elements of prejudice that are hidden to those who do not investigate claims, beliefs, perceptions and assumptions carefully. Therefore, critical thinking should be used in schools as a richly textured approach that not only sharpens the mind but dampens prejudicial thinking in numerous ways.

What is critical thinking?

Evaluative thinking and prejudice

Critical thinking is clearly one avenue to consider in the voyage to reduce prejudice, at least from a cognitive perspective. The word critical comes from the Greek 'kriticos' meaning 'judge'. Therefore, the root of critical thinking is embedded in the idea of judgement.

Traditionally, the notion has been that good judgement is closely related to reason or logical thinking:

> critical thinking is best seen as coextensive with rationality, and rationality is concerned with reasons. For a person to be rational, that person must (at least) grasp the relevance of various reasons for judgments and evaluate the weight of such reasons properly.
>
> *(Siegel, 1985, p. 72)*

> Education aimed at [. . .] critical thinking is [. . .] aimed at the fostering of rationality and the development of rational persons.
>
> *(Siegel, 1988, p. 32)*

Historical portrayal of the idea that judgement should be logical and freed from bias can be found in the icon of blind Justitia – the Roman goddess of justice whose eyes are covered from the vicissitudes and excesses of humanity that cloud judgement.

One might say that whereas prejudice is an a priori or pre-judgement, critical thinking involves a posteriori or reflective judgement. At the outset we can quickly see how critical thinking is, potentially, an antidote to prejudicial thinking.

Knowing how to judge situations and to do so well is essential for a number of reasons, one of them being autonomy: the good judge can think on his or her own feet and take executive decisions for him or herself, 'critical thinking thus liberates as it renders students self-sufficient' (Siegel, 1985, p. 72). This is relevant since much theory of prejudice development relates it to social psychology and the way humans think when in groups. Clearly, there must be some degree of independence of thought for the individual to form an opinion that is not driven by socially embedded and group pressured stereotypes.

Furthermore, critical thinking, unlike prejudiced thinking, involves reflection (Lipman, 2003) and discernment in the face of information overload (Halpern, 1997), both skills that extend thought beyond the narrow parameters of simplistic over-generalisation, particularly when it comes to detecting ideology, propaganda or prejudiced voice in media. Detecting bias in written or iconographic representations of ideas is a core skill that the critical thinker must develop to cut the wheat from the chaff and make informed opinions.

A somewhat nebulous term

Higgins, Miller and Moseley (2003) discuss the difficulty in defining critical thinking as it is a complex matter that cannot be easily extracted from interrelated concepts such as creative thinking, enquiry, reasoning, cognitive processes and self-engagement. Different definitions have been given by Siegel (1988), Facione (1990), Paul (1990, 1992, 2011), Ennis (1986), Halpern (1997, 1999, 2002, 2014), Anderson and Krathwohl (2001), Lipman (2003) and Moseley et al. (2004, 2005) to mention a few.

Halpern (1997) categorises critical thinking into cognitive skills that cover analysis, deduction and problem-solving with an emphasis on the importance of memory and the use of language. She extends the domain of critical thinking somewhat by including decision-making and creativity. One sees how these skills cover the interrelated domains of logical-mathematical intelligence, verbal intelligence and creative thinking with a clear central emphasis on reasoning.

Black (2008) defines critical thinking with an even stronger accent placed on rational processes including the analysis of arguments, claims, explanations and inferences; the ability to sift through information so as to bring out relevant facts and the formation of good arguments and decisions (p. 7).

Paul (1990), on the other hand, subdivides critical thinking into three dimensions: cognitive macro-abilities and cognitive micro-skills but also the affective domain. The former two elements involve typical examples of rational thinking such as 'refining generalizations and avoiding oversimplifications [. . .], clarifying and analysing the meanings of words or phrases, developing criteria for evaluation, generating or assessing solutions [and] analysing or evaluating actions or policies' for macro-abilities and 'making plausible inferences, predictions, or interpretations, giving reasons and evaluating evidence and alleged facts, recognizing contradictions, exploring implications and consequences' for micro-skills (p. 56).

Within the two areas of cognition, Paul extends purely rational thinking into less obvious areas such as 'the art of silent dialogue' and 'contrasting ideal with actual practice' (p. 56). However, it is in the affective dimension that he moves critical thinking away from reason into dispositions. This is explored later in the chapter.

The fact that definitions of critical thinking are plural and far-reaching suggests that responses to prejudiced thinking should be similarly broad in scope and sequence: there can be no one simple approach to the prejudiced mindset that serves as an antidote. This is partly because prejudice as a construct covers numerous domains (the social, cultural, cognitive and ethical, to mention just some). Therefore, an education for critical thinking so as to temper prejudicial thinking should cover the different elements of critical thinking.

However, just as prejudice can be considered a spectrum that ranges from generalisations that are substantiated, contain a kernel of truth and can be defended well, a type of sophisticated prejudice, all the way to emotionally charged sweeping stereotypes with little or no serious thought behind them – what we could call

Automatic processes	Low level prejudice Unsubstantiated Extreme over-generalisation	Sophisticated prejudice Kernel of truth Reasoned bias	Some nuance and discernment Ability to relativise Some level of objectivity	Suspended judgement Cognitive flexibility Discernment

FIGURE 3.1   The cognitive spectrum from prejudicial thinking to critical thinking

raw, low level prejudice – so too can critical thinking be looked at as a spectrum that ranges from a highly discerning, rigorous, cautious viewpoint to a fairly well substantiated, averagely argued and only partially logical position.

Whereas some element of critical thinking might contradict low level prejudice, it will take a high level of critical thinking to diffuse better argued prejudicial stances.

The implications of this continuum are that human thought needs to be pushed to higher levels of reflexivity for judgements to be increasingly reflective. We are not dealing with a sudden transition in thinking that will convert the prejudiced person into a critical thinker with one or two sweeping 'aha' moments the way a learner might achieve some sort of breakthrough and finally understand a scientific concept. This type of conversion might take place at an emotional, empathetic level through contact with other individuals or so-called life-changing experiences (travel, relationships, important events in one's life) but critical thinking is a long journey made up of small steps (Hawley, 1967, p. 277).

If we are to teach critical thinking, then the strategies employed will need to lead the learner out of a series of intuitive, unfounded responses to measured postulates and finally to wise, considered reflections. A key tool for doing this is questioning, hence the prominence of the Socratic dialogue as a method for developing critical thinking. I come back to this strategy later in the chapter.

Higher level critical thinking

In 1956, Benjamin Bloom placed evaluation (essentially judgement) at the top of his famous taxonomy of the cognitive domain. In other words, the capacity to make sound judgement was seen as the highest cognitive function. The taxonomy was reviewed in 2001 and 'creating' was allocated the highest level of the cognitive domain but evaluating was still put in second place and continued to be recognised as a high level of thinking.

The idea that sound judgement is an intellectually demanding enterprise was ratified between the 1950s and the 1980s when psychologists started to identify what is commonly known as the 'executive function' of the brain. Broadbent (1958) identified parts of the brain that were devoted to controlled thought (attention, focus) as opposed to automatic functioning (stimulus response). These notions were further developed by, amongst others, Shiffrin and Schneider (1977), Posner and Snyder (1975), Shallice (1988) and Baddeley (1986) to identify the pre-frontal cortex as a domain of the brain where executive functioning matures through developmental phases of maturation.

So judging is a neurologically and cognitively sophisticated human activity; that is, if it is to be done well by weighing up all the available criteria (from the Greek 'kriterion' meaning standard for judgement). Critical thinking is a higher-level cognitive enterprise.

Since a core aim of any good education is to ensure that students make sound judgements, 'learning to think critically is among the most desirable goals of formal schooling' (Abrami et al., 2009, p. 1102). However, this is not a straightforward or easy goal and suggests that educating for less prejudice is a cognitively challenging enterprise.

Our cognitive architecture's natural disposition to prejudice

Human beings are naturally disposed to prejudiced ways of thinking since they are not inclined to seek disconfirming information, complex multiple identities or exceptions to the rule. 'In everyday life, humans are cognitive misers, spending just enough energy to get the job done' (Dai & Sternberg, 2004, p. 27). Webster and Kruglanski have identified the 'desire for predictability, preference for order and structure, discomfort with ambiguity, decisiveness, and closed-mindedness' as fundamental drivers in thinking (1994, p. 1049). Thus, humans are quick to generalise laws about others so that they can be comforted with the unchallenging notion of predictability. For example, if one were to believe that all snakes were dangerous, it would follow simply to avoid snakes, an easy rule to adhere to, requiring no real thinking or any degree of cognitive conflict. Under this belief, one would simply walk the other way upon seeing a snake in the vein of automatic stimulus response. If, on the other hand, one were to admit that some snakes are dangerous and some are not, it would imply that not all snakes need be avoided and that some could be approached. This is an altogether different state of affairs that activates knowledge of the different types of snake, a tiresome enterprise requiring research and in-depth knowledge, either by learning all the known types of snake by heart or developing the awareness and skills to identify distinctive features of venomous or non-venomous snakes. Under this belief, a snake in the grass could be avoided or approached. Thus, as opposed to a stimulus–response automatism, one would need to evaluate the situation, analyse the snake in question by activating prior knowledge and applying theory and then make a decision: either to avoid the snake or not. In reality, while most people know that some snakes are dangerous and others are not, out of ignorance and to err on the side of safety but also on the side of the least cognitive demand possible, they simply avoid all snakes.

This is a metaphor for stereotype formation: it is a short cut in thinking that involves oversimplification and essentialism rather than careful deliberation, weighing up and informed, conscious decision-making. As such 'the real problem of intellectual education is the transformation of more or less casual curiosity and sporadic suggestions into attitudes of alert, cautious, and thorough inquiry' (Dewey, 1933, p. 181).

Dispositions

Dispositions can be explained in terms of dispositional theory, meaning that humans will only develop their thinking in so far as they are ready to follow the opportunities that allow for such an enterprise. Naturally, for reasons of economy, we are disposed to seek the easier, intuitive and most heuristic paths when seeking solutions. As such, for a person to develop critical thinking habits, he or she must be disposed to take the more difficult, counter-intuitive and cognitively challenging path. For more developed accounts of the dispositional account of thinking see Baron (1985), Dewey (1922), Ennis (1986), Facione et al. (1995), Perkins, Jay and Tishman (1993), Ritchhart (2002) and Stanovich (1999). The dispositional theory implies that educational structures must provide students with opportunities to develop their dispositions to be critical in their thinking.

A more recent expression of this idea can be found in the work of Carol Dweck (2006) who explains through her mindset theory that motivation lies at the heart of potential critical and mindful thinking, the individual embracing the 'growth mindset' being more disposed to evolve in a cognitively challenging climate.

Perkins and Ritchhart (2004) triangulate different approaches to thinking dispositions in a triad of sensitivity, inclination and ability, well represented in the following metaphor:

> [Imagine the] challenge of crossing the turbulent river. To do so by rowboat, you have to notice conditions that recommend a boat, including the boat itself, the state of the weather and such (sensitivity), decide to try the boat, rather than say walking three miles to the bridge (inclination), and be able to row the boat well enough to make it (ability).
>
> *(p. 359)*

The theory applies to prejudice clearly by suggesting that the critical thinker who disentangles prejudiced thoughts will be able to identify the contextual pressures that lead to a prejudiced viewpoint (sensitivity), be prepared to venture into disconfirming situations and explore Otherness so as to potentially contradict it (inclination) and, finally, possess and develop the cognitive flexibility necessary to deal with complexity, ambiguity, polyvalence and exception (ability). This implies that if schools wish to provide students with the dispositions to tackle prejudice then the approach should triangulate these elements.

Emotions

Another point to consider when discussing thinking is the role of emotions. Paul sees the mind as an expression of the interrelated issues of thinking, feeling and seeking. He sees emotion as a predicate of thinking: 'emotions, feelings, and passions of some kind or other underlie all human behavior' (Paul, 1990, p. 348).

Derryberry and Tucker (1994) suggest that, rather than emotions predicating thought, cognitive processes involve an interrelationship between various parts of the brain through which emotions play an important role: the frontal cortex (executive function and evaluation) interacts with limbic (emotion-arousing) and subcortical (regulatory) systems as the brain processes information into thought.

Other neurobiological approaches to the role of emotions on thinking include those of Allman et al. (2001), Posner and Peterson (1990) and Posner and Rothbart (1998), who identify the anterior cingulate cortex as responsible for self-regulation, controlling emotions and other processes often associated with the prefrontal cortex such as focus, adaptability and problem solving.

Without going into more detail, we can see that the relationship between thinking and emotions is salient and needs to be reflected upon when designing educational interventions to moderate or reduce prejudicial thinking. As such, learning experiences should not try to isolate cognitive functions from emotional drivers but rather embrace the two as inextricably linked. A history lesson on slavery, the holocaust or colonisation, for example, is more likely to become meaningful to the learner if the limbic system is aroused and some emotional connections can be made rather than approaching the subject matter in a dispassionate, dry and purely intellectual fashion. Without falling into melodrama and over-simplification, enemies of the true critical thinker, the teacher must find the delicate balance between thinking and feeling to ensure that meaning-making enterprises are developed and stored.

From logical thinking to wisdom

Critical thinking as a term is not only used to describe evaluative or judgemental thinking as some authors have situated it not only in the strictly cognitive domain but also as a series of attitudes and dispositions. The philosopher Richard Paul describes a series of affective dimensions as part of critical thinking. These include

> thinking independently, developing insight into egocentricity or sociocentricity, exercising fair-mindedness, exploring thoughts underlying feelings and feelings underlying thought, developing intellectual humility and suspending judgment, developing intellectual courage, developing intellectual good faith or integrity [and] developing intellectual perseverance.
>
> *(Paul, 1990, p. 56)*

Hence, one might associate with the highest levels of critical thinking ways of responding to the world that transcend logical thought and enter into the areas of wisdom and humility.

The idea that judgement relates to more than rational thought can be found in the biblical judgement of Solomon (1 Kings: 16–28) whereby the famous wise King tests two women's claim to be the true mothers of a child by suggesting that they cut the child in half, hereby unveiling the true motives of each claim. We see how judgement involves psychology, empathy, hypothetical causation and motivation and much more than pure reason.

Critical thinking in the service of prejudice

Artful, logical argument can be put to the services of a prejudiced mindset and is no guarantee in and of itself of a reduction in prejudicial thinking. Some of the more sophisticated, well-argued levels of prejudicial thinking that are published and endorsed publicly are demonstrated with fine-tuned logical postulation, substantiation and evidence. This shows that the narrow definition of critical thinking as logic is not enough to grapple with prejudice.

The rationalisation of strong antipathetic sentiments can be witnessed in recent examples of what are arguably xenophobic, sexist, homophobic, racist, anti-Semitic and/or Islamophobic discourses published by journalists and academics in France such as Eric Zemmour's *Le Suicide français* (2014) and, to a lesser extent, *L'identité malheureuse* (2013) and *La seule exactitude* (2015) by Alain Finkielkraut. Zemmour's and Finkielkraut's texts bemoan the decline of Western society, arguing that mass immigration has spoilt European culture and identity. Both authors also argue against same-sex marriage and feel that Islam represents a civilisational contradiction to Western values.

This form of academic discourse positions itself against political correctness and argues for intellectual freedom as a hallmark of critical thinking. Indeed, some would argue that the French satirical newspaper *Charlie Hebdo*, the victim of bombing and attacks in 2011 and shootings in 2015, was practising a high level of critical thinking through their provocative portrayals of Mohammed. This viewpoint is premised on the notion that critical thinking must involve enough intellectual freedom for ideas, beliefs and habits to be criticised openly. Similarly, Salman Rushdie's novel *The Satanic Verses* (1988), for which the author was placed under a Fatwah, or Theo Van Gogh's film *Submission* (2004), for which the producer was assassinated, can be considered polemical, provocative elements of critical thinking. This approach to critical thinking plays out some of its more affirmative and provocative elements such as critiquing text, questioning beliefs, intellectual courage and recognising contradictions (Paul, 1990, p. 56). This approach to critical thinking is in line with Karl Popper's idea of 'the open society [. . .], one in which men have learned to be to some extent critical of taboos' (Popper, 1945, p. 202) and the antithesis of the totalitarian, ideological state.

Critical thinking put to the services of prejudice was particularly blatant in some of the literature around the Second World War where more salient, openly anti-Semitic literature bestsellers logically demonstrated arguments against Judaism. These included *Bagatelles pour un massacre* (1937), *L'école des cadavres* (1938) and *Les Beaux Draps* (1941) by Louis Ferdinand Céline in France and Adoph Hitler's *Mein Kampf* (1925) in Germany, which by the end of the Second World War had sold over 10 million copies. One could argue that the essentialising of Jews in these tracts make them anything but examples of critical thinking but the point is that they all put forward logically constructed arguments and meet some of the criteria of basic logical thought in their exposition.

However, what is clearly missing in these literary productions is a sense of humanity or any shared societal legacy: arguments in the name of hate are missing the vital components of empathy and open-mindedness needed to create a balanced, emotionally intelligent view of the world. If we are to embrace a more wide-spread appreciation of critical thinking that tends towards wisdom more than mere logical criticism, with notions of suspending judgement, humility and cultural sensitivity at the centre, a quite different picture can be painted and the above-mentioned artistic productions can be cited as insensitive, unwise without careful analysis of potential social consequences. Critical thinking for less prejudice must involve some gauge of sensitivity with it and cannot be considered uniquely in the narrow sense of pure logical argument.

Educational strategies to enhance critical thinking for less prejudice

What do we know about the use of critical thinking strategies in the classroom to reduce prejudice?

At the most abstract level, by synthesising the work of Diane Halpern (1997, 2002, 2014), Matthew Lipman (2003) and King and Kitchener (1994), approaching the prejudiced mindset through critical thinking can happen at four fundamental levels: memory, analysis, evaluation and decision-making. These higher-order cognitive processes can be enhanced by the use of questioning (the Socratic method), argument and debate, stereotype disconfirmation and instances that evoke some realisation or understanding. Running through these processes and strategies is what Vygostsky called 'scaffolding', in other words, a series of cues designed to iteratively take the learner to successively higher levels of less prejudicial thinking. This can be considered against cognitive maturation of the individual in the vein of Piaget's theory of cognitive development and, more generally, genetic epistemology (whereby learners accommodate and assimilate new ideas through steps of equilibration) with more recent extrapolations on cognitive development by King and Kitchener (1994), Biggs and Collis (1982) and Perry (1970).

Levels			
Memory	Analysis	Evaluation	Decision-making
Strategies			
Questioning ──▶			
Debate ──▶			
Stereotype disconfirmation ──────────────────────────▶			
Understanding ───────────────────────────────────────▶			
Principles			
Scaffolding			
Cognitive development			

FIGURE 3.2 General principles for critical thinking strategies to reduce prejudice

Memory

Halpern (1997) situates within memory, a fundamental constituent of all cognition, core processes that are distinctly linked to prejudicial thinking such as 'developing an awareness of the influence of stereotypes and other beliefs on what we remember [and] developing an awareness of biases in memory' (from Moseley et al., 2005, p. 142).

So learning experiences that teach students to become aware of the fallibility of their memory is a metacognitive step to take to ensure a more cautious approach to information storage, allowing for more self-doubt and reserve in making strong claims about others. This can be done by exposing students to the alarming weakness of working memory by having them discuss and analyse various games that require high performing working memory (memory games such as Mastermind or Cluedo or certain card games such as Memory), or discussing research on memory such as Loftus's work on the misinformation effect (Weingardt et al., 1994), showing how people tend to reinvent the past in the light of more recent information.

A more detailed account of memory is discussed in Chapter 4 on metacognition.

Analysis

The word analysis comes from the Ancient Greek 'luein', meaning to loosen and 'ana' meaning up, so literally to loosen up. The etymology helps us understand the fundamental premise of analysis, which is to reflect on something and in doing so to open it up or examine it in more detail.

Analysis, as a higher order thinking process, clearly has a role to play in deconstructing prejudice as it involves paying attention to detail and not following assumptions without some degree of careful thought.

Halpern discusses under the banner of analysis 'thought and language skills', 'deductive reasoning skills' and 'argument analysis skills' and makes it clear that numerous elements of analytical thinking involve detecting and unravelling prejudicial thinking. These include 'recognising and defending against the use of emotional and misleading language [. . .], detecting misuse of definitions and reification [. . .], understanding the difference between opinion, reasoned judgment, and fact [and] recognising and avoiding common fallacies' (from Moseley et al., 2005, pp. 142–143).

Classroom learning experiences that stimulate analytical thinking must involve textual commentary, particularly of historical sources or information presented by mass media, analysis of propaganda and political speeches and/or discourses. Questions that incur analytical thinking include 'what if' hypothesis testing questions, questions seeking elaboration ('could you please explain that in more detail', 'what do you mean?') and questions pushing for substantiation ('could you give some examples to explain what you mean?').

Evaluation

As previously discussed, evaluation is at the heart of critical thinking and must, therefore, play a central role in critical thinking protocols. Students need to learn at once how to make valid evaluations of situations (and this can include making inferences, drawing conclusions, imagining consequences) and understanding what some of the main criteria for good judgement are – some of these are included above under what Halpern describes as analysis but could include understanding the context of a situation, thinking through the reasons why the people involved position themselves the way they do, knowing whether something is fair or unfair and being able to choose one position over another all things considered.

Ennis (1996) explains that in order to 'judge the basis for a decision', individuals should '1. judge the credibility of a source, 2. observe and judge observation reports' (Moseley et al., 2005, p. 153). One might add to this, in particular for the case of prejudice, 3. suspend hasty judgement and be prepared to carry a suspended judgement until more information is available and 4. ensure that you are not overgeneralising your judgement of an individual to an entire group.

Classroom strategies to enhance evaluational thinking would include selection tasks such as ranking exercises (see, for example, diamond ranking, Clark, 2012), debates, peer evaluation of work, student-written assessment criteria and assessed items asking students to judge the quality or pertinence of an idea or artwork.

Cues

Norris (2002) found that students responded well to critical thinking cues. In an experiment where students were given the *Ennis-Weir critical thinking essay test* (Ennis & Weir, 1985) but with clear prompts to ensure that students were reflecting critically as they made their way through the test (for example 'think of other explanations for the results' (p. 322)), he found that the treatment group scored over 60 per cent higher than the non-treatment group. This suggests that teachers should use cues to move students along to the next level of critical thinking as they make their way through tasks.

Teachers should ensure that the quality of students' critical thinking is carefully scaffolded with checkpoints and stimuli that are positioned at different conceptual thresholds and/or stages of cognitive development. Discussing these with students and using them actively in reporting will allow for recognisable progress through goal-setting.

Staged development

If we are to consider critical thinking as a response to prejudiced thinking, some idea of the way that ideas progress through cognitive maturation needs to be considered. In the various models of this idea, thinking increases in sophistication as it entertains notions of application, generalisability, multiplicity and relativism, moving from literal, absolutist views of the world to conceptual, abstract thinking.

Piaget's model of cognitive development

Piaget's theory of cognitive development has been criticised for underplaying social elements of learning (Vygotsky, 1986), focussing uniquely on logico-mathematical intelligence (Moseley et al., 2005, p. 193), assuming overarching structures of thought that have been shown by others to be domain (subject area) specific (Bidell & Fischer, 1992) and insisting on a fairly rigid series of steps as opposed to a continuum or modal fashion of learning. At the outset, therefore, one might argue that it is not a suitable model to apply to prejudice reduction.

However, his model is still the most influential representation of developmental patterns in human intelligence and allows for specific types of educational intervention to reduce prejudicial thinking at different levels of thought. Furthermore, researchers in prejudice such as Allport and Nesdale have borrowed Piaget's structure to analyse the way that prejudice might develop in individuals as they grow.

Piaget's milestone 1950 publication, *The Psychology of Intelligence*, drew up the model so familiar today:

- *sensorimotor stage (0 to 2 years)*: profound egocentrism, reality exists uniquely within the field of physical perception.
- *pre-operational stage (2 to 7 years)*: symbols and language become apparent to the young learner.
- *concrete operational stage (7 to 11 years)*: decentration, ability to entertain abstract thought in the absence of physical markers, learner begins to tolerate complex ideas such as reversibility. Physical manipulation of objects is needed to formulate thoughts well.
- *formal operational thought (11 onwards)*: not necessarily mastered by all, including adults, an ability to reason in purely abstract, internal ways.

If we are to turn to prejudice, the implications of Piagetian theory are that the processes needed to deal with the higher order thinking elicited by prejudice deconstruction become apparent at the concrete operational stage. This is essentially because complex notions such as reciprocation, multiple identities, relativity and (accurate) generalisability are needed to activate stereotype disconfirmation and acceptance of ambiguity.

Nesdale (2004), one of the most prominent authors of the developmental patterns of ethnic prejudice in children, outlines four basic developmental levels that resonate clearly with Piaget's stages of cognitive development:

- *Phase 1 (0 to 2/3 years) – undifferentiated*: here the child can differentiate colours but does not differentiate human beings by ethnicity.
- *Phase 2 (2/3 to 6/7) – ethnic awareness*: children start to accommodate ethnic categories into their lexical and perceptual repertoire. An important part of this phase is ethnic self-identification.
- *Phase 3 (6/7 to 11/12) – ethnic preference*: the child learns and understands that (s)he is part of a particular ethnic group. This tends to lead to an ingroup bias

but does not necessarily entail an outgroup dislike. Nesdale points out that social group preference is far more salient for gender than ethnicity at this stage.

- *Phase 4 (11/12 onwards) – ethnic prejudice*: here children shift the positive ingroup sentiments that have been kindled in phase 3 towards antipathy and negative stereotyping for a given outgroup.

In sum, Nesdale uses Piaget's levels of cognitive development to chart the growth of prejudice. In a sense, therefore, he maintains Piaget's categories but contradicts the spirit of cognitive development in them by suggesting that the natural inclination is to go from an unprejudiced to a prejudiced mindset whereas Piaget's model suggests a steady decrease in prejudicial thinking (see, for example, his work with Weil on developmental approaches to reciprocity (Piaget & Weil, 1951)).

Other researchers such as Aboud (1988) are more in line with traditional Piagetian thought and suggest a decline in prejudiced thinking as cognition matures.

King and Kitchener (1994), summarising more than 30 different studies and working off Dewey's notions of reflective thought (1933, 1938) and Piaget's theory of genetic epistemology, propose a seven-stage model that was originally intended for college level students but could be used in schools. The steps take learners from pre-reflective to reflective thought in successive steps that can be used to assess and monitor progress.

TABLE 3.1 King and Kitchener's seven-stage model of reflective judgement (1994)

Stage 1	Knowledge is extremely limited and consists essentially of literal belief in unchecked observations.	Pre-reflective thought
Stage 2	The knower discovers right and wrong and categorises information systematically in this simplistic binary system.	
Stage 3	Knowledge begins to become more subtle – it is understood that 'in some areas, knowledge is certain and authorities have knowledge. In other areas, knowledge is temporarily uncertain; only personal beliefs can be known' (Moseley et al., 2005, p. 232).	
Stage 4	The knower realises that knowledge in general is not always certain but nonetheless struggles to differentiate knowledge and justification.	Quasi-reflective thought
Stage 5	Knowledge is still limited to the perspective of the knower but there is some realisation that it is defined by context, as is justification.	
Stage 6	Still holding on to the thought that knowledge is uncertain, the knower realises that it is constructed to a large extent by evidence and opinion and that these elements are not absolute or stable but vary across contexts.	Reflective thought
Stage 7	Knowledge, while being provisional, is constructed by reason and inquiry – an idea that can be generalised across contexts and domains.	

TABLE 3.2 Applying King and Kitchener's (1994) staged model to prejudice reduction

Stage	Description	Implications for prejudice reduction	Level
Stage 1	Knowledge is extremely limited and consists essentially of literal belief in unchecked observations.	Over-generalisations created from narrow base of empirical evidence	Pre-reflective thought
Stage 2	The knower discovers right and wrong and categorises information systematically in this simplistic binary system.	Grouping of individuals into camps based on over-generalisations.	
Stage 3	Knowledge begins to become more subtle – it is understood that 'in some areas, knowledge is certain and authorities have knowledge. In other areas, knowledge is temporarily uncertain; only personal beliefs can be known' (Moseley et al., 2005, p. 232).	Some exceptions admitted, partial acceptance of the idea that some individuals might belong to more than one camp.	
Stage 4	The knower realises that knowledge in general is not always certain but nonetheless struggles to differentiate knowledge and justification.	Admission of the tentative nature of grouping and the real possibility of individuals not belonging too rigidly to certain groups. Fairly frequent questioning of labelling but still persists in the belief that humans can be grouped socially in absolute terms.	Quasi-reflective thought
Stage 5	Knowledge is still limited to the perspective of the knower but there is some realisation that it is defined by context, as is justification.	Understanding that grouping is contingent on context and that individuals can be seen through different lenses accordingly and hence grouped differently.	
Stage 6	Still holding on to the thought that knowledge is uncertain, the knower realises that it is constructed to a large extent by evidence and opinion and that these elements are not absolute or stable but vary across contexts.	Significant deconstruction of the ideas of social categories altogether and the need for rigorous evidence before committing to labelling into generalised camps.	Reflective thought
Stage 7	Knowledge, while being provisional, is constructed by reason and inquiry – an idea that can be generalised across contexts and domains.	The notion of social categories is deconstructed and understood as a convention that stands on flimsy premises. Consistent challenging of labelling, desire to see each individual on the merits of character and not physical or social identity.	

King and Kitchener's (1994) model lends itself naturally to prejudice reduction as it maps well on the idea that reflection is needed to undo initial, hasty generalisations that may be prejudiced. Table 3.2 shows how this might be done in a school environment.

King and Kitchener's (1994) model resembles Perry's (1970) developmental scheme in that it maps the development of thought from single observations and essentialism to pluralistic, relativist postulates. The implications for education against prejudice are that educators should aim to take learners up the various stages of cognitive ability that allow for increasing tolerance of relativism.

Research conducted by Guthrie, King and Palmer (2011) using a sample of 48 university students in American colleges found, by using the reflective judgement model, that there was an inverse correlation between levels of intellect and levels of prejudice. They identified stage 4 of the reflective judgement model as the turning point where, on the one hand, participants started to search for stronger and more diverse forms of evidence to warrant their claims and on the other, they started to grapple with information at a more abstract, conceptual level.

Another taxonomy of reflective or critical thinking that can be used in the classroom to assess and monitor levels of critical thinking is Biggs and Collis's SOLO taxonomy (Structured Observation of Learning Outcomes) (Biggs & Collis, 1982). For Biggs and Collis, increasingly complex levels of thinking can be tracked on a continuum that goes from simplistic, 'unistructural' thoughts whereby single pieces of information are identified and taken at face value with little thinking behind the relationships the items may or may not have, to 'multistructural' (where two or more pieces of information are understood), then 'relational' thinking where pieces of information are structured in a coherent structure and finally 'extended abstract' thinking whereby items are considered in a large, conceptual framework and successful generalisations are made. In the SOLO taxonomy, on the way from unistructural to extended abstract thinking, learners improve the complexity of their thinking by engaging in increasingly dynamic and polyvalent categorisations (see Hattie & Brown, 2004).

The implications of this taxonomy for prejudiced thinking are somewhat different from those associated with King and Kitchener and Perry. The SOLO taxonomy allows educators checkpoints to consider as they evaluate thinking towards rather than away from generalisation. Indeed, it is not because prejudice is an overgeneralisation that the notion of generalisation should be seen as intellectually poor; on the contrary, it stands at one of the highest levels of conceptual understanding. To generalise is to apply laws, make connections, see associations and categorise members of groups, and it lies very much at the core of logical thinking as Aristotle's famous core categorical syllogism ('all men are mortal, Socrates is a man, therefore Socrates is mortal').

The critical thinker will not be afraid to make generalisations about people but, if following a logical suite that is valid, will do so in a justified, moderate and accurate manner. For example, to say 'my neighbour is a woman, she listens to loud music, therefore all women listen to loud music' is a poorly configured generalisation and could be considered a prejudiced over-generalisation. On the other hand, to say 'my neighbour is a woman, she listens to loud music, therefore some women listen to loud music' would be more tempered.

Perry's developmental scheme

Perry (1970) developed a checklist of educational views that he used through a series of interviews with nearly 500 university students (Moseley et al., 2004, p. 200) to chart levels of thinking. Perry was especially interested in learners' responses to relativism and pluralism, working off the premise that increasingly sophisticated levels of thinking would involve development from simplistic dualism to various levels of multiplicity and interrelations and finally to self-awareness and commitment to some cause or project. Perry's framework spans the cognitive and affective domains whilst taking motivation and sense of purpose into account.

His qualitative research showed that learners follow a clear sequence of development as they grow in their tolerance of multiplicity and understanding of personal agency. This sequenced development is mapped in a chart detailing nine positions: 'strict dualism [...]; dualism with multiplicity perceived [...]; early multiplicity [...]; late multiplicity [...]; relational knowing [...]; anticipation of commitment [...]; initial commitment [...]; multiple commitments [and] resolve' (Perry, 1970, pp. 10–11). As learners develop their thinking and move up the different positions, they grow out of pure thinking and understanding into action. The taxonomy is interesting because it adds a praxis to critical thinking, insisting that it is not merely a passive act of critiquing or describing but a dispositional way of reacting to and acting within the world.

The nine positions can be applied to prejudiced thinking since the prejudiced mindset tends to struggle with the concept of multiplicity on the one hand and how to respond effectively and coherently to social networks and/or social causes on the other. Perry's developmental stages allow educators to monitor and advance thinking about others in increments, taking learners from essentialism to heterogeneity and finally positive action in successive steps. Table 3.3 suggests how Perry's work might be adapted to combat prejudice.

Perry's nine stages were originally conceived for students in American liberal arts colleges and one might wonder on the extent of their generalisability to other domains such as prejudice. Indeed, Zhang found that Perry's stages did not apply fluidly to students in China (Zhang, 1999) although, on the other hand, Finster found that they applied well to students studying chemistry and technology (Finster, 1989, 1991).

Despite the identification of these thinking taxonomies and the implications for classroom practice that will elicit higher order thinking, critical thinking and thinking that moves away from prejudice, studies have shown that most classroom questioning and classroom talk tends to gravitate around lower-order declarative knowledge (Gall, 1984; Torrance & Pryor, 1998; Wade & Moje, 2000).

TABLE 3.3 Perry's (1970) chart of development applied to prejudiced thinking

Perry's position	Main cognitive elements	Application to prejudiced thinking	Classroom strategies
1	Absolutism, dualism, over-simplified representation	Essentialism, adherence to stereotypes and prejudicial thinking	Identifying the stereotypes and prejudices that students hold
2	Recognition but caution of multiplicity	Recognition but caution of disconfirmation (counter-examples)	Providing counter-examples
3	Partial acceptance of multiplicity	More acceptance of the role and veracity of counter-examples	Discussing and exploring counter-examples
4	Simplistic relativism	Surface-level breakthrough: acceptance that the prejudiced belief might be inaccurate	Allowing students articulation and reflection on their breakthrough
5	Deeper relativism, appreciation of interrelations	Identification of features unifying humanity and deconstructing difference	Learning about conceptual frameworks that transcend differences, further deconstructing divisive prejudicial ideas
6	Dawning of the notion of commitment	Feeling of personal implication in areas of social justice	Moving from identifying parts of thought as prejudice to feeling responsible for addressing areas of prejudice
7	Initial commitment	Acting on social injustice related to prejudice (such as discrimination)	Making available projects in which students can engage (community service)
8	Exploration of commitment and responsibility	Reflecting on action taken to address some form of social injustice related to prejudice (such as discrimination)	Scaffolding reflection on project-based action
9	Affirmation of identity among multiple responsibilities	Discourse and/or discursive production	Student production (research, artistic, portfolio) showing stance on values and identity in the light of learning experience

Implications of staged development models for educational practice

Educators can either refer to a particular model and consider educational strategies that are appropriate or reflect upon similarities between models and design educational experiences that are aligned with the general spirit of developmental theory.

The models discussed tend to share these core elements:

1   An initial phase that involves low levels of differentiation, nuance or weighed up criteria for categorisation. This first phase of pre-social categorisation corresponds to young ages (Piaget's sensorimotor) or baseline cognitive abilities. Educational strategies to reduce prejudice at this cognitive level are perhaps not particularly worthwhile or realistic. As this is very much the stage of discovery and initiation, educators should be careful not to plunge learners into scenarios that are either too essentialised or complex. Some simple ground rules to enhance a climate of tolerance, such as those evoked in Chapter 2, Understanding beyond the Other, would be helpful here, such as:

    a   Respecting one another in the playground.
    b   Encouraging mixed play environments to stimulate basic principles of heterogeneity.

2   An early stage of differentiation that is essentialised, simplistically dichotomous with a tendency to overgeneralise. This second stage, similar to Piaget's pre-operational, is when learners will be tempted to make judgements quickly by cutting corners and not bothering with elaborating criteria for evaluative positions or decisions. This need to judge quickly and easily is natural and part of the human mind's search to lessen cognitive load. At this stage, educational strategies should focus on guiding students through categorisations, ensuring that the students are making those categorisations themselves but ensuring that this is done in an appropriately evaluative manner, discussing criteria for categories and entertaining notions of sub-groups and shared group members. Some examples of how this can be done include:

    a   Basic work on set theory (categorical syllogisms).
    b   As part of set theory, using Venn diagrams to illustrate different types of categories and how they might intersect.
    c   Discussion groups on similarities and differences between people that explore – at an appropriate level – core identifying features and accidental or non-essential differentiating features – of gender, ethnicity, age and culture. The purpose of this should be to guide learners towards conclusions that are less systematically 'all Xs are Ys' to postulates such as 'some Xs are Ys'.

3   A more considered set of social categories begins to anchor in the student as (s)he becomes aware of societal labels erected by media, family, culture and language. Generalisations are less crude and tend to be based on empirical evidence that is still, however, often overgeneralised. This corresponds roughly to Piaget's concrete operational phase of development where the maturation of the cognitive architecture is such that general principles can be established but only through the manipulation of real-life, concrete elements. As such, learners in this phase of development are at a fairly literal level of social categorisation

('every X I have met has been a Y, therefore all Xs are Ys' or 'my teacher/the news/scientists/a documentary says that Xs are Ys') and need to be guided towards a more abstract approach to making knowledge claims. Educational strategies to develop more nuanced thinking at this stage of cognition include:

a   Discussion groups that allow students to share their personal, socially related experiences and draw conclusions from them. If groups are structured in a balanced, diverse manner, this should allow for fruitful interaction, gentle disagreement and reconsideration. Teachers should be careful to scaffold these discussions subtly.

b   Reflection on facts drawn out of humanities, particularly in subjects such as history, economics and geography where stereotype formation can grow easily if not tempered by some healthy scepticism and deliberate analysis.

c   Media analysis with a strong emphasis on audience manipulation, persuasion by argument, statistics and image, vested interests, emotive language and iconography and how the media loads on stereotypes. Students should analyse texts and images in the classroom on a regular basis and be awarded for the degree of critical thinking they are able to evoke in this analysis.

d   Some work on the idea of social categories being human constructs that are not entirely immutable. This can be done through the reading of carefully selected literature and the arts (see Chapter 2).

e   Some work towards the understanding that mathematical axioms are not pure, natural, Platonic truths but system-enabling mechanisms or givens that must be erected for consequent operations to work. Similarly, a movement towards the idea that science is not simply a series of 'whats' and 'hows' with laws that represent truth but more a socially constructed community of individuals that erects, through peer-reviewed research, certain arguments above others, that what we call scientific evidence is a socially valued argument connecting data (that are not stable or error-free) and theory. This is to steadily unpack unbridled, absolutist beliefs in knowledge and to move towards relativism.

4   An abstract or theoretical level of critical thinking that allows students to make valid generalisations, temper hasty judgements, evaluate various criteria for or against categorisation, and to do so in the absence of immediate empirical data but rather on principle and through deductive critical thinking. At this stage of thinking, as we see in Perry's model, the student is also moving to action and feels directly concerned by the way that society has categorised individuals. In other words, at this final, most sophisticated stage of critical thinking for less prejudice, the student has moved away from a merely theoretical approach to social categorisation ('some Xs are Ys') to applied knowledge involving empathy whereby he or she is ready to be engaged in social justice ('Xs in this community are being treated badly because of a prejudiced belief and I want to

do something about it'). This last stage, like Piaget's formal operational level of thinking, is a glass ceiling and can extend to high levels of thinking and being. Educational interventions that can enhance good thinking and action at this stage include:

a   Lessons in psychology on the nature of generalisations and how they are erected cognitively and socially, therefore an understanding of the mind's predisposition to prejudice but at a high level of analysis.
b   Drawn-out, challenging debates/discussions/conferences on the construct of social identity, politics and global affairs with opportunities for interaction and sharing of ideas, opinions and positions.
c   Community service projects that allow for action.
d   Pure logic (truth tables).
e   Interdisciplinary and comparative studies that allow for synthesis and comparison across historical movements and social phenomena.

Ultimately, these four generic levels of critical thinking lead towards metacognitive thought. This is because the most salient way of combatting prejudice at the individual level is through a constant effort at self-regulation, self-knowledge and healthy self-doubt. The next chapter deals with the question of metacognition in detail.

Conclusion

The literature on critical thinking has been translated into numerous educational programmes that are well known and mediatised. Amongst these are:

*   Philosophy for Children (Lipman, 2003): a programme that involves students discussing texts as a community of inquirers whereby they can choose topics that are of interest to them and express themselves freely so as to develop competencies in three core areas (critical thinking, caring thinking and creative thinking). The main idea behind this programme that has its roots in Deweyan notions of the democratic classroom is to ensure that students are engaging in genuinely philosophical discussions as opposed to studying philosophers but not necessarily thinking for themselves. Philosophy for Children has gained success in numerous universities and schools in the UK, USA and Australia.
*   Instrumental Enrichment (Feuerstein, 1980). With an emphasis on learners with special needs, this programme 'uses abstract, content free, organisational, spatial, temporal and perceptual exercises that involve a wide range of mental operations and thought processes' (Begab, 1980, p. xv). There are over 80 Instrumental Enrichment training programmes in 26 countries across the globe (Feuerstein Academy, 2016).
*   The Cognitive Acceleration through Science Education (CASE) programme (Adey, Shayer & Yates, 1989), with an emphasis on learning scientific concepts scaffold with carefully posited questions from a minimally invasive teacher.

This approach has currency in many schools as does the ACTS project (Activating Children's Thinking Skills) for upper primary level (McGuinness et al., 1997), which has influenced the curriculum in Northern Ireland.

More examples could be given but the point to be made is that these approaches tend to focus on cognitive acceleration in general with an emphasis on academic or philosophical issues, most often with a focus on scientific thinking. In general, science tends to play a prominent role in research and theory of cognition, perhaps because as an epistemic domain it is more straightforward to operationalise than critical thinking in the humanities and arts. If schools are to use the tenets of critical thinking to tackle prejudice, then a programme with some focus on social psychology would be useful so that students are constantly brought back to the predilection humans have for bias, over-generalisation, hasty conclusions, lazy thinking, loose associations, unsubstantiated evaluation and stereotype or prejudice confirming thought patterns. At the centre of these fallibilities in thinking is the question of working memory power and the temptation to take short cuts so as to lessen cognitive load. Examples of these could be evoked across all disciplines to allow students to make connections and build up a broad representation of the nature of human psychology as they learn.

What this chapter has shown us is that critical thinking is hard and critical thinking used in the service of thinking for less prejudice is even harder because it pushes the thinker beyond logic to wisdom, decision-making, empathy and metacognition. Schools are faced with a challenge to create learning environments that push students to rise to high levels of thinking if prejudicial thinking is to be deconstructed and reduced.

Despite the implications of critical thinking for prejudice reduction and the numerous strategies available to activate critical thinking in the classroom, experimental work (Levy 1999, Levy et al. 2004) and a handful of field experiments run on North American students (Katz & Zalk, 1978; Katz, 2000) on cognitive training suggest weak effects (Levy Paluck & Green, 2009, p. 356).

This is no doubt related to the general dearth of strong evidence for strategies to reduce prejudice other than the heavily-researched contact hypothesis and remains, therefore, a generic problem very much linked to the difficulty of operationalising prejudice or simulating experimental conditions that allow researchers to measure its presence, development or reduction. However, this should not stop schools from seeing critical thinking as a central avenue leading to prejudice reduction since the unavoidable elements of reflective thought needed to quell prejudice figure prominently in this educational design.

References

Aboud, F.E. (1988). *Children and prejudice*. Oxford: Basil Blackwell.

Abrami, P.C., Bernard, R.M., Borokhovski, E., Wade, A., Surkes, M.A., Tamim, R., & Zhang, D. (2009). Instructional interventions affecting critical thinking skills and dispositions: A stage 1 meta-analysis. *Review of Educational Research*, 78(4), 1102–1134.

Adey, P.S., Shayer, M., & Yates, C. (1989). *Thinking science: Student and teachers' materials for the CASE intervention*. London: Nelson.

Allman, J.M., Hakeem, A., Erwin, J.M., Nimchinsky, E., & Hop, P. (2001). The anterior cingulate cortex: The evolution of an interface between emotion and cognition. In A.R. Damasio, A. Harrington, J. Kagan, B.S. McEwen, H. Moss, & R. Shaikh (Eds), *Unity of knowledge: The convergence of natural and human science* (pp. 107–117). New York, NY: New York Academy of Sciences.

Anderson, L. W, & Krathwohl, D.R. (2001). *A taxonomy for learning, teaching and assessing: A revision of Bloom's taxonomy of educational objectives*. New York, NY: Longman.

Baddeley, A.D. (1986). *Working memory*. Oxford: Clarendon Press.

Baron, J. (1985). *Rationality and intelligence*. New York, NY: Cambridge University Press.

Begab, M.J. (1980). Foreword. In R. Feuerstein, Y. Rand, M. Hoffman and R. Miller (Eds), *Instrumental enrichment: An intervention for cognitive modifiability* (p. xv). Baltimore, MD: University Park Press.

Bidell, T.R., & Fischer, K.W. (1992). Beyond the stage debate: Action, structure and variability in Piagetian theory and research. In R.J. Sternberg and C.A. Berg. (Eds), *Intellectual Development* (pp. 100–140). Cambridge: Cambridge University Press.

Biggs, J.B., & Collis, K.F. (1982). *Evaluating the quality of learning: The SOLO taxonomy (structure of the observed learning outcome)*. New York, NY: Academic Press.

Black, B. (2008). *Critical thinking: A definition and taxonomy for Cambridge Assessment*. Paper presented at 34th International Association of Educational Assessment Annual Conference, Cambridge.

Broadbent, D.E. (1958). *Perception and communication*. Oxford: Oxford University Press.

Céline, L.F. (1937). *Bagatelles pour un massacre*. Paris: Denoel.

Céline, L.F. (1938). *L'école des cadavres*. Paris: Denoel.

Céline, L.F. (1941). *Les beaux draps*. Paris: Denoel.

Clark, J. (2012). Using diamond ranking as visual cues to engage young people in the research process, *Qualitative Research Journal*, 12(2), 222–237.

Dai, D.Y., & Sternberg, R.J. (Eds). (2004). *Motivation, emotion, and cognition: Integrative perspectives on intellectual functioning and development*. Mahwah NJ: Lawrence Erlbaum Associates.

Derryberry, D., & Tucker, D.M. (1994). Motivating the focus of attention. In P.M. Niedenthal and S. Kitayama (Eds.), The heart's eye: Emotional influences in perception and attention (pp. 167–196). San Diego, CA: Academic Press.

Dewey, J. (1922). *Human nature and conduct*. New York, NY: Holt.

Dewey, J. (1933). *How we think: A restatement of the relation of reflective thinking to the educative process*. Boston, MA: D.C. Heath and Company.

Dewey, J. (1938). *Experience as education*. New York, NY: Collier Books.

Dweck, C.S. (2006). *Mindset: The new psychology of success*. New York, NY: Random House.

Ennis, R.H. (1986). A taxonomy of critical thinking dispositions and abilities. In J.B. Baron and R.S. Sternberg (Eds), *Teaching thinking skills: Theory and practice* (pp. 9–26). New York, NY: Freeman.

Ennis, R.H. (1996). *Critical thinking*. Upper Saddle River, NJ: Prentice-Hall.

Ennis, R.H., & Weir, E. (1985). *The Ennis-Weir critical thinking essay test*. Online. Available at: http://faculty.education.illinois.edu/rhennis/tewctet/Ennis-Weir_Merged.pdf (accessed 12 April 2016).

Facione, P.A. (1990). *Critical thinking: A statement of expert consensus for purposes of educational assessment and instruction. Executive summary, The Delphi Report*. Millbrae, CA: California Academic Press.

Facione, P.A., Sanchez, C.A., Facione, N.C., & Gainen, J. (1995). The disposition toward critical thinking. *Journal of General Education*, 44(1), 1–25.

Feuerstein, R. (1980). *Instrumental enrichment: An intervention program for cognitive modifiability.* Baltimore, MD: University Park Press.

Feuerstein Academy. (2016). Online. Available at: http://acd.icelp.info/training-centers.aspx (accessed 28 April 2016).

Finkielkraut, A. (2013). *L'identité malheureuse.* Paris: Stock.

Finkielkraut, A. (2015). *La seule exactitude.* Paris: Stock.

Finster, D. (1989). Developmental instruction part 1: Perry's model of intellectual development. *Journal of Chemical Education*, 66, 659–661.

Finster, D. (1991). Developmental instruction part 2: Application of the Perry model to general chemistry. *Journal of Chemical Education*, 68, 752–756.

Gall, M. (1984). Synthesis of research on teachers' questioning. *Educational Leadership*, 42, 40–46.

Guthrie, V.L., King, P.M., & Palmer, C.J. (2011). Higher education and reducing prejudice: Research on cognitive capabilities underlying tolerance. Online. Available at: www.diversityweb.org/digest/sp.sm00/tolerance.html (accessed 28 April 2016).

Halpern, D. (1997). *Critical thinking across the curriculum: A brief edition of thought and knowledge.* Mahwah, NJ: Lawrence Erlbaum Associates.

Halpern, D. (1999). Teaching for critical thinking: Helping college students develop the skills and dispositions of a critical thinker. *New Directions for Teaching and Learning*, 80 (Winter), 69–74.

Halpern, D. (2002). *Thinking critically about critical thinking.* Mahwah, NJ: Lawrence Erlbaum Associates.

Halpern, D. (2014). *Thought and knowledge: An introduction to critical thinking* (5th edn). New York, NY: Psychology Press.

Hattie, J.A.C., & Brown, G.T.L. (2004). *Cognitive processes in asTTle: The SOLO taxonomy.* AsTTle Technical Report #43, University of Auckland/Ministry of Education.

Hawley, W.E. (1967). Programmed instruction. In R.L. Craig and L.R. Bittel (Eds), *Training and development handbook* (pp. 225–250). New York, NY: McGraw Hill.

Higgins, S., Miller, J., & Moseley, D. (2003). Taxonomies. *Teaching Thinking.* Online. Available at: www.teachthinking.com (accessed 28 April 2016).

Hitler, H. (1925). *Mein kampf.* Germany: Franz Eher Nachfolger.

Katz, P., & Zalk, S.R. (1978). Modification of children's racial attitudes. *Developmental Psychology*, 145, 447–461.

Katz, P. (2000). Research summary. *Intergroup relations among youth: Summary of a research workshop.* New York: Carnegie Corp.

King, P.M., & Kitchener, K.S. (1994). *Developing reflective judgment: Understanding and promoting intellectual growth and critical thinking in adolescents and adults.* San Francisco, CA: Jossey-Bass.

Levy, S.R. (1999). Reducing prejudice: Lessons from social-cognitive factors underlying perceiver differences in prejudice. *Journal of Social Issues*, 55, 745–765.

Levy, S.R., West, T. L, Ramirez, L.F., & Pachankis, J.E. (2004). Racial and ethnic prejudice among children. In J. Chin (Ed.), *The psychology of prejudice and discrimination: Racism in America* (Vol. 1) (pp. 37–60). Westport, CT: Praeger.

Levy Paluck, E., & Green, D.P. (2009). Prejudice reduction: What works? A review and assessment of research and practice. *Annual Review of Psychology*, 60, 339–367. doi: 10.1146/annurev.psych.60.110707.163607

Lipman, M. (2003). *Thinking in education* (2nd edn). Cambridge: Cambridge University Press.

McGuinness, C., Curry, C., Greer, B., Daly, P., & Salters, M. (1997). Final Report on the ACTS project: Phase 2. Belfast: Northern Ireland CCEA.

Moseley, D., Baumfield, V., Elliott, J., Gregson, M., Higgins, S., Miller, J., & Newton, D. (2005). *Frameworks for thinking: A handbook for teaching and learning.* Cambridge: Cambridge University Press.

Moseley, D., Baumfield, V., Higgins, S., Lin, M., Miller, J., Newton, D., [. . .] Gregson, M. (2004). *Thinking skill frameworks for post-16 learners: an evaluation. Learning and Skills Research Centre.* Wiltshire: Cromwell Press.

Nesdale, D. (2004). Social identity processes and children's ethnic prejudice. In M. Bennett and F. Sani (Eds), *The development of the social self* (pp. 219–246). Hove: Psychology Press.

Norris, S.P. (2002). The meaning of critical thinking test performance: The effects of abilities and dispositions on scores. In D. Fasco Jr. (Ed.), *Critical thinking: Current research, theory, and practice* (pp. 315–330). Cresskill, NJ: Hampton Press.

Paul, R. (1990). *Critical thinking: What every person needs to survive in a rapidly changing world.* Santa Rosa, CA: Foundation for Critical Thinking.

Paul, R. (1992). Critical thinking: What, why and how? *New Directions for Community Colleges,* 20(1), 3–24.

Paul, R. (2011). Reflections on the nature of critical thinking, its history, politics, and barriers and on its status across the college/university curriculum. Part I. Inquiry: Critical Thinking Across the Disciplines, 26(3), 5–24.

Perkins, D.N., Jay, E., & Tishman, S. (1993). Beyond abilities: A dispositional theory of thinking. *The Merrill-Palmer Quarterly,* 39(1), 1–21.

Perkins, D.N., & Ritchhart, R. (2004). When is good thinking? In D.Y. Dai and R.J. Sternberg (Eds), *Motivation, emotion, and cognition: Integrative perspectives on intellectual functioning and development* (pp. 351–384). Mahwah, NJ: Erlbaum.

Perry, W.G., Jr. (1970). *Forms of intellectual and ethical development in the college years: A scheme.* New York, NY: Rinehart and Winston.

Piaget, J. (1950/2001). *The psychology of intelligence.* London and New York: Routledge.

Piaget, J., & Weil, A.M. (1951). The development in children of the idea of the homeland and of relations to other countries. *International Social Science Journal,* 3, 561–578.

Popper, K. (1945). *The open society and its enemies.* London: Routledge.

Posner, M.I., & Peterson, S.E. (1990). The attention system of the human brain. *Annual Review of Neuroscience,* 13, 25–42.

Posner, M.I., & Rothbart, M.K. (1998). Attention, self regulation and consciousness. *Philosophical Transactions of the Royal Society of London B,* 353, 1915–1927.

Posner, M.I., & Snyder, C.R.R. (1975). Attention and cognitive control. In R.L. Solso (Ed.), *Information processing and cognition: The Loyola symposium.* Hillsdale, NJ: Lawrence Erlbaum Associates.

Ritchhart, R. (2002). *Intellectual character: What it is, why it matters, and how to get it.* San Francisco, CA: Jossey-Bass.

Rushdie, S. (1988). *The Satanic verses.* London: Viking.

Shallice, T. (1988). *From neuropsychology to mental structure.* Cambridge: Cambridge University Press.

Shiffrin, R.M., & Schneider, W. (1977). Controlled and automatic human information processing: II: Perceptual learning, automatic attending, and a general theory. *Psychological Review,* 84(2), 127–190. doi: 10.1037/0033-295X.84.2.127

Siegel, H. (1985). Educating reason: Critical thinking, informal logic, and the philosophy of education. Part two: Philosophical questions underlying education for critical thinking. *Informal Logic,* 7, 2–3.

Siegel, H. (1988). *Educating reason.* New York, NY: Routledge.

Stanovich, K.E. (1999). *Who is rational? Studies of individual differences in reasoning.* Mahwah, NJ: Lawrence Erlbaum Associates.

Torrance, H., & Pryor, J. (1998). *Investigating formative assessment: Teaching, learning and assessment in the classroom.* Philadelphia, PA: Open University Press.

Van Gogh, T. (2004). [Film]. *Submission.* Netherlands. VPRO.

Vygotsky, L.S. (1986). *Thought and language* (A. Kozulin, Trans. and Ed.). Cambridge, MA: MIT Press.

Wade, S.E., & Moje, E.B. (2000). The role of text in classroom learning. In M.L. Kamil, P.B. Mosenthal, P.D. Pearson and R. Barr. (Eds), *Handbook of reading research* (Vol. III) (pp. 609–627). Mahwah, NJ: Lawrence Erlbaum Associates.

Webster, D.M., & Kruglanski, A.W. (1994). Individual differences in need for cognitive closure. *Journal of Personality and Social Psychology*, 67(6), 1049–1062.

Weingardt, K.R., Toland, H.K., & Loftus, E.F. (1994). Reports of suggested memories: Do people truly believe them? In D. Ross, J.D. Read and M.P. Toglia (Eds), *Adult eyewitness testimony: Current trends and developments* (pp. 3–26). New York, NY: Springer-Verlag.

Zemmour, E. (2014). *Le Suicide français*. Paris: Albin Michel.

Zhang, L.F. (1999). A comparison of U.S. and Chinese university students' cognitive development: The cross-cultural applicability of Perry's theory. *The Journal of Psychology*, 133(4), 425–439.

4

METACOGNITION AS A STRATEGY FOR RECOGNISING AND CONTROLLING PREJUDICE

Introduction

If critical thinking is an important step for the individual to take to reduce prejudicial thinking, then the next step, a consummation of critical thinking and meaningful application of its constituents, is metacognition. This chapter discusses metacognition by defining what it is, how it relates to critical thinking, what its relevance for prejudice reduction is and, finally, how educators can design learning experiences to ensure that metacognitive learning is activated towards the reduction of prejudice.

What is metacognition?

The prefix 'meta' means 'after' or 'beyond' in Ancient Greek, coined famously by Aristotle (2004) in his *Metaphysics*, a book that he composed after (hence 'meta') his work entitled the *Physics*. However, 'meta' has come to be associated not so much with something that happens after a phenomenon but more at a higher level, describing the structural fundaments and essential properties of the thing in question. Hence, when we speak of a metalanguage, we mean a technical language that describes everyday language.

The term metacognition was coined by Flavell in 1976:

> Metacognition refers to one's knowledge concerning one's own cognitive processes and products or anything related to them. . . . For example, I am engaging in metacognition (metamemory, metalearning, metaattention, metalanguage, or whatever) if I notice that I am having more trouble learning A than B; if it strikes me that I should double-check C before accepting it as a fact . . . if I sense that I had better make a note of D because I may

forget it. . . . Metacognition refers, among other things, to the active monitoring and consequent regulation and orchestration of these processes . . .
usually in the service of some concrete goal or objective.

(Flavell, 1976, p. 232)

Hence metacognition involves two movements: on the one hand it is thinking about
thinking, more precisely knowing how to describe one's own thinking processes,
and on the other hand it involves acting on thinking: self-regulation or knowing
how to self-correct thinking processes. The latter can only happen if the former is
in place – in other words, one cannot self-regulate and correct cognitive strategies
if one does not have a mental representation of how one learns in the first place.

More recent definitions (Demetriou, 2000; Zimmerman, 2000) have not
changed much since Flavell although there have been inroads into the area of
metacognition to give more granularity to the concept. Frith, for instance, has dis-
tinguished between explicit, deliberate and more implicit, automatic forms of self-
regulation (Frith, 2012, p. 2214) to show how implicit, automatic metacognition
tends to be heavily biased and egocentric (p. 2215). This suggests that a conscious
effort needs to be made if one is to consider not only how one learns and knows,
but how others might view the world.

There has been much debate as to whether metacognition should be situated
within cognition – as part of critical thinking – and whether the two movements
entitled in metacognition described above (self-knowledge and self-regulation) can
be dissociated (for more discussion see Zeidner, Boekaerts and Pintrich (2000),
Ashman and Conway (1997) and/or Zimmerman (2000). For the purposes of
this chapter, metacognition will be considered as distinct from critical thinking
because the emphasis is on self-knowledge and the capacity to act on thinking
strategies, both vital for prejudice reduction and entirely worthy of separate, dedicated discussion.

The importance of metacognition for effective learning has been pointed out by
numerous studies going back to the 1970s (for example, Chase & Simon, 1973; Chi,
Glaser & Rees, 1982; Chi & Koeske, 1983; Glaser, 1992). Upon studying the way
that different learners go about organising information, researchers have identified
patterns that lead us to believe that some approaches are more efficient and productive than others. In essence, the process of learning can be divided into techniques
that are termed novice or expert (Pellegrino, Chudowsky & Glaser, 2001).

Novice learners will not have any particular strategy to learn and will make
their way through new information intuitively, through trial and error, with more
or less success as they deal with isolated facts with no experience of any repertoire
from which to draw examples. Critically, novice learners will struggle to organise
information into schemata (conceptual frameworks) and will therefore spend much
more psychic energy as they try to learn seemingly dissociated elements one by
one rather than connected parts of a system. Information will therefore be encoded
and retrieved with some difficulty, placing increasing cognitive load on working
memory. Expert learners, on the other hand, have developed mental schemata that

allow for rapid, fluent information encoding and retrieval (see Hatano, 1990 and Pellegrino et al., 2001, p. 73).

Therefore, educational practice should lead students to strategies that allow for fluent, expert-type information encoding and retrieval. These involve

> knowing when to apply a procedure or rule, predicting the correctness or outcomes of an action, planning ahead, and efficiently apportioning cognitive resources and time. This capability for self-regulation and self-instruction enables advanced learners to profit a great deal from work and practice by themselves and in group efforts.
>
> *(Pellegrino et al., p. 78)*

The implications of expert learner strategies for problem solving are that they tend to be linked to a domain and are not generic, subjectless skills: examples of expert practice tend to come from specialists in well-defined fields that incorporate a set of epistemic approaches (physicists, chess players, musicians, athletes). It is for this reason that many researchers suggest that generic courses in critical thinking are less effective than critical thinking assessments embedded in specific domains (for more discussion on this, see NRC, 1999).

Furthermore, evidence has been drawn up to suggest that metacognitive skilfulness, as opposed to lower-order natural maturation, develops over the time spent at school (Karmiloff-Smith, 1979) and that it can be taught at school.

When it comes to greater metacognitive fluency to deal with issues related to prejudice (strategies to deal with over-generalisation, hasty conclusions, unwarranted judgement of others, bias, refusal to encode disconfirming information, strong emotional responses to social situations, feelings of threat and insecurity, rigidity and a compulsion to hold on to beliefs about other people), educational practice should aim to empower students so that they can embed instruction well into meaningful units of understanding (schemata) while nonetheless retaining some level of flexibility, open-mindedness and a sense of relativity. The goal is to educate students to become expert learners in the field of social psychology so that they understand the dynamics of prejudice well and can act upon their own inclinations with meaningful strategies.

These skills can be taught through traditional subjects (for example, making students aware of overgeneralising in mathematics, in science, in the humanities or teaching students to detect bias in history etc) with the aim to equip students with the skills and knowledge to generalise what has been learnt and apply it to real-life situations, or through a course with a focus entirely dedicated to the construction of others such as social psychology, cultural studies, sociology or ethnology.

Relevance for prejudice reduction

If prejudice is to be reduced then the learner must find ways of standing outside of his/her own thinking to realise how thinking itself happens so as to self-regulate.

This must involve a deeper reflective process than mere suppression justification (where suppressed prejudice incubates and then manifests itself in a less polemical or socially judged arena).

Whatever the approach, it is clear that if individuals are to temper prejudicial thoughts when they arise in the mind, they will need a repertoire of concepts to identify, understand and act on their own thinking. To recognise prejudice within oneself, a high level of self-awareness is needed with particularly acute knowledge of cognitive architecture and the dynamics of information processing. 'Self-regulation involves cognitive, motivational, affective and behavioural components that enable individuals to adjust their actions and/or their goals in order to achieve desired results in changing environmental circumstances' (Moseley et al., 2005, p. 14).

There are numerous parallels to be drawn between the design of prejudice reduction and the enterprise of metacognition. First, metacognitively fluent problem solvers will be open to try different strategies if any one does not work whereas novice learners will push their thinking more emphatically into a single strategic approach even after it has failed (Pellegrino et al., 2001, p. 78).

A parallel can be drawn here as a prejudiced mindset will tend to hold on to a belief about a group rigidly and show reluctance to change position, even in the light of disconfirming evidence (Stephan, 1989). To illustrate, we might imagine someone trying to understand how the great pyramid was built. A metacognitive thinker would systematically run through different options (pulleys, hydraulic pressure, gradients, scaffolding) and not merely settle on one hypothesis and insist on that no matter what disconfirmation was produced. Similarly, if someone were exposed to displeasing behaviour by a member of a group and was a poor metacognitive thinker, he or she would generalise quickly and attribute the behaviour to all members of the group and reject any disconfirmation whereas a metacognitive thinker would seek various explanations for the behaviour in question (individual temperament, provocation, situation, context, point of view, etc).

Therefore, educational strategies that encourage cognitive flexibility and the willingness to approach knowledge issues from different perspectives will equip learners with the means to consider people and groups from more than one single, entrenched position, hereby opening less monomaniac and more heterogeneous, less prejudice-prone paths of judgement and decision-making.

Second, metacognition involves the ability to stand back from oneself so to speak and evaluate one's own thinking and progress: the metacognitively apt learner will have some understanding of the way that he or she thinks and solves problems and, if operating at a high level of metacognition, will be able to continually reflect on the way that he or she thinks, recognising and evaluating thinking strategies. When considering prejudice, the individual working towards a reduction in prejudicial thinking should be cognisant of the way that he or she approaches situations and should be able to evaluate the extent to which his or her assumptions are prejudiced or not.

To give an example of this parallel, an expert mathematics learner will be able to analyse his/her performance on an assessment by judging the accuracy and relevance of his/her working ('here I was trying to solve the problem through arithmetic rules and struggled to find the correct response whereas here I was working at a more elegant level by designing an equation and could thus check my answers easily and therefore came up with the correct answer more effectively). Similarly, if we turn to social interactions that might incur a prejudiced response, someone operating at face value might say 'I saw an X and wanted to get away because I don't like Xs' whereas a metacognitive thinker might say 'I saw X and wanted to get away because I don't like Xs but this was a prejudiced reaction on my part and I should have exercised more open-mindedness. I think that the reason why I responded that way was because . . .'.

An important element of metacognition is motivation. When dealing with prejudice, individuals need to go further than merely think about situations or understand the underpinnings of logical constructions as they do so, they need to employ a certain desire to overcome emotionally driven and socially influenced temptations, look inwards and formulate opinions that are sound. As such, metacognition implies a more active part of critical thinking that leads to decision-making. Metacognition is more than the passive activity of judging information, ranking phenomena or arguments, it involves emotional self-regulation.

In Pintrich's model of self-regulated learning (2000), much emphasis is placed on motivation as a part of metacognition: part of the enterprise of knowing oneself as a learner is understanding the role of motivation in the learning process and believing in one's ability to tackle and solve a problem (Bandura, 1997). A significant difference between the enterprise to reduce prejudice and mastering a more traditional, academic domain such as a subject (mathematics/sciences, languages, etc) is the question of motivation since there are extrinsic pressures on learners to learn subjects and perform well on assessments but there is no real impetus to reduce one's prejudice other than the importance placed on such a design by society or an institution. This therefore leaves schools with the supplementary challenge of raising student motivation to wrestle with prejudice without this necessarily being recognised as a socially important objective.

The desire to improve one's thinking is also a question of patience as it has been argued that arriving at the most elegant problem-solving techniques is by no means a straightforward process but one that requires time and a certain necessary amount of trial and error. Kaiser, Proffitt, and McCloskey (1985) have shown that children go through a number of stages of thinking before they cross the bridge from erroneous to efficient and productive problem-solving. Fay and Klahr (1996) suggest that this involves learners employing strategies that are partially correct or only operate in a specific context as they make their way to better thinking. In order to correct the mistakes in thinking strategies, practice and time are needed.

Time and practice are also needed before young learners are able to see how one strategy can be transferred to a different type of problem. Siegler's study of transfer (1998) has shown how practice not only allows children to get better at generalising problem-solving strategies but that it leads to them developing new, untaught strategies.

This implies that teachers should be willing to let students approach problems not only in different ways but over an extended series of applications. This is to ensure that enough time is being put aside for problem-solving strategies to crystallise in the learner's mind.

In a similar vein, if educational systems are to support students as they discover ways of reducing prejudice and disentangle stereotypes and over-generalisations, effort and patience must be put into the process so that students are able to go back over their experiences reiteratively as they begin to employ a balanced approach to others and become metacognitively aware of this. There can be no quick-fix solution to reducing prejudice, most especially if this is to be anchored in deep understanding of system, concept and process – the metacognitively reflective approach to prejudice is a drawn-out process and educational scaffolding must take this into account.

Know thyself

For students to undo some of their prejudiced thoughts, they need to be aware of them in the first place. Some experiments requiring participants to reflect consciously on instances of their own prejudiced thinking have yielded results. For example, Son Hing, Lee and Zanna (2002) found a positive correlation between participants' implicit association test scores on prejudice to Asians and feelings of guilt over memories of prejudiced behaviours towards those groups.

> Whereas high-prejudice persons are likely to have personal beliefs that overlap substantially with the cultural stereotype, low-prejudice persons have decided that the stereotype is an inappropriate basis for behavior or evaluation and experience a conflict between the automatically activated stereotype and their personal beliefs. (Devine, 1989).

Suppression-justification

However, becoming aware of one's prejudices or stereotypic beliefs is an extremely complex affair since few are happy to admit such thinking patterns in their own profiles. Crandall and Eshleman (2003) have shown how many stereotypes are not socially acceptable (racist, sexist or homophobic stereotypes in particular) and therefore lead subjects to suppress their prejudiced inclinations. This in turn leads to one of three possible scenarios: either a type of systematic prejudice-suppression or self-imposed thought control (see Yzerbyt & Demoulin, 2010) or, more complex, a need to expiate the frustration caused by such externally forced self-suppression through other, more socially accepted forms of prejudice, for example, generalisations or hate speech against child abusers (see Dovidio & Mullen, 1992; Esses, Dietz & Bhardwaj, 2006; Norton, Vandello & Darley, 2004). To give an example of this phenomenon, we might imagine someone harbouring strong anti-Semitic feelings realising that such a position is not socially acceptable and therefore suppressing these sentiments, becoming overwhelmed at the frustration of keeping these views quiet and consequently erupting into excessive judgement of less polemical targets of prejudice such as drug addicts or criminals. This form of suppression-justification is, in effect, a form of prejudice that hides another. This reminds us of the difficulty of attempting to measure prejudice since its manifestations will often either be hidden or redirected.

Suppressing prejudiced feelings is not a metacognitive solution, however, as it implies a type of politically correct thought control that is disingenuous and unsustainable. The aim of a deep educational response to prejudice is not merely to lead to systematic inhibition or occulting but for individuals to have the cognitive strategies at their disposal to make sufficiently reflective judgements and to endorse their thoughts and beliefs fully.

In order to deconstruct prejudicial thinking deeply, it must be approached at a structural, metacognitive level that allows the thinker to identify decision making, trait association, prediction of human behaviour and human categorisation in an abstract, metacognitive manner. This is important because on the one hand it allows a generalisable, conceptual framework that enhances understanding of prejudice at a profound level (as opposed to a superficial level dealing with effects rather than causes) and, on the other hand, means that individuals make judgements about other people with some degree of hindsight, self-criticism and awareness of their own perspective.

In a detailed discussion of the role of metacognitive reasoning in stereotype and prejudice formation, Yzerbyt and Demoulin (2010) point to entity (Lickel et al., 2000; Hamilton, 2007) versus incremental (Chiu, Hong & Dweck, 1997; Dweck, Hong & Chiu, 1993) theories of personality traits as playing a fundamental role:

> Whereas entity theorists believe that personal attributes are fixed, incremental theorists are convinced that traits are malleable. Several studies found that entity theorists make stronger trait inferences from behavior and use traits or trait-relevant information to make stronger future behavioural predictions than incrementalists. [. . .] People's implicit theories about the fixedness versus malleability of human attributes predict differences in social stereotyping.
>
> *(Yzerbyt & Demoulin, 2010, p. 248)*

The idea is similar to Dweck's (2006) model of growth versus fixed mindsets, which suggest that more prejudiced ways of thinking tend to be rigid and essentialist whereas a more open-minded disposition that accepts challenge, change and risk will be more likely to undo or relativize prejudiced thinking.

Educational strategies that allow students to look back at their own thinking and identify elements of incremetalist or entitative processes will be dealing with the root cognitive causes of stereotype formation rather than the surface, symptoms and manifestations. This suggests educating students to use a repertoire of concepts and terms that will allow them to critique their own thinking and identify their own styles of thinking and assumption-making tendencies.

Houghton (2010) conducted a 9-month long action research project with 36 Japanese university students in which they were guided through various steps to not only better understand the nature of stereotypes but to reflect on them in written and oral tasks, designing questionnaires to administer to 'a foreigner about their values' (p. 187).The main idea behind this qualitative research methodology was for participants to build up an understanding of stereotypes iteratively through different pathways (written composition, reading of theory, questionnaire design, interview) and to come back to their own stereotypic formations constantly throughout the process.

Houghton concludes by pointing out the centrality of 'the awareness of one's own cognitive processes and the ability to take conscious control of one's own cognitive tendencies in the process of understanding stereotypes' (p. 194). Much of this is done through comparing and contrasting mental representations with reality and hereby gaining metacognitive awareness of the relationship between the two.

This leaves education with the challenge of designing learning experiences that will lead students to reflect on the way that categorising tendencies in thinking quickly lead to stereotypes. Students should be aware of stereotype formation in order to master and relativise it when it takes place in their own thinking.

Metacognition and feelings of prejudice against the self

Up until now, this book has focused on prejudice as a way of thinking about other groups or individuals. However, an important part of the universe of prejudice is how one perceives oneself and to what extent one believes that a prejudiced view is being used to define and categorise oneself. Indeed, one of the more pernicious effects of prejudice is self-denigration, lack of confidence and even self-hatred that can be caused by 'buying in' to prejudiced beliefs and either believing that they exist (when they might not or in any case might exist to a lesser degree than what is believed) or, at a more radical level, turning them against oneself.

To break this down into two workable concepts, I will turn to research on stereotypes: on the one hand, there is what are known as 'meta-stereotypes', namely stereotypes about stereotypes or more clearly, a generalisation about a view others purportedly have about the self ('All Xs think that I'm Y just because I'm a Z.This is because all Xs think that Zs are Ys'). Meta-stereotypes can lead to feelings of paranoia and victimisation. On the other hand, there is what is called 'stereotype threat', meaning the perception that one is being viewed or assessed in a stereotypical manner and acting accordingly, usually with heightened anxiety and sensitivity and, consequently, less efficacy.

Investigating various facets of this complex psychological interplay suggests educational pathways to take so as to bring the victims and/or perceived victims of prejudice to a higher level of metacognitive awareness and therefore, intellectual freedom. A metacognitive approach (in other words, an approach that makes the phenomena of meta-stereotypes and stereotype threat salient and, further, allows the individual strategies to act on this knowledge) can lead to a more mindful, focused and emotionally satisfying approach.

Meta-stereotypes

Sigelman and Tuch (1997) introduced this term to describe people's beliefs about outgroup members' stereotypes concerning their ingroup. If students are to engage with prejudice at a sophisticated level, some understanding of how individuals and groups relate to prejudice against themselves is necessary.

Although one might assume identical stereotype representations when perceived by ingroup members of themselves and in relation to outgroups (for example, 'I'm an X, I believe that Xs are Ys, therefore people outside my group also believe that Xs are Ys'), in reality this is rarely the case. Coherent with Social Identity Theory (Tajfel & Turner, 1979) and studies by Cuddy, Fiske and Glick (2008) and van den Bos and Stapel (2009), more negative valence is attributed to outgroup members than ingroup members. This leads to contradictions whereby ingroup members will be less prone to endorse stereotypes supposedly held by an outgroup about their own ingroup when these are negative but will be more prone to accept them if they are positive. So the relationship between meta-stereotypes and stereotypes is not a linear or positive one.

Furthermore, as shown by Frey and Tropp (2006), there is a general tendency to assume that stereotypes of ingroups from the outside (or outgroups) are systematically negative. Judd et al. (2005) have synthesised numerous studies that show how individuals tend to exaggerate prejudiced generalisations about themselves when generated by outgroups. There is, perhaps, something of a tendency for the victims of prejudice to assume a maximum amount of prejudiced thinking about them when in reality the phenomenon may be more dispersed and fragmented than one would assume. Lammers, Gordijn and Otten (2008) have shown how low-status minority groups tend to perceive negative stereotypes against them to a greater degree than other groups do.

Meta-stereotyping can lead to more polarisation, avoidance, less communications and a taller, sturdier wall of division between groups. On the other hand, it can also lead to 'impression management strategies' (Yzerbyt & Demoulin, 2010, p. 259) whereby members of groups (Yzerbyt & Demoulin discuss racial groups to elucidate the theory), when in the company of members of another group, will act up to assumed stereotypes by seeking to disconfirm them in the way they behave: they 'spontaneously frame the interaction in terms of how they are perceived by outgroup members' (Vorauer et al., 2000, p. 691).

Educational strategies aimed at reducing prejudice need to lead students away from the assumptions they have about outgroups' prejudices of themselves as these may or may not be true and are worthy of the same critical investigation and evidence-based argumentation as direct acts or utterances of prejudice.

At a metacognitive level, therefore, prejudice should be viewed as a dynamic phenomenon involving two parties whereby assumptions are made on either side of the interaction: prejudice is by no means a simple one-way street with a prejudiced person on one end and a victim of prejudice on the other. One powerful metaphor to unpack the complex interplay involved in the act of perception and how this can affect prejudice is Lacan's (1955) 'Schema L' (Lacan, 1977) to represent imaginary and unconscious relations. Lacan's schema describes just how complex human interaction is. While intuitively we might think that one person perceives another in a relatively straightforward manner, the schema suggests that perception is actually made up of multiple components. The real self ('Me' with a capital 'M') and his/her interlocutor (the 'Other' with a capital 'O') have an unconscious relation that is primarily out of awareness, driven by impulses, desires or fears. While this 'real' relation is subconscious, people communicate through an imaginary relation whereby the ego (or 'me' with a small 'm') responds not to a real Other but to the imaginary other in his or her world view (an 'other' with a small 'o'). This imaginary relationship takes place through a communication line that is in awareness and is made up of language, stereotypes and cultural norms. In other words, two people never communicate directly but always through the representations they have of one another in their minds.

A metacognitive analysis of prejudice and stereotypes should involve some understanding that each individual in a conversation or interaction holds on to stereotypic and possibly prejudiced representations of one another that may or may not be true and that this interactive set-up takes place against more oblique, sub-conscious modes of interaction. This also means that humans can be prejudiced in subconscious and conscious ways.

In order to accept this complex representation of human interaction, the student must be willing to tolerate high levels of ambiguity, paradox, uncertainty and double meaning.

Stereotype threat as an inhibitor to performance

Studies by Steele and Aronson (1995), Marx (2011) and Schmader et al. (2008) – to mention a few – have shown how individuals can perform below par if they feel threatened by stereotypes. Furthermore, research has shown that individuals tend to avoid admitting to stereotypic behaviours when operating in pressurised environments. For example, Steele and Aronson have reported that when blacks are involved in intelligence testing scenarios, and therefore feel subjected to a certain amount of pressure and scrutiny, they tend to report less openly on stereotypic behaviours involving sports and music. Similarly, Pronin, Steele and Ross (2004) have shown that when women are majoring in traditionally male-dominated high-stakes subjects such as science and maths, they report dressing in less obviously feminine ways.

A number of neuroscientific experiments have confirmed that minority groups will react particularly, usually with heightened sensitivity and anxiety, when under the belief that they are being assessed on stereotype-related phenomena (Forbes, Schmader & Allen, 2008; Gehring et al., 1993; Hajcak, McDonald & Simons, 2003). It is important to note that this usually occurs subconsciously.

Therefore, part of the mission of an education for less prejudice is to empower students to free themselves of the performance inhibiting affects caused by anxiety so that they can become more metacognitively aware of them and develop strategies to counter such underperformance.

Interestingly, increasing effort in the face of stereotype threat does not necessarily increase performance, especially when tasks are subtle and cognitively demanding.

Jamieson and Harkins (2007) conducted research on women involved in an antisaccade task (meaning that they were meant to detract their vision from a distractor on a computer screen). They found that when the women were told that the test was a measure of visuospatial and mathematical ability, results were lower than when they were not told. However, the tendency to autocorrect after an initial distraction was higher in the treatment group. This suggests that stereotype threat creates an anxiety that impedes on performance but at the same time leads to a higher level of self-regulation.

Further research by Schmader and Johns (2003), Beilock, Rydell and McConnell (2007) and Croizet et al. (2004) shows that working memory is impaired in subjects under stereotype threat. More specifically, the central executive of working memory tends to become saturated, hence depleting that function's ability to make connections between information held in phonological loops, the visual sketchpad and long-term memory (see Baddeley's (2000) multicomponent model of working memory). In other words, subjects under stereotype threat experience cognitive overload. Some research suggests that impairment is particularly acute in verbal working memory (Miyake & Shah, 1999; Rapee, 1993).

In reference to work conducted by Cadinu et al. (2005), Inzlicht and Schmader (2011) point out that 'women performing difficult math problems after being told that gender differences in math exist had more negative math-related thoughts and performed more poorly than did women who did not receive this information' (p. 7).

Implications for educational strategy

The research on stereotype threat points out a number of directions for educational institutions to consider. In the first place, scores on psychometric tests, admissions assessments and other ego-related tests should be considered with the hindsight offered by the literature: we know that minority groups or individuals belonging to groups that suffer from prejudice have to cope with supplementary cognitive load created by stereotype threat. This is not to say that fear and anxiety are the exclusive domain of victims of prejudice but nonetheless, test scores on assessments that might entail stereotype threat cannot be taken at face value alone.

Second, research findings on the relationship between stereotype threat and impaired performance should be broadcast more widely so that students are aware of them and can be coached to develop coping strategies. Merely knowing about the effects of stereotype beliefs on performance can improve results: Johns, Schmader and Martens (2005) have shown how women taught about stereotype threat effects on performance performed better on mathematical assessments because they were able to relativize their anxiety and approach tasks with more mindfulness.

Third, at the broadest level, students need to be taught to approach anxiety and stress as drivers and not distractors, to learn to live with them and harness them so that performance does not suffer because of subconscious corollaries. Again, the act of knowing about cognition (metacognition) gives learners more control over their learning, more self-confidence and greater serenity when engaged in tasks.

The role of the teacher in teaching metacognitive prejudice reduction

For the teacher's role in guiding students towards self-aware, self-monitoring strategies to monitor and reduce prejudice, an innovative approach to instruction and assessment is needed. Four core instructional techniques should be considered.

Modelling metacognition as a co-learner

'If teachers are to help students become self-regulated learners, their own self-regulation has to be unleashed as well. Traditional design theories of instruction run the risk of interfering with rather than supporting this goal' (Corno & Randi, 1999, p. 296). Teachers should be willing to share their own thoughts, assumptions, beliefs and how they are not only willing to put these in parentheses, doubt and questioning but share with students examples of how they were able to change their thoughts, shift strategy and deconstruct prejudicial thoughts at a personal level, through lived experiences.

A 'sage on the stage' approach whereby the theory of prejudice formation is lectured and moral lessons are given on why one should not be prejudiced might lead students to feel disconnected from the importance of the subject and, worse, resentful of it as it will appear as a homily given in an unappetising ex-cathedra manner. The co-constructivist model suggests that learning to learn is 'a complex mix of dispositions, lived experiences, social relations, values, attitudes and beliefs that coalesce to shape the nature of an individual's engagement with any particular learning opportunity of individual students' (Deakin Crick, Broadfoot & Claxton, 2006).

Therefore, an education that stimulates metacognition for less prejudice should involve a collaborative ethos whereby experiences are shared and reflected upon by the group. A clear example of this type of practice is Matthew Lipman's 'community of inquiry' used to develop philosophy for children:

> the teacher's main role is that of a cultivator of judgment who transcends rather than rejects right–wrong answers in the sense of caring more for the process of inquiry itself than the answer that might be right or wrong at a given time. It is the behaviour of such a teacher ... that is especially cherished ... it has an integrity they are quick to appreciate.
>
> *(Lipman, 2003, p. 219)*

This co-constructivist strategy to reduce prejudice where the teacher is there to guide reflection rather than teach subject matter explicitly has been investigated in the form of cooperative learning, a philosophy of education whereby 'lessons are engineered so that students must teach and learn from one another' (Levy Paluck & Green, 2009, p. 352). Johnson and Johnson (1989) conducted meta-analyses on the effects of cooperative learning and found positive outcomes for behaviours related to prejudice-reduction such as positive peer relationships and helpfulness.

At a broad, structural level, a learning environment whereby students discuss the way they build up knowledge will allow for a free exchange of learning strategies, beliefs and mental constructs, enabling students to learn from each other and to reflect upon their own learning strategies in the light of their peers' experiences. Constructivist educational philosophy postulates that this manner of building up knowledge is more effective at consolidating learning amongst students than more traditional didactic methods. This is particularly relevant for learning related to prejudice given the fact that each learner appropriates representations of other groups and individuals that are anchored in experience and individual context – as such students should share their thoughts as a community of learners to at once articulate their beliefs and learn from others' examples.

Think-aloud protocols

Think-aloud protocols (Ericsson & Simon, 1984) mean that when the learner is engaged in a task (s)he verbalises the different steps that are being taken so that the teacher or peer who is listening gets an idea of the thought processes behind the actions that are taken.

For example, a student using a think-aloud protocol when engaged in a simple chemistry experiment would tell the teacher what (s)he was doing as (s)he went along, saying things like 'Now I'm rinsing each cup with distilled water to make sure there is no distortion of the pH value due to what was in there before. I'm labelling each cup and now I'm pouring ½ a cup of distilled water into each cup. Next I take ½ a teaspoon of ammonia in this cup, ½ a teaspoon of vinegar in this one and I leave the third one with the distilled water. The reason why I do this is because I want to test the comparative pH values of each of these liquids. Oh yes and I make sure that the spoon is clean, etc.'.

The teacher's role in think-aloud protocols is to intervene when the student does something unusual or incorrect with questions such as:

- Why would you do that?
- What would you want to show by doing that?
- What if you did it another way?

The think-aloud protocol can be managed in different ways: it may be too time-consuming for the teacher to go through the steps with each individual student, in which case students could be organised in small groups and, one by one, be asked to explain to the rest of the group what they were doing. The students in the group would ask questions and give feedback to the student doing the think-aloud thought processes, the teacher would roam and observe the groups, adding questions where appropriate. The student doing the think-aloud would change each time the teacher would make a signal (clap hands, say something or ring a bell).

To use this method for the services of metacognitive prejudice-reduction, teachers could organise discussion groups centred on particular themes evoked in a stimulus (for example, an advert, piece of writing, website, image or extract from a film). Students could discuss how they reacted to the stimulus by breaking down their thoughts through a think-aloud protocol. Alternatively, students could explain the different levels of stereotyping and/or prejudice evocation embedded in the stimulus by sharing their thoughts verbally ('I noticed that X is represented in such and such a way, that such and such an argument is made to discredit him/her, that such and such a series of fears/anxieties about X is triggered through the use of such and such a type of language/imagery' etc.).

Levy Paluck and Green (2009) report that 'training in complex thinking and in statistical logic, with the hypothesis that this will help individuals avoid faulty group generalizations [. . .] claim modest success' but go on to cite Gardiner (1972) and Schaller et al. (1996) to explain that 'after training, students are more likely to write positive stories about a picture depicting an interracial encounter, to report friendliness toward racial and ethnic out-groups [. . .] and to avoid stereotyping fictitious characters presented in a vignette' (p. 347).

As is the case with metacognition in general as opposed to domain-specific performance, what is of particular importance is not so much the mental product created at the end of the learning encounter (in this instance 'complex thinking') but the process used to achieve such an aim and the extent to which this process is verbalised, conceptualised and understood.

Classroom discussion

Think-aloud protocols can be put to the service of prejudice reduction by ensuring that students discuss their experiences, beliefs and fears concerning prejudice. The simple act of discussing prejudice freely is a productive step towards its reduction.

Studies by Rokeach (1971) showed how no more than half an hour of open discussion about prejudice-related matters such as attitudes, beliefs and social justice by university students led to them demonstrating awareness and support for civil rights as much as a year later. For more details see Plous (2002, p. 23).

This is part of the educational philosophy that sees talk as the foundation of learning. When a teacher asks a question and the students answer, there needs to be careful follow-up to make sure that ideas are fully expressed and justified. One of the simplest principles of metacognitive learning is making sure that there is genuine conversation in the classroom, what we could call 'dialogic teaching' (Alexander, 2006), meaning that talk is valorised and recognised as the main foundation of learning.

Swan and Pead (2008) suggest cues that teachers can use to ensure that students are clarifying their thoughts: to 'ask pupils to repeat their explanation' for example, teachers would ask 'Can you just say that again?' or to 'invite pupils to elaborate', teachers would say 'Can you just say a little more about that . . .'. Taking Swan and Pead's thinking further and applying it to intergroup perception, in order to ensure that students reflect more transparently and self-consciously on their own reasoning within the parameters of prejudice, the following questions might be asked in the classroom:

TABLE 4.1 Cues to clarify thinking about prejudice

Cues that drive students to restate prejudiced positions and hence to clarify their thoughts	'Could you please repeat what you said about Xs (a social group)?' Or 'You said that all Xs are Ys, could you please go through that again?'
Cues that push students to elaborate their prejudiced positions and therefore further argue their case	'Could you please say more about that idea that all Xs are Ys … what else could you say about that idea?'
Cues that require students to justify prejudiced thinking	'Could you please explain what it is that makes you think that all Xs are Ys? Please say what makes you feel that.'
Cues that drive students to seek out alternative approaches to a prejudiced view	'You said that all Xs are Ys, is there any other way of looking at the situation? Can you think of situations where all Xs might not be Ys?'
Cues that drive students to turn prejudiced postulates they might have formulated on themselves	'What do you think it's like being an X? You said that all Xs are Ys; how would you feel if we said you were an A and that all As are Bs?'
Provocative cues that illicit reasoned responses to prejudiced statements	'Someone in this group said that Xs are Ys, would anyone like to respond? Is this a reasonable statement or does anyone disagree?'
Cues that push students to discuss prejudiced postulates amongst themselves	'In groups (of two or four), please discuss the statement that all Xs are Ys and feed back to the whole class on what you think.'
Cues that push students to question prejudiced beliefs	'Is there anyone in the class who would like to ask the student about his or her feelings concerning Xs?'
Protocols that require students to think aloud and therefore uncover the process behind their prejudiced thoughts	'Could you please go through that idea – that all Xs are Ys – step by step?'

Transfer of knowledge

One of the core purposes of metacognition is to give students sufficient mental representation of knowledge construction and the way they learn in different domains for them to become adequately self-regulatory to not only self-correct in specific domains but transfer problem-solving strategies from one domain to the next. This is particularly important when it comes to reducing prejudice since prejudiced views can emerge in many different guises and contexts. A metacognitively aware student combatting prejudice should be able to recognise its fundamental tenets whether expressed in the well-known forms of racism, homophobia, sexism and religious bigotry or more subtle forms such as class snobbery, ageism and positions held against political groups, professions or levels of education.

However, research has shown that knowledge does not transfer easily (Lave, 1988; Bassok & Holyoak, 1993; Cognition and Technology Group at Vanderbilt, 1997; Ritchhart & Perkins, 2005) and does not happen of its own accord. Concretely, if students are taught to master a discipline, they will not necessarily transfer what they have learnt to other domains. Transfer needs to be taught discretely and purposefully.

A recognised teaching method for the transfer of concepts and knowledge is concepts-focused instruction. For more discussion of this, see this book's discussion of concepts in Chapter 7.

A way of testing metacognitive mastery of concepts related to prejudice is through assessments that require students to apply their knowledge and skills to new situations. Some examples are suggested in the table below.

TABLE 4.2 Concepts that can be transferred from domains to the world of prejudice

Domain	Concepts learnt	Transfer to prejudice formation
Mathematics	Set theory	Accurate criteria for categorising people; good syllogistic thinking as opposed to fallacious categorisation
Science	Falsification	Only holding on to a generalisation about a group if it cannot be falsified
Humanities	Bias	Recognising bias in assumptions, statements and judgements about other people
Physical education	Team spirit	Relating to others as part of a social network rather than as aggressive competitors in a zero-sum game
Languages	Expressions/idioms	Recognising socially and culturally embedded stereotypes
Art	Symbol	Understanding the relationship between symbolic representation of groups and real-life exceptions to this
Literature	Characterisation	Seeing the stereotypic nature of 'stock' characters in works of fiction

Conclusion

This chapter has explored metacognition as an extension of critical thinking and a vital conjugation of cognitive processes to ensure a self-aware, self-regulatory approach to prejudice, be it perceptions of prejudiced thoughts against the self, recognition of prejudiced behaviour and verbalisations by others towards third parties or prejudiced behaviours by the self towards others.

It is clear that metacognition is not a simple state of affairs and is to be situated within Piaget's fourth, abstract stage of cognitive development. This is because metacognition comes after cognition, in the literal sense of the word 'meta': it is a superstructural way of looking back at one's own thinking and metaphorically stepping out of the self to observe, evaluate, monitor and control thinking processes and products.

Education for metacognition operates at a high level of reflection and implies subtle pedagogical strategies whereby the teacher must constantly come back to the individual and group's mental representations of reality. Four components of teaching for metacognitive prejudice reduction are: co-constructivism, the use of think-aloud protocols, recognising the centrality of talk in learning and the importance of mental schemata that allow for the transfer of knowledge and skilfulness.

Finally, a helpful representation of the learning continuum that should be mastered within domains and applied to social categories if teaching for prejudice reduction is to be successful at the metacognitive level, is the spectrum between novice and expert learners. Teachers will know that they have equipped their students well to reflect critically on prejudice if students do so using strategies that are effective, efficient, well-known, contextualised, conceptual and fluent.

References

Alexander, R. (2006). *Towards dialogic teaching: Rethinking classroom talk.* Thirsk: Dialogos.

Aristotle. (2004). *The metaphysics.* London: Penguin.

Ashman, A.F., & Conway, R.N.F. (1997). *An introduction to cognitive education: Theory and applications.* London: Routledge.

Baddeley, A.D. (2000). The episodic buffer: A new component of working memory? *Trends in Cognitive Sciences*, 4, 417–423.

Bandura, A. (1997). Self-efficacy: Toward a unifying theory of behaviour change. *Psychological Review*, 84, 191–215.

Bassok, M., & Holyoak, K.J. (1993). Pragmatic knowledge and conceptual structure: Determinants of transfer between quantitative domains. In D.K. Detterman and R.J. Sternberg (Eds), *Transfer on trial: Intelligence, cognition, and instruction.* Norwood, NJ: Ablex.

Beilock, S.L., Rydell, R.J., & McConnell, A.R. (2007). Stereotype threat and working memory: Mechanisms, alleviations, and spillover. *Journal of Experimental Psychology: General*, 136, 256–276.

Cadinu, M., Maass, A., Rosabianca, A., & Kiesner, J. (2005). Why do women underperform under stereotype threat? Evidence for the role of negative thinking. *Psychological Science*, 16, 572–578.

Chase, W.G., & Simon, H.A. (1973). Perception in chess. *Cognitive Psychology*, 1, 33–81.

Chi, M.T.H., & Koeske, R.D. (1983). Network representation of a child's dinosaur knowledge. *Developmental Psychology*, 19, 29–39.

Chi, M.T.H., Glaser, R., & Rees, E. (1982). Expertise in problem-solving. In R.J. Sternberg (Ed.), *Advances in the psychology of human intelligence (Volume 1).* Hillsdale, NJ: Erlbaum.

Chiu, C., Hong, Y., & Dweck, C.S. (1997). Lay dispositionism and implicit theories of personality. *Journal of Personality and Social Psychology*, 73, 19–30.

Cognition and Technology Group at Vanderbilt. (1997). *The Jasper Project: Lessons in curriculum, instruction, assessment, and professional development.* Mahwah, NJ: Erlbaum.

Corno, L., & Randi, L. (1999). A design theory for classroom instruction. In C.R. Reigeluth (Ed.), *Instructional design theories and models: A new paradigm of instructional theory, Vol. II* (pp. 293–318). Hillsdale NJ: Lawrence Erlbaum Associates.

Crandall, C.S., & Eshleman, A. (2003). A justification-suppression model of the expression and experience of prejudice. *Psychological Bulletin*, 129, 414–446.

Croizet, J.C., Despres, G., Gauzins, M., Hugeut, P., & Leyens, J. (2004). Stereotype threat undermines performance by triggering a disruptive mental load. *Personality and Social Psychology Bulletin*, 30, 721–731.

Cuddy, A.J.C., Fiske, S.T., & Glick, P. (2008). Warmth and competence as universal dimensions of social perception: The stereotype content model and the BIAS Map. *Advances in Experimental Social Psychology*, 40, 61–149.

Deakin Crick, R., Broadfoot, P., & Claxton, G. (2006). *What is the ELLI Research Project?* Online. Available at: www.ellionline.co.uk/research.php (accessed 28 April 2016).

Demetriou, A. (2000). Organization and development of self-understanding and selfregulation: Toward a general theory. In M. Boekaerts, P.R. Pintrich and M. Zeidner (Eds), *Handbook of self-regulation* (pp. 209–251). London: Academic Press.

Devine, P.G. (1989). Stereotypes and prejudice: Their automatic and controlled components. *Journal of Personality and Social Psychology*, 56(1), 5–18.

Dovidio, J.F., & Mullen, B. (1992). *Race, physical handicap, and response amplification.* Unpublished manuscript. Colgate University, Hamilton, NY.

Dweck, C.S. (2006). *Mindset: The new psychology of success.* New York, NY: Random House.

Dweck, C.S., Hong, Y., & Chiu, C. (1993). Implicit theories: Individual differences in the likelihood and meaning of dispositional inference. *Personality and Social Psychology Bulletin*, 19, 644–656.

Ericsson, K.A., & Simon, H.A. (1984). *Protocol analysis: Verbal reports as data.* Cambridge, MA: MIT Press.

Esses, V.M., Dietz, J., & Bhardwaj, A. (2006). The role of prejudice in the discounting of immigrant skills. In R. Mahalingam (Ed.), *The cultural psychology of immigrants* (pp. 113–130). Mahwah, NJ: Erlbaum.

Fay, A., & Klahr, D. (1996). Knowing about guessing and guessing about knowing: Preschoolers' understanding of indeterminacy. *Child Development*, 67, 689–716.

Flavell, J. (1976). Metacognitive aspects of problem solving. In L. Resnick (Ed.), *The Nature of Intelligence* (pp. 231–236), Hillsdale, NJ: Lawrence Erlbaum Associates.

Forbes, C., Schmader, T., & Allen, J.J.B. (2008). The role of devaluing and discounting in performance monitoring: A neurophysiological study of minorities under threat. *Social Cognitive Affective Neuroscience*, 3, 253–261.

Frey, F.E., & Tropp, L.R. (2006). Being seen as individuals versus as group members: Extending research on metaperception to intergroup contexts. *Personality and Social Psychology Review*, 10, 265–280.

Frith, C.D. (2012). The role of metacognition in human social interactions. *Philosophical Transactions of the Royal Society of Biological Sciences*, 306, 2213–2223. doi: 10.1098/rstb.2012.0123

Gardiner, G.S. (1972). Complexity training and prejudice reduction. *Journal of Applied Social Psychology*, 2, 326–342.

Gehring, W.J., Goss, B., Coles, M.G.H., Meyer, D.E., & Donchin, E. (1993). A neural system for error detection and compensation. *Psychological Science*, 4, 385–390.

Glaser, R. (1992). Expert knowledge and processes of thinking. In D.F. Halpern (Ed.), *Enhancing thinking skills in the sciences and mathematics* (pp. 63–75). Hillsdale, NJ: Lawrence Erlbaum Associates.

Hajcak, G., McDonald, N., & Simons, R.F. (2003). Anxiety and error-related brain activity. *Biological Psychology*, 64, 77–90.

Hamilton, D.L. (2007). Understanding the complexities of group perception: Broadening the domain. *European Journal of Social Psychology*, 37, 1077–1101.

Hatano, G. (1990). The nature of everyday science: A brief introduction. *British Journal of Developmental Psychology*, 8, 245–250.

Houghton, S. (2010). Managing stereotypes through experiential learning. *Intercultural Communication Studies*, XIX(1), 182–198.

Inzlicht, M., & Schmader, T. (Eds). (2011). *Stereotype threat: Theory, process, and application.* New York, NY: Oxford University Press.

Jamieson, J.P., & Harkins, S.G. (2007). Mere effort and stereotype threat performance effects. *Journal of Personality and Social Psychology*, 93, 544–564.

Johns, M., Schmader, T., & Martens, A. (2005). Knowing is half the battle: Teaching stereotype threat as a means of improving women's math performance. *Psychological Science*, 16, 175–179.

Johnson, D.W., & Johnson, R.T. (1989). *Cooperation and competition: Theory and research*. Edina, MN: Interaction Book Co.

Judd, C.M., Park, B., Yzerbyt, V.Y., Gordijn, E., & Muller, D. (2005). They show more intergroup bias and have stronger stereotypes than do I: Evidence from ethnic, gender, and nationality intergroup contexts. *European Journal of Social Psychology*, 35, 677–704.

Kaiser, M.K., Proffitt, D.R., & McCloskey, M. (1985). The development of beliefs about falling objects. *Perception & Psychophysics*, 38(6), 533–539.

Karmiloff-Smith, A. (1979). Problem-solving construction and representations of closed railway circuits. *Archives of Psychology*, 47, 37–59.

Lacan, J. (1977). *Ecrits: A selection* (A. Sheridan, Trans.). London: Tavistock.

Lammers, J., Gordijn, E.H., & Otten, S. (2008). Looking through the eyes of the powerful. Power (or lack thereof) and metastereotyping. *Journal of Experimental Social Psychology*, 44, 1229–1238.

Lave, J. (1988). *Cognition in practice: Mind, mathematics and culture in everyday life*. Cambridge: Cambridge University Press.

Levy Paluck, E., & Green, D.P. (2009). Prejudice reduction: What works? A review and assessment of research and practice. *Annual Review of Psychology*, 60, 339–367. doi:10.1146/annurev.psych.60.110707.163607

Lickel, B., Hamilton, D.L., Wieczorkowska, G., Lewis, A., Sherman, S.J., & Uhles, A.N. (2000). Varieties of groups and the perception of group entitativity. *Journal of Personality and Social Psychology*, 78, 223–246.

Lipman, M. (2003). *Thinking in Education* (2nd edn). Cambridge: Cambridge University Press.

Marx, D.M. (2011). Differentiating theories: A comparison of stereotype threat and stereotype priming effects. In M. Inzlicht and T. Schmader (Eds), *Stereotype threat: Theory, process, and application*. New York, NY: Oxford University Press.

Miyake, A., & Shah, P. (1999). *Models of working memory: Mechanisms of active maintenance and executive control*. New York, NY: Cambridge University Press.

Moseley, D., Baumfield, V., Elliott, J., Gregson, M., Higgins, S., Miller, J., & Newton, D. (2005). *Frameworks for thinking: A handbook for teaching and learning*. Cambridge: Cambridge University Press.

NRC (National Research Council). (1999). Evaluation of the voluntary national tests, year 2: Final report. Committee on the Evaluation of the Voluntary National Tests, Year 2. '/images/interface/clear.gif'. In L.L. Wise, R.J. Noeth and J.A. Koenig (Eds), *Commission on Behavioral and Social Sciences and Education*. Washington, DC: National Academy Press.

Norton, M.I., Vandello, J.A., & Darley, J.M. (2004). Casuistry and social category bias. *Journal of Personality and Social Psychology*, 87, 817–831.

Pellegrino, J.W., Chudowsky, N., & Glaser, R. (2001). *Knowing what students know: The science and design of educational assessment*. Washington, DC: National Academy Press.

Pintrich, P.R. (2000). The role of goal orientation in self-regulated learning. In M. Boekaerts, P.R. Pintrich and M. Zeidner (Eds), *Handbook of self-regulation* (pp. 451–502). San Diego, CA: Academic Press.

Plous, S. (2002). *Understanding prejudice and discrimination*. New York, NY: McGraw-Hill.

Pronin, E., Steele, C.M., & Ross, L. (2004). Identity bifurcation in response to stereotype threat: Women and mathematics. *Journal of Experimental Social Psychology*, 40, 152–168.

Rapee, R.M. (1993). The utilization of working memory by worry. *Behavioral Research Therapy*, 31, 617–620.

Ritchhart, R., & Perkins, D. (2005). Learning to think: The challenges of teaching thinking. In K.J. Holyoak and R.G. Morrison (Eds), *The Cambridge Handbook of Thinking and Reasoning*. New York, NY: Cambridge University Press.

Rokeach, M. (1971). The measurement of values and value systems. In G. Abcarian (Ed.), *Social psychology and political behavior* (pp. 611–640). Columbus, OH: Charles Merrill.

Schaller, M., Asp C.H., Rosell, M.C., & Heim, S.J. (1996). Training in statistical reasoning inhibits the formation of erroneous group stereotypes. *Personality and Social Psychology Bulletin*, 22, 829–844.

Schmader, T., & Johns, M. (2003). Converging evidence that stereotype threat reduces working memory capacity. *Journal of Personality and Social Psychology*, 85, 440–452.

Schmader, T., Johns, M., & Forbes, C. (2008). An integrated process model of stereotype threat effects on performance. *Psychological Review*, 115, 336–356.

Siegler, R.S. (1998). *Children's thinking* (3rd edn). Upper Saddle River, NJ: Prentice Hall.

Sigelman, L., & Tuch, L.A. (1997). Metastereotypes – Blacks' perceptions of Whites' stereotypes of Blacks. *Public Opinion Quarterly*, 61, 87–101.

Son Hing, L.S., Li, W., & Zanna, M.P. (2002). Inducing hypocrisy to reduce prejudicial responses among aversive racists. *Journal of Experimental Social Psychology*, 381, 71–78.

Steele, C.M., & Aronson, J. (1995). Stereotype threat and the intellectual test performance of African Americans. *Journal of Personality and Social Psychology*, 69, 797–811.

Stephan, W.G. (1989). A cognitive approach to stereotyping. In D. Bartal, C.F. Graumann, A.W. Kruglanski and W. Stroebe (Eds), *Stereotyping and prejudice: Changing conceptions* (pp. 37–58). Berlin: Springer.

Swan, M., & Pead, D. (2008). Professional development resources. Bowland Maths Key Stage 3, Bowland Charitable Trust. Online. Available at: www.bowlandmaths.org.uk (accessed 28 April 2016).

Tajfel, H., & Turner, J.C. (1979). An integrative theory of intergroup conflict: The social identity theory of intergroup behaviour. In W.G. Austin and S. Worchel (Eds), *The social psychology of intergroup relations* (pp. 33–47). Monterey, CA: Brooks/Cole.

Van den Bos, A., & Stapel, D.A. (2009). Why people stereotype affects how they stereotype: The differential influence of comprehension goals and self-enhancement goals on stereotyping. *Personality and Social Psychology Bulletin*, 35, 101–113.

Vorauer, J.D., Hunter, A.J., Main, K.J., & Roy, S.A. (2000). Meta-stereotype activation: Evidence from indirect measures for specific evaluative concerns experienced by members of dominant groups in intergroup interaction. *Journal of Personality and Social Psychology*, 78, 690–707.

Yzerbyt, V.Y., & Demoulin, S. (2010). Intergroup relations. In P. Briñol & K.G. DeMareee (Eds), *Social metacognition* (pp. 243–262) New York, NY: Psychology Press.

Zeidner, M., Boekaerts, M., & Pintrich, P.R. (2000). Self-regulation: Directions and challenges for future research. In M. Boekaerts, P.R. Pintrich and M. Zeidner (Eds), *Handbook of self-regulation* (pp. 750–769). London: Academic Press.

Zimmerman, B.J. (2000). Attaining self-regulation: a social cognitive perspective. In M. Boekaerts, P.R. Pintrich and M. Zeidner (Eds), *Handbook of self-regulation* (pp. 13–39). San Diego, CA: Academic Press.

5

EMPATHY AND THE SEARCH FOR COMMON HUMANITY IN THE FACE OF PREJUDICE

Introduction

When considering the role of the individual in the educational combat against prejudice, I have discussed the matter from the perspectives of cognition and metacognition – so effectively the realms of reason and thinking and from those of historiography and culture – what I have called 'educating beyond the Other' in this book. These approaches are intellectual in nature and hinge on the all-important notion of critical thinking. Indeed, much prejudicial thinking comes from a lack of critical thought, an inability to temper bias or deal with complexity, leading the knower to opt for a short cut bent on over-generalisation and quick, unprocessed judgement.

However, knowing and thinking is not enough for humans are sentient beings and relate to the world not only in cold abstractions but through emotions, sensations, temperament, desires and physical experience. The twenty-first century is focussing more and more on emotional and social intelligences as critical facets of learning as we move away from the old Cartesian idea of a separation between the body and the mind, premised on Plato's suspicion of the emotions and a 2,500-year-old Western paradigm structured on reason over passion towards character education (Berkowitz & Bier, 2005; Bialik et al., 2015), mindsets (Dweck, 2006, 2012), emotional intelligence (Goleman, 1995; Salovey, Mayer & Caruso, 2004) and empathy (Gordon, 2005).

This chapter takes the reader through the construct of empathy by discussing what it is, how it relates to prejudice, how educational interventions can trigger greater empathy and, finally, how this information can be yoked together in a model of empathy for less prejudice in the classroom.

What is empathy?

Empathy as a word has its roots in the Ancient Greek *empatheia*, a term used by Aristotle in the *Rhetoric* to mean 'being profoundly moved or touched' (Maxwell, 2008, p. 27) or 'empathes' used by Aristotle in *De Insomniis* to mean 'in a state of emotion' (Griswold & Konstan, 2012, p. 37).

The term is also closely related to pathos ('pity and fear' or, for Liddell & Scott, 1940, 'passion' or 'suffering'), fundamental for ancient Greek theatre. The protagonists of the works of the Attic poets (Sophocles, Aeschylus and Euripides), either by their fate or deeds, would move the audience to a state of pathos at the sight of others' suffering, which would allow them to expunge their emotions through catharsis. At the origin therefore, pathos and empathy are related to the core idea that strong feelings run through people and must be evoked to maintain a balanced appreciation of the human condition. It is also connected to the notion that life involves suffering and through the medium of suffering some common understanding or fundamental recognition is evoked.

The modern use of the word empathy was coined by the German philosopher Robert Vischer in the late nineteenth century (see Mallgrave & Ikonomou, 1994). His term 'Einfühlung', meaning 'feeling into' evokes the idea that one relates to another person's inner state by understanding what he or she is going through and can imagine and relate to their suffering (see, for example, Pijnenborg et al., 2012; Snyder, Lopez, & Pedrotti, 2011).

Katz's (1963) study gives an eloquently phrased account of how it makes itself apparent in human interactions:

> triggered by cues in the conversation or by impressions we receive of the state of mind or feeling of the other person. We assimilate this information without being aware of doing so. We pick up the signals through a kind of inner radar and certain changes in our own emotional states make themselves felt. We mimic the other person and in the excitement of our spontaneous response our attention is almost completely absorbed.
>
> *(Katz, 1963, p. 5)*

Indeed, empathy is something that happens primarily through emotional facets that may or may not be in primary awareness and they will manifest themselves in physical ways, often through strong feelings, laughter or tears, fear or hope. This means that empathy is not something that will necessarily translate immediately into measurable domains such as language or other mental products. Testing someone's mathematical reasoning or knowledge of history is relatively straightforward whereas testing someone's empathy is more subjective and challenging as I argue further in this chapter.

There is some debate as to what it is exactly that causes empathy within different individuals. Some studies suggest that it is an innate quality that can be measured in neural activity. Carr et al. (2003) conducted an experiment using magnetic resonance imaging (MRI) on 12 subjects, the results of which suggested that heightened inferior frontal cortical activity took place during the observation of an empathy-inducing action – this related to humans' predispositions to learn through mimesis or repetition – in so-called 'mirror neurons'. Another set of MRIs conducted on 19 participants by Moll et al. (2006) implied that while altruism is tied to the systematic activation of a neural system that is generic to mammalians, triggering reward or aversion; when altruism is related to 'abstract moral beliefs', the anterior prefrontal cortex of the human brain is activated, a uniquely human phenomenon.

Earlier work by Hogan (1969), Davis (1983) and Duan and Hill (1996) suggested that a tendency to empathise is fairly stable in individuals regardless of contextual factors although this view has been challenged by researchers such as Rogers (1975) and Ogle, Bushnell and Caputi (2013), who see it as related to independent variables such as stimuli and environment.

A study by Paro et al. (2014) in which 1,350 randomly assigned medical students responded to a series of questionnaires showed that female students manifested higher levels of empathy and were more distressed at the sight of discomfort to others than males. The idea that females are more prone to empathy than males has been confirmed by Gilligan (1982).

Much of the recent research on empathy has been conducted in the field of medicine, counselling and psychotherapy where doctors and nurses are frequently put in circumstances requiring empathy as patients are often in states of anxiety, discomfort or suffering and, at an emotional level, desire some recognition and understanding. However, it has been argued that the importance of empathy goes well beyond the medical field:

- Research on social workers has shown correlations between levels of empathy and burnout prevention. For example, Wagaman et al. (2015) conducted a study on 173 social workers using an empathy assessment index and found that 'components of empathy may prevent or reduce burnout and STS while increasing compassion satisfaction, and that empathy should be incorporated into training and education throughout the course of a social worker's career' (abstract).
- Empathy has been recognised as a core leadership quality: 'Empathy is particularly important today as a component of leadership for at least three reasons: the increasing use of teams; the rapid pace of globalization; and the growing need to retain talent' (Goleman, 1998). The view that empathy is a vital part of good leadership has been reiterated by others such as Yukl (1998), George (2000) and Kellet, Humphrey and Sleeth (2002).
- Pilling and Eroglu (1994) have pointed out the centrality of empathy in the professional profiles of salespersons.
- Ellis (1982) ran a controlled trial on 332 delinquents (with 64 controls) and found that the nondelinquent group showed a significantly higher level of

empathy, suggesting that antisocial thought and behaviour correlates negatively with empathy. This implies that if society does not nurture empathy in individuals, they will be more prone to drift into delinquency.

At the broadest level, since much human activity is social and there is increasing recognition and valorising of social intelligence in the workplace, empathy is rightly regarded as a fundamental and extremely relevant facet of character. At a deeper, ethical level, if humans are to learn to live together, to respect and care for one another, some sensitivity is required. Recognising someone else's humanity comes through a feeling of oneness.

In the light of these findings, I would suggest that an appropriate twenty-first century definition of empathy would be: a set of responses to the suffering of sentient beings that is values-driven and recognises the interconnectedness and precious value of life.

It should be noted that, like so many areas within the domains of social psychology related to prejudice, including prejudice itself, empathy is a difficult construct to measure and operationalise and is frequently grasped through nonexperimental or quasi-experimental methods, including often unreliable self-reported measures (see Batson, 1987 and Mayer, Caruso & Salovey, 2000).

Some of the more recent research in empathy has operationalised it by examining neural activity captured through magnetic resonance imaging that suggests empathetic reactions to various stimuli (usually images or films of subjects experiencing discomfort). Specific neural responses that suggest this include the anterior cingulate cortex – supplementary motor area – insula circuit that relates to pain and other sensorimotor contagion, often recorded through facial electromyography. As evidence, this motor mimicry shows that reactions occur, but the extent to which one can interpret the specific meaning of those reactions for each individual is the subject of some discussion.

Empathy and prejudice

The philosophy of life that is implied by empathy is clearly related to reducing prejudice. Prejudice is a type of objectification whereby a person's individuality is not recognised and he or she is seen as part of a whole, a type of stock character defined by pre-ordained traits that are, in effect, a set of clichés, stereotypes and over-generalisations.

To get beyond this, the first step is to recognise another person's individuality, the fact that he or she stands outside of a set of stereotypic definitions, that he or she can be related to in terms of the universal themes that unite humanity (desires, feelings, family, belief, culture, the body and so on). Admitting a person's likeness is a gesture that moves in the opposite direction of prejudice.

A philosophy of empathy goes further than admitting someone else's identity and implies a network or system of values that can be seen in certain African *weltangshauungs* such as that coined in the Nguni phrase 'Ubuntu', which comes from the longer statement 'umuntu ngumuntu ngabantu', meaning 'a person is a person because of other people'. In this case, empathy is not so much admitting someone else's individuality but doing away with the notion of individualism and seeing all humans as interconnected. Eze explains the concept:

> It is a demand for a creative intersubjective formation in which the 'other' becomes a mirror (but only a mirror) for my subjectivity. This idealism suggests to us that humanity is not embedded in my person solely as an individual; my humanity is co-substantively bestowed upon the other and me. Humanity is a quality we owe to each other. We create each other and need to sustain this otherness creation. And if we belong to each other, we participate in our creations: we are because you are, and since you are, definitely I am. The 'I am' is not a rigid subject, but a dynamic self-constitution dependent on this otherness creation of relation and distance.
>
> *(Eze, 2010, p. 90)*

Todd et al. (2011) ran five experiments requiring participants to take on the perspective of subjects of other ethnic origin in simulations of racial prejudice and found that perspective taking can reduce automatic racial bias.

However, feeling empathy for another does not necessarily in and of itself offer an antidote to prejudice as empathy can be heightened for ingroup members and dampened for outgroup members. Avenanti, Sirigu and Aglioti (2010) ran an experiment where magnetic resonance imaging would detect motor cortex stimulation in subjects. They showed how, what they describe as empathetic resonance in participants, was heightened when faced with an ingroup member's hand being pricked but absent when the hand belonged to an outgroup member. In this case, the specific sign of empathetic resonance was muscle twitching in the participant's hand at the sight of another hand being pricked. Xu et al. (2009) found similar results in a study on racial in- and outgroup empathy.

Mathur et al. (2010) showed that black and white American participants showed similar empathetic responses when shown black and white subjects in pain but that only the black participants showed heightened empathy-related neural activity when shown images of other blacks in pain whereas the white participants did not show heightened empathy-related neural activity when shown images of other whites in pain. This suggests that members of groups that have traditionally suffered prejudice (what we could call minority groups) have a heightened sense of empathy for their own group. For a synthesis of studies suggesting that empathy is not necessarily an antidote to prejudice but in many circumstances might actually reinforce it, see Cikara et al. (2014).

These findings would suggest that educational interventions that focus on empathy need to be conducted in careful conjunction with knowledge of the dynamics of prejudice formation: it is not enough to heighten empathy within individuals – empathy should be nurtured within a framework of perceptions and feelings about in-groups and out-groups and directed in such a way that it serves to build care for other people.

Galinsky and Moscowitz (2000) ran three experiments to show that perspective-taking reduces stereotyping. More specifically, 'perspective-taking can reduce the accessibility and application of stereotypic responding because of increased overlap between representations of the self and representations of the out-group' (p.708). This means that as people begin to feel connected to another group and experience the 'overlap' of self and other, they no longer hold the group as an outgroup and start to identify external factors as responsible for certain dictates. The study pointed out that stereotype suppression was not a meaningful solution as participants who did this tended to re-enact prejudicial acts or thoughts on other groups: perspective taking should be done deeply and critically so that learners are able to genuinely associate with the member of the outgroup.

In a similar vein, Finlay and Stephan (2000) ran a study whereby black and white participants were instructed to read essays supposedly written by black college students describing experiences of discrimination. The experimental group was asked to read the essays with empathy, imagining what it would be like to be the person writing whereas the control group was instructed to read the essays more objectively. They found that the experimental group demonstrated lower levels of prejudicial white on black bias in their subsequent evaluations than the control group. Hence, reading testimonies with the instruction to apply feeling to the reading can have a positive effect on empathy development.

Batson et al. (1997) and Batson et al. (2002) showed how when participants are instructed to focus on a subject's feelings rather than the situation they are in, higher levels of empathetic concern are generated. These studies used polemical subjects such as murderers and drug-addicts and found that even here the wall of socially acceptable prejudice would begin to crumble when the focal point was feeling.

How can educational interventions trigger greater empathy?

At the most obvious, empirical level, evoking what it must be like to be another person in a given situation is something that is done often in educational discourses that ask students to imagine that they are someone else (a character in a work of literature, a historical figure or member of a group). Common learning experiences that activate this type of feeling include role-play, theatrical productions, 'hot seating' (when a student pretends to be a character and must answer questions as that character would), perspective-taking through different types of production (literary, discursive, artistic) and representing positions that may or may not be one's own in debates.

Paluck and Green (2009), relating to evidence found by Galinsky and Moscowitz (2000) and Vescio et al. (2003) state: 'writing an essay from the perspective of an elderly person decreased subsequent stereotypes about the elderly; writing an essay from the perspective of the opposite [. . .] group led to more positive ratings of the out-group's personality characteristics' (Paluck & Green, 2009, p. 348).

At a deeper, and potentially more transformative level, there is the idea of putting students in the same or similar situations to those that are potential objects of prejudice. This can range from field trips to other countries, cultures and socio-cultural environments to exchanges whereby students live with members of another group or are hosted by families of other groups.

Finally, at the most radical level, educational environments can simulate real-life scenarios where students have to experience literally what it is to be another person by plunging the student in a typical other group-member settings (often work related) or making them endure what another person has to go through. This last model is less frequent in schools as it is risky and might cause extreme discomfort. However, common sense tells us that the greatest levels of empathy that lead to the most meaningful contributions to the plights of those suffering under such conditions are borne out of experience: one empathises with the poor if one has known poverty; one can understand redundancy empathetically if one has been made redundant.

The studies by Finlay and Stephan (2000) and Galinsky and Moscowitz (2000) cited earlier in this chapter suggest that classroom instruction should incorporate the idea of empathy consciously and purposefully by instructing students to approach situations with empathy. Hence, instructions such as 'read this passage and focus on the feelings of the protagonist', 'watch this extract and consider what it must have been like for X to experience Y', 'in analysing this work of art, consider what might be going through the head of such-and-such a character' or 'retell this passage from the perspective of X' would be more effective than detached, objective accounts. These interventions could take place at an early level of cognitive development (in fact, they resonate naturally with pre-operational phases of development), would be easy to carry out in the classroom and would represent level 1 of empathy-evoking learning experiences.

If we are to consider a higher level of empathy development (level 2), numerous educational interventions to decrease prejudice have been developed in the past decades using the premises of contact and communication with others. A fairly well-known one is 'Roots of Empathy', a Canadian-based classroom programme for children from kindergarten to the equivalent of grade 8, which claims to have 'shown significant effect in reducing levels of aggression among schoolchildren by raising social/emotional competence and increasing empathy' (Roots of Empathy, 2015). The guiding principle of this approach is to stimulate empathy through the observation of a baby interacting with its mother and to consider reality from the

TABLE 5.1 Three levels of empathy-evoking experiences

Level 1	Level 2	Level 3
Empathy through imagination and production	Empathy through contact and communication	Empathy through direct experience of conditions

baby's perspective and then to generalise and apply the sentiments gleaned in such an experience to the outside.

The programme aims to develop emotional literacy in students (a term coined by the psychotherapist Claude Steiner, meaning 'the ability to understand your emotions, the ability to listen to others and empathise with their emotions, and the ability to express emotions productively' (Steiner & Perry, 1997, p. 11). A reasonable amount of research has substantiated the effectiveness of the programme (Mac-Donald et al., 2013; Schonert-Reichl et al., 2012; Santos et al., 2011; Rolheiser & Wallace, 2005; Jaramillo, Buote & Schonert-Reichl, 2008).

Roots of Empathy is an example of an educational design to heighten empathy that lies within the affective rather than cognitive domain. It is part of a vision of education that seeks to stimulate responses not only through discursive stimuli (lectures, readings and theory) but through real-life experiences, although it is still a dynamic whereby students observe situations and draw conclusions from them that will be internalised, conceptualised, generalised and then later applied to other situations. These higher-order processes cannot be expected to take place of their own accord and will require some pedagogical scaffolding.

To turn to the highest level of empathy development (level 3 whereby real-life phenomena experienced directly by the subject are used as building blocks for learning), Goleman (1998) explains how interventions to stimulate emotional intelligence should focus on stimulating the limbic rather than the cortical system: 'emotional intelligence is born largely in the neurotransmitters of the brain's limbic system, which governs feelings, impulses, and drives. Research indicates that the limbic system learns best through motivation, extended practice, and feedback'. Goleman contrasts this type of learning with the colder, analytical function of the neocortex that tends to express more activity on intellectual tasks. The point is that deep learning experiences that will stimulate empathy require emotional arousal rather than pure theory or technical information. He goes on to lament that most training programmes are centred on neocortex rather than limbic activity, hereby doing little to arouse emotions, proving to be not only inefficient but with potentially negative effects for job performance.

Just as Goleman (1998) has argued that 'to enhance emotional intelligence, organizations must refocus their training to include the limbic system', I would argue that education must place students in situations where they make emotional connections with the world around them and learn deeply through active experiences rather than second- or third-hand information alone. A powerful manner in which this can be done is by ensuring that students actually live out directly what others have to go through in their lives.

This brings us back to the core idea that effective learning for more empathy is learning by doing. The famous lines by the fictional character Atticus Finch in Harper Lee's novel *To Kill a Mocking Bird* (1960) sum it up clearly: 'You never really understand a person until you consider things from his point of view . . . until you climb into his skin and walk around in it.'

Empathy for less prejudice

Thus far, the following points about learning for more empathy have been established:

1   Learning experiences that evoke empathy have been shown to lessen prejudicial attitudes.
2   Empathy is not in itself necessarily an antidote to prejudice as it can be directed towards ingroups and dampened for outgroups, it requires scaffolding.
3   One can consider a developmental spectrum of empathy ranging from passive to active to experiential episodes: empathy becomes more meaningful as we move into the realm of actual lived experience.

In the light of this information, we can consider some classroom projects that unite these points as examples of empathy-evoking learning experiences that have the potential to lessen prejudice. Examples will be given according to the levels established earlier:

Level 1: Empathy through imagination and production

The main concept to be developed at this first level is empathy through mental products such as art works, narrative, films, music, historical anecdotes, eye-witness testimonies and biographies. By having students engage with material that describes the plight of others and then reflect on those empathetically, a bridge is built between the self and the other.

Autobiographies are commonly used to evoke a feeling of empathy in the reader. Anne Frank's *The Diary of a Young Girl* (1952), used with young children to stimulate thoughts on what it must have been like to be a Jewish child during the Holocaust, is an example. Kirshenblatt-Gimblett and Shandler (2012, pp. 184–185) describe the structure of empathy in the novel as a process whereby the readers are less focused on Anne's fate as a Holocaust victim and more on the universal themes of humanity that she evokes. This hinges on the idea that whereas sympathy is related to explicit recognition of a condition in time and place, empathy is related to connections that transcend social categories.

Therefore, in order to evoke an empathetic reading of *The Diary of a Young Girl*, instructors would do well to concentrate less on the historical dimension of the author's experience and more on the human themes of happiness, fear and innocence that characterise her and give her universal credence.

One Day in the Life of Ivan Denisovich (1963) by Alexander Solzhenitsyn is a book that opens students' minds about the realities of being a prisoner of war in a Soviet Gulag but, more universally, is about the plight of someone in extreme discomfort whose very humanity is threatened by the cruelty and harshness of life in prison. The protagonist and narrator, Shukhov, muses 'can a man who's warm understand one who's freezing?'.

The Long Journey of Poppie Nongena (1978) by Elsa Joubert takes the reader through the events that mark the life of a woman living under Apartheid and allow for instances of empathetic identification.

Works of literature that use the first person narrative or narratological techniques to plunge readers into the psychic reality of a character can, arguably, evoke greater empathy than accounts told from the outside, so to speak: 'If an author wants intense sympathy for characters who do not have strong virtues to recommend them, then the psychic vividness of prolonged inside views will help him' (Booth, 1983, pp. 377–378). Booth goes on to give an example from Jane Austen's novel *Emma* (1815): 'By showing most of the story through Emma's eyes, the author insures that we will travel with Emma rather than stand against her' (1983, p. 245).

Works of art that are commonly used to evoke feelings of empathy include Picasso's *Guernica* (1937), a painting that renders palpable the fear and distress of the victims of the German bombing of the Spanish town in 1937 and stimulates empathy for the victims of fascism in general. Grade 11 classroom teacher Katherine Joyce describes how she used the painting in conjunction with historical artefacts and pieces of information to evoke not only empathy but philosophical discussions about war:

> The students clearly saw the painting as representing the horror of war. They felt that viewing this painting and then exploring it more in depth gave them a sense of the horror that people in and connected to Guernica reacted to the bombing, and that using this in connection with other sources, such as newspaper reports and letters, gave a fuller picture of the event. This empathy, this ability to take a more nuanced historical perspective, allowed us to delve further into the question of why people fight wars, and more specifically allowed us to explore more fully cause and consequence, because we could now bring an understanding of personal and collective emotion into the discussion.
>
> *(Joyce, 2015)*

Another famous artwork that can be used to evoke empathy is Goya's *The Shootings of May Third 1808* (1818) where the facial expressions and symbolic posture of the victims of the shootings evoke strong feelings of empathy for victims of war.

Films that develop empathy for the protagonists through the use of focalisation or a first person narrative include David Lynch's *The Elephant Man* (1980), which discusses disfigurement; Steve McQueen's *12 Years a Slave* (2013), allowing for a harrowing, closely focalised experience of slavery; Steven Spielberg's *The Color Purple* (1985), evoking the reality of black America in Georgia at the beginning of the twentieth century; Jim Sheridan's *My Left Foot* (1989), allowing for empathy with people suffering from physical handicaps or Ang Lee's *Brokeback Mountain* (2005), a film that plunges viewers into the realities of homosexual love in a world that is repressively heterosexual. Batson et al. have pointed out that *The Elephant Man* and *The Color Purple* are particularly effective in the way that they induce feelings strongly related to empathy such as compassion, sympathy and tenderness (1997, p. 105).

Works of art have the potential to evoke empathy not only by inducing strong emotional responses to the plight of others but also by drawing attention to areas that are not often discussed or problematised, hereby raising awareness as well as empathy. Fraser writes of works that dramatise violence such as *One Day in the Life of Ivan Denisovich* and *Guernica* 'if one is made to feel more or less deeply uncomfortable, it is because one is being confronted with facts that one hadn't known, or hadn't thought carefully enough about, or is still reluctant to feel intensively about' (Fraser, 1974, p. 47).

Level 2: Empathy through contact and communication

The central idea behind this level of empathy evocation is to have students reflect on what it must be like to be another person by placing them in simulations of situations where they endure through role-play what another person would have to in real life. Learning experiences tend to be symbolic or staged so as to tease out the core elements of the experiences affecting those with whom the students are to empathise.

Model United Nations

In 1953 the International School of Geneva initiated a simulation of the United Nations General Assembly and called it the Students' United Nations. By having students aged between 15 and 20 draft, debate and vote for resolutions the experience was meant to stimulate higher-order thinking through debate and to familiarise students with the realities of diplomacy. Since then the learning experience has continued and grown considerably at the International School of Geneva, currently known as The Student League of Nations.

Crucially, the rules stipulate that students are not to represent their own countries in the simulation, hereby ensuring that the enterprise would put them in situations where they had to defend ideas that were not their own, represent different countries and positions and research issues and national standpoints on such issues as preparation for the debate: 'the objective is to participate in a realistic simulation of the United Nations' General Assembly in the role of delegates. The rules stipulate that each delegation is composed of two students who may not represent their own country' (Ecolint, 2016).

The rules of the General Assembly further ensure that students discover and reinforce knowledge of situations other than their own national concerns: 'Each delegation must have adequate general knowledge of the country or international organization which it is representing, as well as of the subjects which will be debated in the General Assembly' (Ecolint Student League of Nations, 2014, p. 11).

Since then, the Model United Nations system as it has come to be known has grown considerably and is practised in most international schools. Many cite empathy as a fundamental goal of the simulation: Nyborg Gymnasium cites as goals 'insight, empathy, responsibility, unity' (Nyborg, 2016); London International Model United Nations states that it

> aims to extend cultural empathy, understanding of international affairs and knowledge of the United Nations among young people through the medium

of Model United Nations. By equipping youth with mediation, analytical and leadership skills, while stressing the interdependence of the modern world, it is hoped that the next generation of global leaders will face issues of common concern with the spirit of international cooperation.

(LIMUN, 2016)

The Schutz American School points out that 'participation in MUN leads to the development of empathy, tolerance, and a broadening of perspective' (Schutz, 2016), while Mickolus and Brannan (2013) explain that Model United Nations stimulate 'the skills of diplomacy, the value of empathy, and looking at international issues from multiple points of view' (p. 2).

By engaging students in Model United Nations programmes, schools will be taking a step towards empathy-developing skills and experiences.

Simulations

To be included in the repertoire of activities that operate at level 2 of empathy development, we can mention games that emphasise symbolically the experience of suffering prejudice. These simulations follow a number of different formats, often involving a separation of the class into two categories (those who are 'dots'; those who are 'non-dots', for example), students categorised with a symbol that the teacher has attributed to them.

In general, the idea is to treat one group more favourably than the other and then to scaffold some discussion on what it felt like to be on either side of the iniquity.

Some simulation games go far and evoke the literal substance of discrimination rather than a symbolic representation. For example, world history teachers might use slavery simulations in lessons where students would take on the roles of slave and slave master in order to evoke deeper understanding. Activities such as this are dangerous as they risk traumatising students and/or trivialising the event simulated.

Educators who oppose the use of simulations for emotionally vulnerable subjects generally point to three main concerns: the effects of simulations on children's psychological development, the ability of simulations to over-simplify history and oppression, and the fact that few teachers possess the appropriate training to facilitate simulations successfully.

(Teaching Tolerance, 2008)

Blue eyes/brown eyes exercise

Possibly the most famous of these empathy-evoking simulations is the 1968 'blue eyes/brown eyes exercise' invented by the classroom teacher Jean Elliott. The now well-known story comes from a third-grade classroom in Riceville, Iowa on the day after the assassination of Martin Luther King Jr.

Elliot was asked by her students why King had been assassinated and her response was to sensitise them to racial prejudice by simulating a climate of discrimination. She divided the blue-eyed and brown-eyed students, gave armbands to the blue-eyed students and stated 'the browneyed people are the better people in this room [. . .] they are cleaner and they are smarter' (Bloom, 2005). Elliott went further to give a pseudo-scientific explanation for the division, telling her students that melanin was an intelligence-enhancing chemical that could be found in greater concentrations in brown-eyed children. She later reversed the participants so that the blue-eyed children were given special privileges that the brown-eyed were not.

Elliot made a number of observations during the activity, notably a lack of self-esteem and performance in the discriminated group and heightened confidence in members of the privileged group.

Scientific evidence on the effectiveness of the blue eyes/brown eyes activity is not particularly strong. A study by Byrnes and Kiger (1990) on non-black teachers' attitudes to blacks showed moderate statistical improvement in attitudes although qualitatively participants reported that the experience was meaningful to them even though it caused high levels of stress.

Williams and Giles (1992) criticised the method due to ethical issues such as the level of consent, the stress and levels of coercion implied. Byrnes and Kiger (1992) responded to this by suggesting that the downsides of the method were outweighed by the gains.

Weiner and Wright (1973) ran a controlled experiment with third-grade non-black schoolchildren over 3 days and found more willingness to blend with black students on the third day of the experiment and 3 days later.

The blue eyes/brown eyes activity is often described as an experiment but it is more properly a quasi-experiment since the conditions for true experimental work (randomisation, control groups, masking) are not used and the analysis tends to be fairly anecdotal. Like all level 2 empathy learning experiences involving simulation, extreme caution and sensitivity is needed and the emphasis should be on the quality of reflection and unpacking that takes place afterwards.

A repertoire of level 2 type learning experiences can be found in the toolkit and case studies developed by the Ashoka organisation (Ashoka, 2016).

Level 3: Empathy through direct experience of conditions

Exchanges

Examples of the highest level of empathy-evocation would be those that plunge students not only into strong simulations of others' experiences but ensure that they live under those conditions directly for a period of time.

An instance of this is the 'radical empathy' programme that took place in 2014 between University Heights High School (situated in the South Bronx) and Ethical Culture Fieldston School, a prestigious '$43,000-a-year tuition' school in New York (Lovell, 2014). The programme, centred around four pairs of students from either school, saw visits, focus group discussions and sharing of stories between students over an 8-year period.

A specific and highly important part of this learning experience was the so-called Narrative 4 project whereby students from schools in radically different socioeconomic areas were paired up and each asked to write a story that described who they were. The next step was for each student to take ownership of his or her partner's story and tell it in a first-person narrative, in this way '"shattering stereotypes by walking in each other's shoes," as one of the Narrative 4 facilitators put it' (Lovell, 2014). Narrative 4 has reached out to schools across the globe to extend the model to South Africa, Ireland, Afghanistan and many American states (Narrative 4, 2016).

Another example of level 3 empathy building is the Arava Institute for Environmental Studies situated in a kibbutz in the Negev desert in which 'groups of Israeli, Palestinian, Jordanian and overseas students – cumulatively numbering by 2011 about 600' created 'a network of regional environmentalists who are able and willing to work together' (Schoenfeld et al., 2014, p. 171). Schoenfeld et al. interviewed 38 participants who had experience of the institute's work and, based on the outcome of this qualitative inquiry, compiled the following six empathy-building strategies that are seen as particularly effective as used by the Arava Institute (Schoenfeld et al., 2014):

1   Using 'Arab and Jewish "Program Associates." Older, more mature students, similar to university dons or housemasters, live in student residences. They are problem solvers, advisors and role models in a setting where academic study and the cultivation of empathy go together' (p. 172).
2   '[T]he intimacy of a small group living together for months in an isolated setting – talking over meals, engaging in recreation activities and in small classes – is a major aspect of learning to understand each other and developing sympathy and trust' (p. 172).
3   Fieldtrips and projects (by overseas students travelling to the Middle East).
4   Working together on practical work (in this example, dry lands agricultural projects).
5   '[S]taff and students taking responsibility for restoring relations after difficult interactions' (p. 181).
6   Seminars on Peacebuilding and Environmental Leadership.

At the core of this programme is the idea of putting oneself in someone else's shoes. As one participant explained:

> I invited several of the non-Israeli students to stay with us in Jerusalem. . . .
> We went sightseeing, visited the famous Ben Yehuda Midrahov, and even sat in a cafe. Several days or weeks later . . . a suicide attack in Jerusalem hit the same cafe where we were sitting just a few days earlier. That was a shocking moment to my Jordanian friend. . . . He could much more easily identify with

the Israelis after he could relate to the location, the time and the place. He realized that had the attack been just a few days before, he could have been there too.

(p. 180)

Approaching problems collectively

If communities, such as schools, break down the individualistic dimension of conflict and consider it as a communal problem that is not merely a question of aggressors and victims but shared responsibility, each person shares the situation and therefore the strategies to remediate it. This also means that many people feel affected by the phenomenon in question and thus can empathise with the individuals involved collectively. Schools should be clear about the importance of empathy in collective gatherings such as assemblies and special events or presentations, highlighting the general idea of a community respecting each of its members rather than isolating individual cases in any polarising dichotomy of victim and aggressor. Furthermore, schools can use groups of students to develop an ethos of empathy by ensuring that they work together in various configurations that cut across dividing lines of age and ability to work on conflict resolution collectively. Examples of this type of collective approach include the students in a class or whole school setting behavioural rules or a code of conduct together, community events such as debates or interactive workshops on bullying and/or conflict and open discussions on bullying that are scaffolded in such a way that there is consensus at closure. For more detail on collective approaches to bullying in schools, see Rock, Hammond and Rasmussen (2002).

Movements such as these that look at models of collective responsibility, transcend the notion of empathy in a traditional sense of feelings for one person or group by another since a common base of sentiment, response and problem-solving is created in what could be described as intergroup emotions theory (Smith, Seger & Mackie, 2007) in which lowered levels of self-consciousness and increased feelings of unity lead to a collective mindset. Lamm and Silani (2014) point out that:

> lack of self-awareness and self/other distinction is one putative mechanism of collective affective experiences such as the high synchrony between individuals that occurs during mass phenomena, such as at music concerts or at political demonstrations. There, the individual becomes part of a larger crowd, and loses his or her ability for self-awareness and self/other distinction.

(p. 11)

This phenomenon can be explained neurobiologically: the dorsal and anterior medial prefrontal cortex appears to be active in a lessening of influence by others (see Brass, Ruby & Spengler, 2009; Lamm, Meltzhoff & Decety, 2010; Lamm et al., 2007). While the associations one usually makes with groupthink tend to be

Orwellian and negative (suggesting an unthinking tyranny of the masses), if schools are able to create values-driven collective cultures, this facet of human behaviour can be used in a positive sense to allow for collective empathy.

Non-educational examples of collective empathy include those developed by Muller, Pfarrer and Little (2014), who discuss a model of corporate philanthropy whereby approaches to giving are taken collectively. Schools can learn from these as they demonstrate an increasingly necessary collective decision-making ethos to solve world problems.

Indeed, a considerable educational challenge is that of creating practical responses to global problems such as biocapacity, poverty and conflict that necessarily harness shared knowledge and group approaches since they are too complex, interrelated and challenging to be solved by any one person or single lobby. As long as we view these problems as belonging to another person or to some future generation, we will not be in the right mindset to solve them. Therefore, level 3 empathy in education is not only about putting individuals and groups in situations where they can relate to 'others' problems', it means evoking a philosophy that allows them to see themselves as sufficiently connected to those problems in the first place to want to solve them as their own.

The twenty-first century is an era of huge changes to social, political, environmental and economic structures. It is increasingly clear that educational systems that prepare young people to solve these problems need to view them with some degree of sensitivity and empathy so that isolationist, selfish outlooks are not allowed to predominate as these will neither solve these problems or seek out responses for the good of humanity as a whole.

After decades of scientific progress and positivism in the Western world, one might argue that it is time to return to indigenous knowledge systems that have a collective view of the ecosystem. This broadens the notion of empathy from an individual or group, human phenomenon to one where humans are seeking to understand the world around them, feel part of it and respond to the threats that face it as part of a *weltanschauung*: 'It is the common experience of all human societies that these are the elements that constitute the large majority of any members of any social system' (Ayoob, 2002, pp. 40–41).

Conclusion

Theories about empathy as a response to prejudice are difficult to measure, as this chapter has argued. Although neuroscientific advances allow us to measure mimicry and various neural responses to images, mental products or emotional outflows of others, it remains particularly difficult to know the extent to which they represent genuine states of empathy as opposed to biological automatisms that may or may not contain degrees of considered feelings for others. This essentially means that in order to assess empathetic responses from students, qualitative measures are more likely to be successful – those that ask students to express their feelings about a situation in some detail. These would include essays, portfolio assignments, interviews, discussions, works of art, presentations and self-reflections.

Trying to assess levels of empathy in any strictly hierarchical sense would be difficult if not counter-productive since, like creativity, empathy is a subtle, flexible construct. Therefore, schools should aim to develop as many empathy nurturing learning experiences as possible so that an appreciation of the degree of empathy someone is engaging in is based on widespread evidence. To allow empathy to develop, schools should ensure that conversations are happening around those experiences that allow for feedback on degrees of self-reflection, and awareness of other people's predicaments.

Qualitative social science research has shown that engaging students in educational experiences that teach them, show them, model for them or even ensure that they directly experience the plight of others will draw them into more empathetic dispositions. The three stages of empathy evocation that I have developed in this chapter will allow instructors developmental approaches.

For a particularly rich developmental empathetic experience concerning one group or person, students might begin with exposure to literature and/or art works from or about the group or person, then progress into simulating the conditions in which that group/person operates and, through games and classroom learning experiences, try to understand what it might be like to be them. Finally, a field trip or exchange would allow for theory, beliefs, indirectly garnered experience and assumptions to be reinforced or debunked by a real-life experience. Provided that this process is scaffolded with questions that allow the student to progress his/her empathetic understanding ('What was it like to . . . ?', 'How did it feel when you . . . ?', 'Tell me/us about the time when you . . . ?', 'What would you have done in that situation?', 'Can you relate to this or think of something similar that might have happened to you once?'), the experience would be meaningful,

I have also argued that at the highest level of empathetic thinking and being, the entire notion of 'us and them' or 'me and you' should be broken down and de-dramatized so that a common understanding overrides difference and allows for a broad appreciation of what it means to be human.

If a student's sense of empathy were truly developed, it would lead to significant action and a type of moral outrage in the face of social injustice. Indeed, if one of the reasons for an education for less prejudice is to lead to a more peaceful world, then a heightened sense of empathy should lead individuals and groups to act so as to eradicate the ills that befall others wherever possible. An education for peace without social justice would be an education without genuine empathy, as Julius Nyrere stated powerfully, shortly after Tanzania's independence:

> peace by itself is not enough for the human spirit if it means just an absence of violent conflict. . . . . Peace and human justice are interlinked, and should be interlinked. Those of us who are free to develop ourselves and our nation have no right to demand that the oppressed, the victims of discrimination,

the starving and the persecuted, should acquiesce in their present condition. If we do make such a demand we are ourselves becoming their persecutors and their oppressors. The peace which exists while such human conditions prevail is neither secure nor justifiable.

(Nyerere, 1974, pp. 1–2)

Perhaps the best known literary expression of the idea that humanity and commonality represent the highest level of empathy is that in John Donne's famous *Meditation XVII* (1623): 'ask not for whom the bell tolls, it tolls for thee' (Dickson, 2007).

At the root of this is not only a cultural, anthropological issue but an epistemological one. Empathy requires a level of being that goes beyond the cognitive: 'knowledge alone will not reduce prejudice; knowledge is something of a prerequisite to prejudice reduction, not the sole means' (Pate, 1981, p. 288). This mindset can be extended to the environment in general so that sentient and non-sentient beings and artefacts are respected and treated as assets for humanity in general. This way of thinking is necessary for the preservation of the planet and provides educational structures with the significant challenge of creating environments where mindful respect of the entire environment is promoted.

References

Ashoka. (2016). Online. Available at: http://empathy.ashoka.org/ (accessed 28 April 2016).

Austen, J. (1815). *Emma*. London: John Murray.

Avenanti, A., Sirigu, A., & Aglioti, S.M. (2010). Racial bias reduces empathic sensorimotor resonance with other-race pain. *Current Biology*, 20, 1018–1020.

Ayoob, M. (2002). Inequality and theorising in international relations: the case for subaltern realism. *International Studies Review*, 4(3), 27–48.

Batson, C.D. (1987). Self-report ratings of empathic emotion. In N. Eisenberg and J. Strayer (Eds), *Empathy and its development* (pp. 356–360). New York, NY: Cambridge University Press.

Batson, C.D., Chang, J., Orr, R., & Rowland, J. (2002). Empathy, attitudes, and action: Can feeling for a member of a stigmatized group motivate one to help the group? *Personality and Social Psychology Bulletin*, 28, 1656–1666.

Batson, C.D., Polycarpou, M.P., Harmon-Jones, E., Imhoff, H.J., Mitchener, E.C., Bednar, L.L., Klein, T.R., & Highberger, L. (1997). Empathy and attitudes: Can feeling for a member of a stigmatized group improve feelings toward the group? *Journal of Personality and Social Psychology*, 72, 105–118.

Berkowitz, M., & Bier, M. (2005). *What works in character education: A report for policy makers and opinion leaders*. Character Education Partnership.

Bialik, M., Bogan, M., Fadel, C., & Horthavotha, M. (2015). *Character education for the 21st century: What should students learn?* Centre for Curriculum Redesign. Online. Available at: http://curriculumredesign.org/wp-content/uploads/CCR-CharacterEducation_FINAL_27Feb2015.pdf (accessed 28 April 2016).

Bloom, S.G. (2005). *Lesson of a lifetime*. Smithsonian.com. Online. Available at: www.smithsonianmag.com/history/lesson-of-a-lifetime-72754306/?no-ist=&onsite_medium=internal&page=1 (accessed 28 April 2016).

Booth, W.C. (1983). *The rhetoric of fiction* (2nd edn). Chicago, IL: University of Chicago Press.

Brass, M., Ruby, P., & Spengler, S. (2009). Inhibition of imitative behaviour and social cognition. *Philosophical Transactions of the Royal Society of London B: Biological Science*, 364, 2359–2367.

Byrnes, D.A., & Kiger, G. (1990). The effect of a prejudice-reduction simulation on attitude change 1. *Journal of Applied Social Psychology*, 20(4), 1559–1816. doi:10.1111/j.1559-1816.1990.tb00415.x

Byrnes, D.A., & Kiger, G. (1992). Prejudice reduction simulations: Ethics, evaluations, and theory into practice. *Simulations and Games*, 23, 457–471.

Carr, L., Iacoboni, M., Dubeau, M.C., Mazziotta, J.C., & Lenzi, G.L. (2003). Neural mechanisms of empathy in humans: A relay from neural systems for imitation to limbic areas. *PNAS*, 100(9), 5497–5502. doi:10.1073/pnas.0935845100

Cikara, M., Bruneau, E., Van Bavel, J.J., & Saxe, R. (2014). Their pain gives us pleasure: How intergroup dynamics shape empathic failures and counter-empathic responses. *Journal of Experimental Social Psychology*, 55, 110–125.

Davis, M.H. (1983). Measuring individual differences in empathy: Evidence for a multidimensional approach. *Journal of Personality and Social Psychology*, 44(1), 113–126. doi: 10.1037//0022-3514.44.1.113

Dickson, D.R. (Ed.). (2007). *John Donne's Poetry* (Norton Critical Edition). New York: Norton.

Duan, C., & Hill, C.E. (1996). The current state of empathy research. *Journal of Counseling Psychology*, 43(3), 261–274. doi: 10.1037/0022-0167.43.3.261

Dweck, C.S. (2006). *Mindset: The new psychology of success*. New York: Random House.

Dweck, C.S. (2012). *Mindset: How you can fulfill your potential*. London: Constable & Robinson.

Ecolint Student League of Nations. (2014). Online. Available at: www.ecolint.ch/sites/default/files/document_files/sln_handbook_2014.pdf (accessed 28 April 2016).

Ecolint. (2016). Online. Available at: www.ecolint.ch (accessed 28 April 2016).

Ellis, P.L. (1982). Empathy: A factor in antisocial behavior. *Journal of Abnormal Child Psychology*, 10(1), 123–133.

Eze, M.O. (2010). *Intellectual history in contemporary South Africa*. London: Palgrave Macmillan.

Finlay, K.A., & Stephan, W.G. (2000). Improving intergroup relations: The effects of empathy on racial attitudes. *Journal of Applied Social Psychology*, 30, 1720–1737.

Frank, A. (1952). *Anne Frank: The Diary of a Young Girl* (B.M. Mooyaart, Trans.). New York, NY: Doubleday.

Fraser, J. (1974). *Violence in the Arts*. Cambridge: Cambridge University Press.

Galinsky, A.D., & Moskowitz, G.B. (2000). Perspective-taking: decreasing stereotype expression, stereotype accessibility, and in-group favoritism. *Journal of Personality and Social Psychology*, 78(4), 708–724.

George, J.M. (2000). Emotions and leadership: The role of emotional intelligence. *Human Relations*, 53(8), 1027–1055.

Gilligan, C. (1982). *In a different voice: Psychological theory and women's development*. Cambridge, MA: Harvard University Press.

Goleman, D., (1995). *Emotional Intelligence*. New York and London: Bantam Books.

Goleman, D. (1998). What makes a leader? Online. Available at; www.sdcity.edu/Portals/0/CMS_Editors/MESA/PDFs/Generic/WhatMakesALeader.pdf (accessed 28 April 2016).

Gordon, M. (2005). *Roots of empathy: Changing the world child*. Toronto: Thomas Allen.

Griswold, C.L., & Konstan, D. (2012). *Ancient forgiveness: Classical, Judaic and Christian*. Cambridge: Cambridge University Press.

Hogan, R. (1969). Development of an empathy scale. *Journal of Consulting and Clinical Psychology*, 33(3), 307–316. doi: 10.1037/h0027580

Jaramillo, A., Buote, D., & Schonert-Reichl, K.A. (2008). *An evaluation of the implementation of the Seeds of Empathy program*. Report prepared for Roots of Empathy. University of British Columbia.

Joubert, E. (1978). *Die swerfjare van Poppie Nongena (The long journey of Poppie Nongena)*. Cape Town: Tafelberg.

Joyce, K. (2015). Feeling the emotions of war: Developing historical empathy through the visual arts. Then/Hier – The history education network. Online. Available at: http://thenhier.ca/en/content/feeling-emotions-war-developing-historical-empathy-through-visual-arts (accessed 28 April 2016).

Katz, R.L. (1963). *Empathy: its nature and uses*. London: Free Press of Glencoe.

Kellett, J.B., Humphrey, R.H., & Sleeth, R.G. (2002). Empathy and complex task performance: Two routes to leadership. *The Leadership Quarterly*, 13, 523–544.

Kirshenblatt-Gimblett, B., & Shandler, J. (2012). *Anne Frank unbound: Media, imagination, memory*. Bloomington, IN: Indiana University Press.

Lamm, C., & Silani, G. (2014). The neural underpinnings of empathy and their relevance for collective emotions. In C. Scheve and M. Salmella (Eds), *Collective Emotions*. Oxford: Oxford University Press.

Lamm, C., Meltzhoff, A.N., & Decety, J. (2010). How do we empathize with someone who is not like us? A functional magnetic resonance imaging study. *Journal of Cognitive Neurosciences*, 22, 362–376.

Lamm, C., Nusbaum, H.C., Meltzhoff, A.N., & Decety, J. (2007). What are you feeling? Using functional magnetic resonance imaging to assess the modulation of sensory and affective responses during empathy for pain. *PLoS ONE*, 12, e1292.

Lee, A. (2005). [Film]. *Brokeback Mountain*. Focus Features.

Lee, H. (1960). *To kill a mockingbird*. New York, NY: Grand Central Publishing.

Liddell, H.G., & Scott, R. (1940). *A Greek-English lexicon: Machine readable text*. Trustees of Tufts University: Oxford. Online. Available at: http://perseus.uchicago.edu/cgi-bin/philologic/navigate.pl?LSJ.4 (accessed 28 April 2016).

LIMUN. (2016). London International Model United Nations. Online. Available at: http://limun.org.uk/ (accessed 28 April 2016).

Lovell, J. (2014). The tale of two schools. *The New York Times Magazine*. Online. Available at: www.nytimes.com/interactive/2014/05/04/magazine/tale-of-two-schools.html?_r=0 (accessed 28 April 2016).

Lynch, D. (1980). [Film]. *The Elephant Man*. Brooksfilms.

MacDonald, A., Bell, P., McLafferty, M., McCorkell, L., Walker, I., Smith, V., Balfour, A., & Murphy, P. (2013). Evaluation of the Roots of Empathy Programme by North Lanarkshire Psychological Service. *North Lanarkshire Psychological Service Research* (unpublished).

McQueen, S. (2013). [Film]. *12 Years a Slave*. Fox Searchlight Pictures.

Mallgrave, H.F., & Ikonomou, E. (Eds). (1994). *Empathy, form, and space: Problems in German aesthetics, 1873–1893*. Santa Monica: Getty Center for the History of Art and the Humanities.

Mathur, V.A., Harada, T., Lipke, T., & Chiao, J. (2010). Neural basis of extraordinary empathy and altruistic motivation. *NeuroImage*, 51, 1468–1475.

Mayer, J.D., Caruso, D.R., & Salovey, P. (2000). Selecting a measure of emotional intelligence: the case for ability scales. In R. Bar-On, & J.D.A. Parker (Eds.), *The handbook of emotional intelligence: theory, development, assessment, and application at home, school, and the workplace* (pp. 320–342). San Francisco, CA: Jossey-Bass.

Maxwell, B. (2008). *Professional ethics education: Studies in compassionate empathy*. Netherlands: Springer Science & Business Media.

Mickolus, E.F., Brannan, J., & Project Muse. (2013). *Coaching winning model united nations teams: A teacher's guide*. Lincoln, NE: Potomac Books.

Moll, J., Krueger, F., Zahn, R., Pardini, M., de Oliveira Souza, R., & Grafman, J. (2006). Human fronto-mesolimbic networks guide decisions about charitable donation. *Proceedings of the*

National Academy of Sciences, USA, 103, 1562, 3–8. Online. Available at: www.ncbi.nlm. nih.gov/pmc/articles/pmc1622872/ (accessed 28 April 2016).

Muller, A., Pfarrer, M.D., & Little, L.M. (2014). A theory of collective empathy in corporate philanthropy decisions. *Academy of Management Review*, 39(1), 1–21. Online. Available at: http://ssrn.com/abstract=2229122 (accessed 28 April 2016).

Narrative 4. (2016). Online. Available at: www.narrative4.com/mission-vision/vision/ (accessed 28 April 2016).

Nyborg. (2016). Model United Nations of Nyborg. Online. Available at: https://munnyborg. wordpress.com/ (accessed 28 April 2016).

Nyerere, J. (1974). Stability and change in Africa (1969). In J. Nyerere (Ed.), *Man and development*. Nairobi: Oxford University Press.

Ogle J., Bushnell, J.A., & Caputi, P. (2013). Empathy is related to clinical competence in medical care. *Medical Education*, 47(8), 824–831. doi: 10.1111/medu.12232

Paluck, E.L., & Green, D.P. (2009). Prejudice reduction: What works? A review and assessment of research and practice. *Annual Review of Psychology*, 60, 339–367. doi: 10.1146/annurev.psych.60.110707.163607

Paro, H.B., Silveira, P.S., Perotta, B., Gannam, S., Enns, S.C., Giaxa, R.R., Bonito, R.F., Martins, M.A., & Tempski, P.Z. (2014). Empathy among medical students: Is there a relation with quality of life and burnout? *PlosOne*, 9(4):e94133. doi: 10.1371/journal.pone.0094133

Pate, G.S. (1981). Research on prejudice reduction. *Educational Leadership*, 38, 288–291.

Pijnenborg, G.H.M., Spikman, J.M., Jeronimus, B.F., & Aleman, A. (2012). Insight in schizophrenia: associations with empathy. *European Archives of Psychiatry and Clinical Neuroscience*, 263(4): 299–307. doi:10.1007/s00406-012-0373-0

Pilling, B.K., & Eroglu, S. (1994). An empirical examination of the impact of salesperson empathy and professionalism and merchandise salability on retail buyers' evaluations. *Journal of Personal Selling & Sales Management*, 14(1), 45–58.

Rock, E.A., Hammond, M., & Rasmussen, S. (2002). *School based program to teach children empathy and bully prevention.* Online. Available at: www.counseling.org/resources/library/Selected%20Topics/Bullying/School_Based_Program.html (accessed 28 April 2016).

Rogers, C.R. (1975). Empathic – unappreciated way of being. *Counseling Psychology*, 5(2), 2–10. doi: 10.1177/001100007500500202

Rolheiser, C., & Wallace, D. (2005). *The Roots of Empathy Program as a strategy for increasing social and emotional learning. Report prepared for Roots of Empathy.* Ontario Institute for Studies in Education, University of Toronto.

Roots of Empathy. (2015). Online. Available at: www.rootsofempathy.org/en.html (accessed 28 April 2016).

Salovey, P., Mayer, J., & Caruso, D. (2004). Emotional intelligence: Theory, findings, and implications, *Psychological Inquiry*, 15(3), 197–215.

Santos, R.G., Chartier, M.J., Whalen, J.C., Chateau, D., & Boyd, L. (2011). Effectiveness of school-based violence prevention for children and youth: Cluster randomized field trial of the Roots of Empathy program with replication and three-year follow-up. *Healthcare Quarterly*, 14, 80–91.

Schoenfeld, S., Zohar, A., Alleson, I., Suleiman, O., & Sipos-Randor, G. (2014). A place of empathy in a fragile, contentious landscape: Environmental peacebuilding in the eastern Mediterranean. In N. Megoran, F. McConnell and P. Williams (Eds), *The geographies of peace: New approaches to boundaries, diplomacy and conflict* (pp. 171–193). I.B.: Taurus.

Schonert-Reichl, K.A., Smith, V., Zaidman-Zait, A., & Hertzman, C. (2012). Promoting children's prosocial behaviours in school: Impact of the 'Roots of Empathy' program on the social and emotional competence of school-aged children. *School Mental Health*, 4(1), 1–12.

Schutz. (2016). Model United Nations. Online. Available at: www.schutzschool.org.eg/activities/model-un.cfm (accessed 28 April 2016).

Sheridan, J. (1989). [Film]. *My Left Foot*. Granada & Miramax films.

Smith, E.R., Seger, C.R., & Mackie, D.M. (2007). Can emotions be truly group level? Evidence regarding four conceptual criteria. *Journal of Personality and Social Psychology*, 93, 431–446.

Snyder, C.R., Lopez, S.J., & Pedrotti, J.T. (2011). *Positive psychology: The scientific and practical explorations of human strengths*. 2nd edn. Los Angeles, CA: Sage.

Solzhenitsyn, A. (1963). *One day in the life of Ivan Denisovich* (R. Parker, Trans.). New York, NY: Dutton.

Spielberg, S. (1985). [Film]. *The Color Purple*. Warner Brothers Pictures.

Steiner, C., & Perry, P. (1997). *Achieving emotional literacy*. London: Bloomsbury.

Teaching Tolerance. (2008). Online. Available at: www.tolerance.org/magazine/number-33-spring-2008/feature/classroom-simulations-proceed-caution (accessed 28 April 2016).

Todd, A.R., Bodenhausen, G.V., Richeson, J.A., & Galinsky, A.D. (2011). Perspective taking combats automatic expressions of racial bias. *Journal of Personality and Social Psychology*, 100(6), 1027–1042.

Vescio, T.K., Sechrist, G.B., & Paolucci, M.P. (2003). Perspective taking and prejudice reduction: The mediational role of empathy arousal and situational attributions. *European Journal of Social Psychology*, 33, 455–472.

Wagaman, M.A., & Geiger, J.M. (2012). The role of empathy in burnout and compassion satisfaction among social workers. Paper presented at the Council on Social Work Education Annual Program Meeting, 9–12 November 2012, Washington, D.C.

Wagaman, M. A, Geiger, J.M., Shockley, C., & Segal, E.A. (2015). The role of empathy in burnout and compassion satisfaction among social workers. *Social Work*, 60, 3, 201–209.

Weiner, M.J., & Wright, F.E. (1973). Effects of undergoing arbitrary discrimination upon subsequent attitudes toward a minority group. *Journal of Applied Social Psychology*, 3, 94–102. doi: 10.1111/j.1559-1816.1973.tb01298.x

Williams, A., & Giles, H. (1992). Prejudice-reduction simulations: Social cognition, intergroup theory, and ethics. *Simulation & Gaming*, 23(4), 472–484.

Xu, X., Zuo, X., Wang, X., & Han, S. (2009). Do you feel my pain? Racial group membership modulates empathic neural responses. *The Journal of Neuroscience*, 29, 8525–8529.

Yukl, G. (1998). *Leadership in organizations* (4th edn). Upper Saddle River, NJ: Prentice Hall.

PART II

The conditions necessary for prejudice reduction

6

THE CONTACT HYPOTHESIS AS A STRATEGY AGAINST PREJUDICE

Introduction

When discussing the conditions that should be established for prejudice to be reduced between people or groups, the best-known and most thoroughly researched strategy in the school of social psychology is the contact hypothesis. This chapter investigates the contact hypothesis' core principles before turning to the substantial research that has been conducted since its inception in the 1950s to show its effectiveness. The chapter will critically examine the reliability and validity of the case studies mentioned. The second half of this chapter looks at known, tried and tested applications of the theory in classroom settings but also outside of the world of education. This information allows for a synthesis of best practice that can be considered when applying the contact hypothesis in schools.

The fundamentals of the theory

Also known as intergroup contact theory, the contact hypothesis can be attributed to Gordon Allport who put the idea forward in chapter 16 (entitled 'The Effect of Contact') of his seminal *The Nature of Prejudice* (1954). Writing in the newly formed school of social psychology at a time when segregation in the United States was at its height, and in the wake of some initial work to suggest that contact between members of different groups could reduce prejudice (see Williams, 1947; Stouffer et al., 1949), Allport's theory was based on studies done before him, his own observations and research conducted by his own students.

The theory can be thus summarised: prejudice can be reduced if there is contact between people of different ethnic groups provided that the following four prerequisites are respected:

1   There must be equal status between the groups.
2   The groups must share common goals.

3   There must be intergroup cooperation.
4   Authorities, law or custom must support the contact.

It is important to grasp these four pillars for without them contact can lead to animosity. Indeed, there is something of a commonly held belief that diversity will reduce prejudice of its own accord but this is not the case. 'Casual contact [Allport pointed out] has left matters worse than before. [. . .] Theoretically, every superficial contact we make with an out-group member could by the "law of frequency" strengthen the adverse associations that we have' (Allport, 1954, p. 264). Pettigrew goes on to explain how

> more interracial contact can lead either to greater prejudice and rejection or to greater respect and acceptance, depending upon the situation in which it occurs. The basic issue, then, concerns the types of situations in which contact leads to distrust and those in which it leads to trust.
>
> *(Pettigrew, 1971, p. 275)*

So contact should be governed by certain prerequisites for it to have a positive effect on prejudicial thinking.

Since Allport's (1954) formula, other conditions for successful contact have been added; notably the idea that if participation is voluntary (Amir, 1969, 1976), and if contact is intimate (Cook, 1962), the chances of prejudice reduction are even greater.

Dixon, Durrheim and Tredoux (2005) have synthesised 13 points that epitomise some of the prerequisites that researchers have added to the contact theory since Allport's (1954) formula: they point out that contact should be regular, 'should involve a balanced ratio of in-group to out-group members' (Dixon et al., 2005, p. 699), should allow for members engaging in contact to do so to the extent that there is a feeling not only of contact but genuine acquaintance, allowing for friendships to form. Furthermore, contact should not be constrained to one environment but should happen across numerous different settings and should be recognised as important to those involved. Dixon et al. (2005) also reiterate some of Allport's original ideas: 'contact should occur between individuals who share equality of status [. . .]; should be organized around cooperation toward the achievement of a superordinate goal [. . .] should be free from anxiety or other negative emotions' (p. 699), should not take place in interactions that are too competitive and should be socially or institutionally endorsed. Ideas that have been developed subsequent to Allport's (1954) theory include the notion that the contact hypothesis should aim to establish counterstereotypic encounters (in other words, interactions that do not conform to some of the clichés that can be traditionally associated with group encounters such as the workplace) but at the same time, for there to be a disconfirming effect, 'contact should be with a person who is deemed a typical or representative member of another group' (p. 699).

Pettigrew reformulated the contact hypothesis in 1998, adding friendship as an essential factor and pointing out that contact would be more beneficial when added to some learning about the outgroup (Pettigrew, 1998). Pettigrew also pointed out that the changing behaviour of participants, the extent to which they might generate affective ties and the need to reappraise intergroup relations were all important conditions. Pettigrew's revised model stresses a process of decategorisation, salient categorisation, and recategorisation whereby the individual is involved in a reflective thought process while considering members of other groups.

It should be noted that the contact hypothesis was designed with ethnic groups in mind, so some caution should be taken when transferring its tenets to other domains of prejudice such as class, gender or sexuality. Research has shown, however, that the contact hypothesis can be applied to different constituents with success. Herek and Glunt (1993), for example, conducted telephone surveys with 937 participants in the United States and found a strong correlation between interpersonal contact and positive attitudes towards homosexual males. Schwartz and Simmons (2001) conducted research on college students in the United States to test their attitudes towards the elderly and found after self-reported data (which, of course, can be fairly unreliable), that the quality of contact led to more favourable attitudes towards the elderly. Other studies that have extended the realm of contact hypothesis beyond ethnic relations include Adsett and Morin (2004), who have studied its effect on linguistic diversity, and Manetti, Schneider and Siperstein (2001), who investigated its impact on views towards mentally handicapped children. However, Pettigrew (2008) has tempered the idea of contact hypothesis transfer by positing that its effects have been far stronger in lessening traditional prejudicial bounds such as racism, ethnocentrism and homophobia and less effective in reducing less overtly criticised forms of prejudice such as that formed against the mentally ill.

The contact hypothesis is a powerful, extensively researched strategy. It has been described as 'one of psychology's most effective strategies for improving intergroup relations' (Dovidio, Gaertner & Kawakami, 2003, p. 5). In theory, putting the contact hypothesis into practice in schools should be fairly straightforward as there is something of a formulaic repertoire of conditions available for review and the central idea within it is simple to understand.

Putting theory into practice: practicality, anxiety and generalisation

There are a number of concerns to be taken into account before the contact hypothesis can be implemented in schools. Amichai-Hamburger and McKenna (2006) have pointed out that three obstacles stand in the way of contact theory operationalisation:

> (1) practicality – creating a contact situation involves overcoming some serious practical obstacles; (2) anxiety – the anxiety felt by the participants may cause a contact to be unsuccessful or at least not reach its potential; (3) generalization – the results of a contact, however successful, tend to be limited to the context of the meeting and to the participants.
>
> *(p. 825)*

These obstacles can be looked at in more detail:

Practicality

The practical obstacles that experimental conditions can eradicate but that reality might present include participant motivation for contact, environmental conditions that ensure a sufficient valency of contact – the problem here being that this can seem forced and potentially counter-productive if attempted in real-life settings and the extent to which superordinate goals about equality and tolerance will be internalised by members of an institution, something that is practically beyond the control of authorities. There is also, in reality, no ongoing assessment or tracking system as there is in experimental or quasi-experimental settings, meaning that regress into prejudice can take place easily without it necessarily being noticed or acted upon.

The problem of practicality that arises when trying to put the theory into practice, illustrated by Dixon et al. (2005), is premised on the fact that outside of experimental conditions, casual contact between individuals or groups in the real world does not resemble the type of contact that Allport had in mind: optimal contact 'usually takes the form of short-lived laboratory analogues or highly localized interventions in the field' (Dixon et al., 2005, p. 700). In opposition, most human interactions are determined by mundane events and conditions that are often functional and driven less by a desire for there to be fruitful social contact between individuals or groups and more in the name of market-driven productivity or practical, logistical goals. The reality is that it is mostly the workplace that will bring people of radically different backgrounds together in any protracted sense where genuine interaction will be necessary.

While equitable working conditions – where they exist – might ensure that contact takes place under some of Allport's less lofty conditions, for example under the premise that people are of equal value and are working together on a common goal, as Amir (1969) points out, this type of professional encounter 'produces only casual interactions rather than intimate acquaintances' (p. 337).

Informal social gatherings such as parties or other types of non-professional congregations such as church services tend to be self-selecting and do not, therefore, bring people of different orientations, belief systems or groups together but, if anything, run the risk of reinforcing ingroup cohesion and hostility towards outgroups. One could argue for these cases that, while ethnic and social differences might be lessened under a 'broad church' or particularly diverse social setting, denominational differences will be exacerbated, therefore exchanging one form of prejudice with another and merely creating a larger ingroup.

Furthermore, at least when looking to ethnicity, the number of cross-race interactions and friendships that occur in society are few and far between. A survey by Sigelman et al. (1996) showed that over 70 per cent of white Americans had no black friends, while Gibson's (2001) survey in South Africa found that only 6.6 per cent of whites and 1.5 per cent of blacks had friends of another race group.

Anxiety

The second point of anxiety is something to take into account since where there is prejudice there will often be fear and this can make contact unlikely or, if it is to occur, confrontational. In fact, negative contact, a trigger for heightened prejudice or manifestations of prejudice, can ensue in those cases where anxiety peaks so it is crucial to ensure that an atmosphere of relative trust and confidence reigns. However, this becomes difficult if not impossible to instil in an environment where there is prejudice in the first place.

Another problem with the contact hypothesis is the relationship between individual and group prejudice. While the contact hypothesis is essentially designed to quell prejudiced thinking in the individual and affect his/her approach to another individual (since the contact that will be taking place can only really be at an individual level), it does not hold that group-to-group prejudice will be affected in any way. In fact, Dixon et al. (2005, p. 703), referring to Forbes (1997, 2004), point out that a complex counter-productive effect might be created at a group level by contact across boundaries at an individual level. This takes place when individuals within an ingroup reach out to members of an outgroup and therefore transgress the cultural barriers that have been made sacred. As such, interracial or inter-religious relationships can threaten the identity of the larger group and cause violent reactions. This clamping down on intergroup contact at an individual level by group pressures is a well-known phenomenon that can be seen in literary archetypes such as Shakespeare's *Romeo and Juliet* (1597) where the young couple transgress the family feud between the Montagues and the Capulets or its modern incarnations such as Leonard Bernstein's *West Side Story* (1961) where Tony and Maria transgress the division between the American and Puerto Rican gangs.

Educational interventions that break down social boundaries should be wary of the pressure individuals might have to face outside of the classroom in their families and communities. Learning to live together should not be a message that remains within school walls and disappears once the learner is away from them; it is something that must transcend schools by taking wider social pressure into consideration.

Generalisation

The problem of generalisation in contact hypothesis theory is due to a number of issues pointed out by Amir (1976), Ford (1986), Stephan (1987) and Forbes (1997). Pettigrew and Tropp (2006), as a means of leading up to their own research, argue that much of this is due to incomplete sampling and lacunae in research methodology: studies have either been restricted to particular groups (for example, one type of ethnic group) whereas comparative analyses have dealt with relatively low numbers of studies without strict inclusion rules (p. 752).

While these issues can be improved through more rigorous approaches, assuming the data for meta-analysis exists, there is a broader question over the type of research method that would best suit a domain such as prejudice reduction. It should not surprise us to see that quasi-experimental design is prominent in the assessment of prejudice reducing interventions given that degrees of prejudice are highly contextual, subjective instances that cannot be standardised as easily as more straightforward constructs (such as knowledge of an academic domain). Accepting the difficulties of generalisable results in this field is, I would argue, something of a chestnut.

However, these problems are generic to most scientific research and are more methodological than pragmatic in nature. Educational settings will be necessarily contextual and fit-for-purpose according to specifics, which means that measuring their impact will necessarily involve some gauge of relativity.

Indeed, participants in experiments using the contact hypothesis will have their own inner experiences and semantics to define group dynamics and these might deviate substantially from the categories and a priori coding that are used by social scientists:

> explanations as to why particular respondents have experienced attitude change are not derived from a careful examination of their own experiences and perspectives but are simply 'read off' from the presence of particular conditions within the contact (i.e., that it was cooperative, that the participants were of equal status, etc.). Given the context-specific character of racial and ethnic relations, and their highly contingent and contradictory forms, the production of such ungrounded assumptions is highly questionable.
>
> *(Connolly, 2000, p. 176)*

So, for an educational institution, what will matter is how the community in question responds to contact hypothesis conditions on its own terms rather than whether theoretical, textbook conditions can be successfully monitored, measured, standardised and replicated. Hence, the most useful evidence for the contact hypothesis may well come through a series of case studies, each different from the next, as frustrating as this might be for the positivist thrust of certain types of research design seeking, for epistemological reasons, comparability and generalisability.

This is not to say that systematic reviews or meta-analyses have not been conducted to point to generalised findings (see Pettigrew & Tropp, 2000; 2006).

Research by Pettigrew and Tropp

Pettigrew and Tropp (2006) conducted a meta-analysis of 713 independent samples from 515 studies dealing with racial prejudice. This piece of research is commonly considered to be the most comprehensive to date. They screened samples for various elements that might have impeded the reliability of their results, for example, those cases where participants could choose to engage in contact with an outgroup (the argument being that cases where there was no choice would be more salient indicators of genuine contact hypothesis causality), creating a publication bias factor with a confidence interval for inclusion, by eliminating studies where results were generalised beyond the direct treatment group and where they were generalised beyond effect sizes (p. 754).

The researchers used a random effect model to measure effect size because this is 'particularly attractive when considering (1) studies that are quite heterogeneous,

(2) treatments that are ill-specified, and/or (3) effects that are complex and multi-determined' (Cook et al., 1992, p. 310). The following target groups featured among the various studies that were used in the meta-analysis: 'Sexual orientation; Physically disabled; Race, ethnicity; Mentally disabled; Mentally ill; Elderly; Other' (Pettigrew & Tropp, 2006, p. 764). Seventy-two per cent of the samples were from the United States.

The results of the meta-analysis indicated that on average contact reduces prejudice to a small but useful degree: 'the meta-analytic results clearly indicate that intergroup contact typically reduces intergroup prejudice. Synthesizing effects from 696 samples, the meta-analysis reveals that greater intergroup contact is generally associated with lower levels of prejudice' (p. 766).

Although Pettigrew and Tropp's (2006) study shows that the contact hypothesis when put into practice has a statistically significant effect, the correlation is rather low and does not suggest a major impact on prejudice. What is more striking is the number of cases manifesting a negative corollary between contact and prejudice and the fact that the mean effect was higher when studies were experimental: they state 'moreover, the mean effect rises sharply for experiments and other rigorously conducted studies. In addition, 94% of the samples in our analysis show an inverse relationship between intergroup contact and prejudice' (p. 766).

In conclusion, Pettigrew and Tropp (2006) suggest that not all of Allport's conditions for prejudice-reducing contact need to be respected for a successful outcome. They give two examples from Apartheid South Africa and segregated American neighbourhoods that show how contact led to a reduction in prejudicial thinking despite the fact that local authorities' positions on these matters were clearly directed elsewhere. The implications of this for schools are important as they suggest that institutional ethos alone might not be as effective as one might think for the reduction of prejudicial thinking.

They posit that an important factor in successful contact hypothesis scenarios is intergroup anxiety. Quoting the research done by Brown and Hewstone (2005), they argue that reducing intergroup anxiety is an important factor since much contact, if not carefully mediated, can heighten anxiety and load on to prejudice.

The meta-analysis ends with a confident assessment of the place of the contact hypothesis in strategies to reduce prejudice. They are sufficiently confident to state that further demonstration is not needed to prove its validity:

> Given the current state of the research literature, there is little need to demonstrate further contact's general ability to lessen prejudice. Results from the meta-analysis conclusively show that intergroup contact can promote reductions in intergroup prejudice. Moreover, the meta-analytic findings reveal that contact theory applies beyond racial and ethnic groups to embrace other types of groups as well. As such, intergroup contact theory now stands as a general social psychological theory and not as a theory designed simply for the special case of racial and ethnic contact.
>
> *(Pettigrew & Tropp, 2006, p. 768)*

Pettigrew and Tropp's comprehensive analysis leaves the reader with useful tips on what works in contact theory. In 2008 they conducted a meta-analytic test of the three most researched mediators (increasing knowledge of the outgroup, the reduction of anxiety related to intergroup contact and increasing perspective taking and empathy). Their analysis led them to the conclusion that, perhaps not surprisingly, empathy and perspective taking along with anxiety reduction were more important mediators than knowledge of the outgroup (Pettigrew & Tropp, 2008).

Examples of studies

While the classical route for contact theory is institutionalised, physical contact between members of different ethnic groups, other studies have been conducted to investigate different types of contact. Those mentioned here suggest different avenues for contact work.

Schiappa, Gregg and Hewes (2005) have developed the Parasocial Contact Hypothesis. The idea is that 'If people process mass-mediated communication in a manner similar to interpersonal interaction, then it is worth exploring whether the socially beneficial functions of intergroup contact have an analogue in parasocial contact' (p. 93). Essentially, the authors posit, 'knowing' someone through a televised setting can have similar effects on outlooks on the group that they represent as 'knowing' them in real life would.

Allport himself acknowledged the power of the media to influence people's prejudices (1954, pp. 200–202) and it stands to reason that in a media-saturated twenty-first century, positions will be altered by exposure to media. Schiappa et al. take the idea quite far:

> One can learn about a minority group from mediated messages and representations, and if one has a positive experience, one's behavior is altered in that one normally will seek out additional (parasocial) contact rather than avoid it. One can develop affective ties with persons known only through mediated communication, and, whether one reappraises one's beliefs about one's ingroup or not, the resulting parasocial relationships could encourage a change in prejudicial attitudes about the outgroups to which minority characters belong.
>
> *(2005, p. 97)*

The authors explain how in five studies analysed in a meta-analysis, 'parasocial contact is positively correlated with perceived homophily' (Schiappa et al., 2005, p. 100). They registered a mean effect size of .48 for an overall sample of over 600 participants. They went on to conduct their own research on 174 college students who were shown 10 episodes of the television show 'Six Feet Under' (in which the protagonist is homosexual). After pre-and post-testing using Likert-type scales to measure attitudes towards homosexuality, selecting only those respondents who had never seen an episode of the programme before, they found that 'the post-test measure of prejudice toward gay men (ATG) was lower than the pre-test mean after parasocial contact with the gay characters of Six Feet Under' (p. 105).

Schiappa et al. (2005) conducted similar quasi-experiments using other television programmes and generally found that these had an effect on views towards homosexuality, supporting the Parasocial Contact Hypothesis. However, they admit shortcomings in their experimental methodology: the studies were not randomised and did not use control groups.

Amichai-Hamburger and McKenna (2006) suggest that the Internet provides a solution to the problems of practicality and anxiety among participants by creating a neutral environment where many of the physical facets, cues and symbols suggesting group belonging are not discernible. The argument is also that such environments are comparatively simple to design, unlike the logistically challenging and potentially artificial physical contexts that must be etched out for the contact hypothesis to be enacted.

This argument goes some way but I would argue that without face-to-face contact, the extent and sincerity of the exchange can be put into question. Furthermore, it becomes almost impossible to determine institutional values through the medium of the Internet as there is no controlling agency or buy-in factor for users. A quick survey of most online fora, chats or responses to online postings shows how quickly dialogue can degenerate into outbursts of prejudice expiation and misuse by Internet trolls.

The contact hypothesis and prejudice against immigrants – research on the effect of knowledge of the outgroup

McLaren (2003) has shown how contact has reduced the feeling of threat Europeans harbour towards immigrants, pointing out in particular that friendships between participants and members of immigrant minority groups lead to less willingness to see illegal immigrants expelled. His studies have also shown that contact dampens anxiety about mass immigration, leaving participants feeling less insecure about large groups of migrants arriving in their countries.

A problem with this assertion, something that is common to the literature on prejudice, is the assumption that views on immigration can be attributed to prejudiced or open-minded mindsets based on the intrinsic value of statements about decisions to host or expel immigrants. I would argue that this is an indirect and potentially inaccurate representation of the degrees of prejudice a person might hold about a group. It is not inconceivable, for instance, that someone harbouring significant prejudices against immigrants might believe that expulsion is not an answer while, on the other hand, someone with a relatively low level of prejudiced sentiment towards immigrants, still believes that expulsion is a better political solution.

Part of this complexity can be felt in the modern-day state of right-wing and left-wing political discourses in Western Europe in which anti-immigration views are not necessarily and systematically the sole property of the right but can be felt in populist, traditionally leftist quarters too. This is clear in France where the traditional extreme right National Front party has well-known left-wing politicians or socialists joining its ranks fairly frequently.

So while contact might lead to a relaxed position on immigration as a socio-political, demographic phenomenon, this does not in and of itself mean that it will lead to less prejudice against immigrants as human beings.

Novotny and Polonsky (2011) correlated the amount of contact Czech and Slovak students had with Muslims with their knowledge of Islam through 716 interviews and found that less knowledge of Islam correlated with more fear and prejudice of that religion and that more contact with Muslims correlated positively with knowledge and understanding of Islam. Findings were modest and addressed with a strong cautionary note from the authors about the limits of generalisability. Nonetheless, they were able to strengthen their hypothesis that some knowledge of the outgroup is needed for prejudiced positions to be dampened. It stands to reason that knowledge of a group will be increased with contact.

The relationship between knowledge of a group and contact with a group is not necessarily positively correlated. Agirdag, Loobuyck and Van Houtte (2012) conducted a study on 620 Flemish teachers in Belgium and found that while more educated (4 years college degree and more) teachers had a positive approach to Muslims, teachers working in schools with more than half enrolled Muslims held less positive attitudes.

Negative intergroup contact

A variant of the contact hypothesis that has been tested is negative intergroup contact. Paolini, Harwood and Rubin (2010) ran an experiment in which 49 white Australians were interviewed after meeting with a woman from Sri Lanka who was briefed to act in positive or negative experience conditions (in other words, in an engaging, friendly manner for the former and a terse, cold manner for the second). The findings showed that participants referred to the woman's ethnicity in the second instance. This would suggest that negative experiences with people from other groups tend to highlight or exacerbate prejudicial thinking.

A study with a similar hypothesis was conducted by Barlow et al. (2012) to investigate white Australians' attitudes towards black Australians alongside white Americans' views of black Americans. The reflections of 1,560 participants on contact quantity and valence were correlated with prejudice indices. The authors determined two types of racism in their study: modern racism whereby race issues were discarded in the vein of an 'everything is fine for blacks' manner of thinking and old-fashioned racism whereby blacks were associated with undesirable stock characteristics.

The results of the comparative study were rather surprising: in the Australian sample, where white Australians mainly manifested a modern type of racism, increased negative contact led to an increase in prejudice (against black Australians) as might be expected,. However, less predictably, Barlow et al. (2012) found that an increase in positive contact did not reduce prejudice but actually saw a slight increase.

The American sample, on the other hand, in which whites articulated both old-fashioned and modern forms of racism against blacks, showed that an increase in negative contact correlated with an avoidance to discuss race and a lack of trust of blacks in positions of authority: 'White Americans [. . .] were more skeptical that Obama was born in the United States' (p. 1630).

In essence, the study shows that negative encounters across social group divides are important as they can have a stronger influence on attitudes than positive encounters. Therefore, when building community guidelines to reduce prejudicial thinking through contact, mechanisms should be put in place that allow for negative contact to be analysed and scaffolded with appropriate follow-up.

It is for this reason that when there are situations of conflict, the feelings and conclusions that either interlocutor derives should be discussed and problematized by the authorities presiding over the conflict resolution. In schools this can be done through constructive dialogue, pedagogic questioning ('Why do you think he or she did that?'; 'What makes you say that?'; 'Do you think it might be due to where he or she comes from or what he or she believes in? Why?'; 'What conclusions can you draw from this situation?').

Indeed, although much thinking on reflective dialogue asks participants to reflect on their own thought processes and emotions, I would suggest that it is equally important to ask why someone thinks that another person might have done whatever they did. This can be used as an opening or conversation prompt to lead to a richer understanding of the reasons, possibly prejudiced, that someone might attribute to another's actions.

Application in schools

The contact hypothesis lends itself naturally to the social organisation of schools in that students are already grouped together under superordinate goals and, in theory or at least in what one would hope would be the majority of cases, the values of a school tend to promote equal opportunity for each individual, one of Allport's mediators. Since the contact hypothesis is a widely accepted strategy to reduce prejudice with convincing results, schools should embrace it wholeheartedly. However, it should be noted that the results of studies on attempts to use the contact hypothesis in schools have not been particularly strong (see Stephan, 1985). This is partly due to the fact that it has typically not been implemented according to all of Allport's mediators and has led to negative interactions. For example, the efforts to use the contact hypothesis in the desegregation of American schools brought about contact but not the social, institutional support that is needed to support it and render it productive.

If we are to find institutions that broadcast values of equality and productive human interaction, one might also argue that such mission statements tend to be the reserve of private or international schools in leafy suburbs. Contact in inner-city or under-resourced rural schools might be less likely to enjoy the careful scaffolding required for positive contact. This is in part due to structural issues such as access to resources, unwieldy class sizes and undeveloped professional development programmes. It is also due to the fact that many national education programmes focus more on subject literacy and less on the affective domain.

This much said, whether the school in question is a national, international, public, grammar or independent school, for an institutional discourse to promote superordinate values, school leadership has to position itself boldly and should not behave as a mere bureaucratic management structure but should be ambitiously vocal and open about what it stands for. School leaders are accountable for school spirit and the clear articulation of values.

Therefore, no school should consider itself beyond the need of some careful self-reflection and action using the contact hypothesis. The following themes can be developed in schools to do this.

The jigsaw classroom

The jigsaw classroom (Aronson & Bridgeman, 1979; Aronson & Patnoe, 1997; Aronson, 2000) is one of the best known classroom strategies that uses contact theory to enhance learning and reduce prejudice.

Aronson first used it in 1971 in Houston during the climate of desegregation (1964–1974) as a way of defusing the tension that this caused since little clear scaffolding for intergroup contact had been designed by the government or districts to help socialise the desegregated classroom. Aronson observed classic teaching, with the teacher asking questions and students raising their hands and observed that this was an aggressive, competitive environment that was exacerbating the ambient racial tension; he says 'we realized that we needed to shift the emphasis from a relentlessly competitive atmosphere to a more cooperative one' (Jigsaw, 2016). Subsequent research has confirmed the damaging effect of too much competition on learning (see Elliot & Dweck, 1988; Smiley & Dweck, 1994; Dweck, 2012), suggesting that techniques such as the jigsaw classroom are needed to reduce anxiety.

The method can be best described in eight clear steps (adapted and extended from Jigsaw, 2016):

1   The students should be divided into groups (usually four to six); ideally the groups will be heterogeneous in composition and will cover a range of backgrounds and ability. Each group should comprise an equal number of students.
2   The lesson content should be divided into the number of students per group (so the lesson would be divided into four parts for groups of four, six parts for groups of six, and so on).
3   One student per group is assigned a corresponding part of the lesson (so in groups of four, the lesson parts would be appropriated by each member of the group). This is done for each group, so many students would be appropriating

the same part of the lesson simultaneously in different groups. Students should have access to their part of the lesson only.

4   Students are given time to appropriate the part of the lesson (by reading or researching).

5   'Expert groups' are formed by grouping students for each part of the lesson: each student who is responsible for part 1 sits together, each student in charge of part 2 sits at another table, and so on. The expert groups are given time to discuss the material together and rehearse the way that they will teach it.

6   The students go back to their original groups and each 'expert' teaches his or her section of the lesson to the rest of the group.

7   The teacher roams and facilitates where there are difficulties. As the activity is not only about subject mastery but also social interaction, the teacher should pay particular attention to this to ensure that discussions are supportive and respectful.

8   The class is tested on the lesson.

The overarching idea with the jigsaw classroom is that it increases students' self-esteem, academic performance and perspective taking (Aronson & Patnoe, 1997). The emphasis is on students learning from each other as they work as a team, respecting one another and learning how to listen attentively to one another, respecting each interlocutor in the process. By shifting roles from peer to learner to teacher, students' egocentricity is diminished (Bridgeman, 1981). By making the class end with some formal assessment, the teacher gives importance to the students' teaching role and ensures that the exercise is taken seriously.

Interestingly, while the jigsaw method is widely referenced as a strategy to increase self-efficacy, mastery and tolerance, there are relatively few empirical studies on it. Some studies have been conducted to show how it can reduce prejudice in the classroom. For example, Walter and Crogan (1998) ran a controlled trial on 103 Grade 4–6 students in Australia and found that the jigsaw classroom decreased the stereotyping of Asians and European Australians but, interestingly, increased social distancing between Australian Europeans and Aborigines (p. 391). Like other manifestations of the contact hypothesis, this shows that bringing students together, even in highly structured ways, will not necessarily undo prejudiced thinking and can actually load onto it. In Walter and Crogan's case, their analysis for the increased social distancing is that 'stereotypes about Aborigines are particularly pernicious' (p. 391) and also because there were few Aborigines in the school which meant that interactions were not substantial enough to be generalised.

Darnon, Buchs and Desbar (2012) tested the jigsaw method on 33 male vocational training students in a controlled trial and found that it created higher levels of self-efficacy.

Bratt (2008) ran two quasi-experiments (controlled) on 11-year-olds and 13-to 15-year-olds but found no real impact of the jigsaw method on intergroup relations. Souvignier and Kronenberger (2007) ran a three-way controlled trial on 208 students from the third grade (in three different classes, each studying astronomy and geometry) to test the jigsaw method alongside a jigsaw with supplementary questioning training and a teacher-guided instruction environment. They found that the jigsaw strategy helped novice learners for some classes but that on the whole, teacher-guided instruction yielded better results for stronger students.

While the evidence on the impact and success of the jigsaw classroom is not entirely conclusive, the classroom climate it creates is worth considering and teachers should feel confident enough about it as a strategy to try it in the classroom. In any case, there is no available literature on the notion that the jigsaw classroom increases prejudice.

School events

School events that can enhance contact between students whilst respecting some of Allport's (1954) principles include group projects, spirit or challenge days (where students are grouped in such a way as to increase contact across diversity) and assemblies. Team sports cover many of Allport's (1954) conditions for prejudice-reducing contact: the zero-sum game individual approach to goals is superseded by collective cooperation, team members learn more about each other as they work towards a common goal and the values of team spirit bind the group in an ethical, philosophical stance of togetherness. Brown et al. (2003) surveyed American high school students on attitudes towards blacks and whites by either group in relation to team sports and found that whites who had experienced team sports with blacks were more tolerant towards blacks than those who had not.

Grouping of students

Schools can focus on ensuring that students are grouped in diverse configurations and that the reasons for such diverse settings are made clear. In boarding schools, students can be placed in dormitories so that cliques are broken and students are stretched to learn about others. Shook and Fazio (2008) conducted a natural field experiment in a college dormitory and found that interracial room-mating produced less intergroup anxiety and implicit racial attitudes.

In 1985, Slavin reviewed instances of cooperative learning more broadly and found that 16 of the 19 studies analysed 'had positive effects of interracial friendships' (Parker, 2002, p. 140).

Assessment

If schools use the contact hypothesis to create prejudice-reducing learning opportunities, it will be important to assess not only cognitive and academic progress but the ways in which students have grown in their interactions with others. Behaviours and attitudes need to be recognised and there should be feedback on these to show parents and students what is considered important so as to valorise and build a discussion around working together.

Interestingly, many assessment criteria descriptors focus not on group work but on independence. For example:

> A highly organised, independent learner.
>
> *(Wasely Hills High School, 2016)*

> A highly motivated student who is able to work independently, takes full responsibility for their own learning.
>
> *(The Ferrers School, 2016)*

> Takes full responsibility for his/her learning; Works to the best of his/her ability; Demonstrates an ability to work independently.
>
> *(The Elton High School, 2016)*

> Works independently and takes responsibility for their learning including independent use of success criteria.
>
> *(Sherburn High School, 2014)*

The spirit of academic excellence with its reliance on independent inquiry is perhaps not an encouragement to work together but more an incentive for individualism and competition. Schools need to think carefully about striking a balance between individual performance and learning to live together and work as a team.

An example of assessment criteria celebrating more collaborative dispositions includes the personal development, behaviour and welfare criteria developed by Ofsted:

> Pupils discuss and debate issues in a considered way, showing respect for others' ideas and points of view. Pupils work hard with the school to prevent all forms of bullying, including online bullying and prejudice-based bullying. Staff and pupils deal effectively with the very rare instances of bullying behaviour and/or use of derogatory or aggressive language.
>
> *(Ofsted, 2015)*

Self, peer or formal assessment should focus on team work, collaboration, listening skills, respect and dialogue, much in the vein of social constructivist pedagogical theory (Vygotsky, 1978).

Conclusion

The idea that people can reduce their own prejudice and the prejudice of others through contact does not bear out when looked at intuitively and historically. As Forbes points out,

> tensions between the different nationalities in the Balkans seem to have grown worse during the past century, despite the increasing opportunities

they have had to meet and to form close personal relations. More generally, neighboring peoples – the French and the Germans, for example, or the Indians and the Pakistanis – seem to have the greatest trouble getting along, not those who live farther apart, such as the Peruvians and the Palestinians or the Tamils and the Turks. The more contact, it seems, the more trouble.

(Forbes, 2004 p. 72)

Therefore, mere contact alone is not always a sufficient condition for prejudice reduction – it needs to be structured carefully, in the light of the considerable research on the subject, to ensure that maximal value comes from the contact. Situations can degenerate or ameliorate when there is contact:

More interracial contact can lead either to greater prejudice and rejection or to greater respect and acceptance, depending upon the situation in which it occurs. The basic issue, then, concerns the types of situations in which contact leads to distrust and those in which it leads to trust.

(Pettigrew, 1971, p. 275)

This chapter has shown how optimal conditions for contact might be difficult to replicate in real-life situations and, according to Pettigrew and Tropp's (2006) meta-analysis, might not all be entirely necessary for the successful effects of the contact hypothesis to be felt. However, I would argue that three conditions consistently referred to in the research (e.g. Forbes, 2004, p. 74) that are essential for schools are:

1   The equality or inequality of status of the different groups in contact.
2   Their cooperative or competitive interdependence in the pursuit of common goals.
3   The presence or absence of social norms supporting intergroup contact.

I would add to these the two most significant mediators as researched by Pettigrew and Tropp (2008):

4   Reducing anxiety.
5   Promoting empathy and perspective-taking.

The first point means that schools need to make it clear in their mission statements that they strongly support: that human beings are of equal value; that no person is to be considered intrinsically superior to another; and that each individual's experiences carry equal weight, importance and significance. Though this is not to say that anything goes: respecting people's positions and frames of reference does not mean that ideas should not be debated critically. The point is not for schools to embrace extreme relativism when it comes to ideas but to embrace equality and equity when it comes to human beings.

Schools should stand by the values decreeing human worth as articulated in the Universal Declaration of Human Rights (United Nations, 1948); these values should be reiterated in assemblies, classrooms, through debates, events and assessments for students, teachers and parents to internalise them and realise that they are ideas that the institution will defend and promote. This will be far more important than the mere existence of words on paper. Needless to say, it is the actions schools will take to ensure the human contact that characterises their communities is not segregated and ridden with prejudice that will make a real impact.

The second point is a particularly valuable challenge for schools to consider since high stakes testing, ranking systems, hierarchical admissions policies to programmes and other competitive strategies for social categorisation that are common in schools do not go in the sense of the literature on the contact hypothesis. The zero-sum game approach to social organisation is something that schools should seek to undo as they carve out a vision of society that is built on team-work, shared knowledge, cooperation, empathy, assistance, collective problem solving and solidarity. Pettigrew explains that:

> The groups share common goals and work cooperatively to achieve these goals. Group against group competition in zero-sum games & − in which what one side wins, the other loses − is a certain recipe for increased intergroup hostility and conflict. By contrast, group interdependence builds cross-group bonds; in time it can even create a single, overarching group identity. In this situation, cooperation between the groups wins rewards for both that are unattainable for each group working alone.
>
> *(Pettigrew, 2008)*

Allport's (1954) exhortation for authorities to lead a non-prejudicial culture (point 3 above) remains critical. One cannot hope for a genuinely open-minded ethos to flourish in a setting where strong values of common humanity are not iterated and celebrated. School leadership should model the contact hypothesis and encourage students, parents and teachers of different backgrounds to interact and work together. Preaching against prejudice in a segregated environment is unlikely to go any real distance while expecting contact between individuals in spite of, rather than as a result of, institutional discourse.

Pettigrew (2008) reminds his readers that society at large is essentially segregated, that 'intergroup friendships are limited, and intergroup marriages remain rare and stigmatized'. This would suggest that schools wishing to reduce prejudice face the challenge of going against the tide to produce models of social interaction they would like to see happening in the world: they should engage in diverse recruitment and aim to mirror the type of plurality in their demographic structure that will influence their students' world views. It is perhaps not the quantity of intergroup interactions that is important as the quality and symbolic dimension of those interactions, since there is some evidence that merely knowing that intergroup relations exist whilst not necessarily being directly involved in those relationships can reduce prejudicial thinking (see Wright et al., 1997).

The fact that educationally instigated contact might create tension for participants when faced with patterns of segregation in broader society means that school leaders and teachers should take particular care in scaffolding an anxiety-reducing environment (point 4 above), an essential mediator for contact much advocated by Pettigrew and Tropp (2000), not only so that students are more comfortable to take risks, ask questions and learn productively but so that friendships across social lines are more likely to flourish away from the judgemental views of life outside the educational institution's parameters and values.

At the core of this is the question of identity: with what do students identify themselves and what is the role of the school community in this? Erickson (2011) has pointed out that amongst the more recent iterations and adaptations of Allport's (1954) original hypothesis (for example, Gaertner & Dovidio, 2000 or Kenworthy et al., 2005), an element that has re-shaped the way that many researchers look at intergroup contact is 'the importance of rousing a sense of identity among participants' (Erickson, 2011, p. 11).

The extent to which the contact hypothesis applies to a twenty-first century world, far more interrelated, complex, ambiguous, volatile and unpredictable than the 1950s when Allport first put forward the idea, needs to be problematized. We are living in a world where notions of social identity and cultural capital are not what they used to be. The entire premise of the contact theory is that group identity is fairly stable and individuals will judge it from a clear vantage point, choosing to integrate or reject cultural artefacts and expressions.

However, as Forbes points out saliently:

> As liberal societies become more and more multicultural, it becomes harder and harder to think of their problems of ethnic conflict in the old liberal way – as problems of the relations between individuals rooted in their irrational prejudices and thus amenable to resolution through the promotion of friendly personal contacts. It becomes more and more necessary to see them as problems of the relationships between groups rooted in their cultural differences and conflicting demands for recognition.
>
> *(Forbes, 2004, p. 86)*

This leads us to the fifth essential point about the contact hypothesis – empathy and perspective-taking. For contact to be meaningful, it must allow for students not only to exchange ideas between themselves but to make a concerted effort to see situations from viewpoints other than their own. In this sense, the contact theory put into practice should be less a question of trying to understand other people and imagining the correlations that might be made between what they say and think and where they come from, and much more an expression of the power of diversity and group work where people can learn from one another holistically, with open minds and consider the richness and diversity of human thought as they work together.

References

Adsett, M., & Morin, M. (2004). Contact and regional variation in attitudes towards linguistic duality in Canada. *Journal of Canadian Studies*, 38, 129–150.

Agirdag, O., Loobuyck, P., & Van Houtte, M. (2012). Determinants of attitudes toward muslim students among flemish teachers: A research note. *Journal for the Scientific Study of Religion*, 51, 368–376. doi: 10.1111/j.1468-5906.2012.01637.x

Allport, G. (1954). *The nature of prejudice*. Cambridge, MA: Addison-Wesley.

Amichai-Hamburger, Y., & McKenna, K.Y.A. (2006). The contact hypothesis reconsidered: Interacting via the internet. *Journal of Computer-Mediated Communication*, 11, 825–843. doi: 10.1111/j.1083-6101.2006.00037.x

Amir, Y. (1969). Contact hypothesis in ethnic relations. *Psychological Bulletin*, 71(5), 319–342.

Amir, Y. (1976). The role of intergroup contact in change of prejudice and ethnic relations. In P.A. Katz (Ed.), *Towards the elimination of racism* (pp. 73–123). New York, NY: Plenum Press.

Aronson, E. (2000). The jigsaw strategy: Reducing prejudice in the classroom. *Psychology Review*, 7(2), 2–5.

Aronson, E., & Bridgeman, D. (1979). Jigsaw groups and the desegregated classroom: In pursuit of common goals. *Personality and Social Psychology Bulletin*, 5, 438–446.

Aronson, E., & Patnoe, S. (1997). *The jigsaw classroom* (2nd edn). New York, NY: Longman.

Barlow, F.K., Paolini, S., Pedersen, A., Hornsey, M.J., Radke, H.R.M., Harwood, J., Rubin, M., & Sibley, C.G. (2012). The contact caveat: Negative contact predicts increased prejudice more than positive contact predicts reduced prejudice. *Personality and Social Psychology Bulletin*, 38, 1629–1643. doi: 10.1177/0146167212457953

Bernstein, L. (1961). [Film]. *West Side Story*. Broadway musical first produced in New York.

Bratt, C. (2008). The Jigsaw classroom under test: No effect on intergroup relations evident. *Journal of Community & Applied Social Psychology*, 18, 403–419. doi: 10.1002/casp.946

Bridgeman, D. (1981). Enhanced role-taking through cooperative interdependence: A field study. *Child Development*, 52, 1231–1238.

Brown, K.T., Brown, T.N., Jackson, J.S., Sellers, R.M., & Manuel, W.J. (2003). Teammates on and off the field? Contact with Black teammates and the racial attitudes of White student athletes. *Journal of Applied Social Psychology*, 33, 1379–1403. doi: 10.1111/j.1559-1816.2003.tb01954.x

Brown, R., & Hewstone, M. (2005). An integrative theory of intergroup contact. *Advances in Experimental Social Psychology*, 37, 255–343.

Connolly, P. (2000). What now for the contact hypothesis? Towards a new research agenda. *Race, Ethnicity and Education*, 3, 169–193.

Cook, S.W. (1962). The systematic analysis of socially significant events: A strategy for social research. *Journal of Social Issues*, 18(2), 66–84.

Cook, T.D., Cooper, H., Cordray, D.S., Hartman, H., Hedges, L.V., Light, R.J., et al. (1992). Some generic issues and problems for metaanalysis. In T.D. Cook, H. Cooper, D.S. Cordray, H. Hartman, L.V. Hedges, R.J., Light, et al. (Eds), *Meta-analysis for explanation: A casebook* (pp. 283–320). New York, NY: Sage.

Darnon, C., Buchs, C., & Desbar, D. (2012). The jigsaw technique and self-efficacy of vocational training students: A practice report. *European Journal of Psychology of Education*, 27(3), 439–449. doi: 10.1007/s10212-011-0091-4

Dixon, J.A., Durrheim, K., & Tredoux, C. (2005). Beyond the optimal strategy: A 'reality check' for the contact hypothesis. *American Psychologist*, 60, 697–711.

Dovidio, J., Gaertner, S., & Kawakami, K. (2003). Intergroup contact: The past, present and the future. *Group Processes and Intergroup Relations*, 6, 5–20.

Dweck, C.S. (2012). *Mindset: How you can fulfill your potential*. Constable & Robinson Limited.

Elliott, E.S., & Dweck, C.S. (1988). Goals: An approach to motivation and achievement. *Journal of Personality and Social Psychology*, 54, 5–12.

Erickson, J.A. (2011). Service-learning's impact on attitudes and behavior: A review and update. Online. Available at: http://web.augsburg.edu/~erickson/MCC2012/Erickson_2011.pdf (accessed 28 April 2016).

Forbes, H.D. (1997). *Ethnic conflict: Commerce, culture, and the contact hypothesis.* New Haven, CT: Yale University Press.

Forbes, H.D. (2004). Ethnic conflict and the contact hypothesis. In Y.T. Lee, C. McAuley, F. Moghaddam, & S. Worchel (Eds), *The psychology of ethnic and cultural conflict* (pp. 69–88). Westport, CT: Praeger.

Ford, W.S. (1986). Favorable intergroup contact may not reduce prejudice: Inconclusive journal evidence, 1960–1984. *Sociology and Social Research*, 70, 256–258.

Gaertner, S.L., & Dovidio, J.F. (2000). *Reducing intergroup bias: The Common Ingroup Identity Model.* Philadelphia, PA: Psychology Press.

Gibson, J.L. (2001). Does truth lead to reconciliation? Testing the causal assumptions of the South African Truth and Reconciliation process. Paper presented at the Annual Meeting of the American Political Science Association, San Francisco.

Herek, G.M., & Glunt, E.K. (1993). Interpersonal contact and heterosexuals' attitudes toward gay men: Results from a national survey. *The Journal of Sex Research*, 30(3), 239–244.

Jigsaw. (2016). Online. Available at: www.jigsaw.org/history/ (accessed 28 April 2016).

Kenworthy, J., Turner, R., Hewstone, M., & Voci, A. (2005). Intergroup contact: When does it work, and why? In J. Dovidio, P. Glick, & L. Rudman (Eds), *On the nature of prejudice: Fifty years after Allport* (pp. 278–292). Malden, MA: Blackwell.

Manetti, M., Schneider, B.H., & Siperstein, G. (2001). Social acceptance of children with mental retardation: Testing the contact hypothesis with an Italian sample. *International Journal of Behavioural Development*, 25, 279–286.

McLaren, L.M. (2003). Anti-immigrant prejudice in Europe: Contact, threat perception, and preferences for the exclusion of migrants. *Social Forces*, 81(3), 909–936. doi:10.1353/sof.2003.0038

Novotny, J., & Polonsky, F. (2011). The level of knowledge about Islam and perception of Islam among Czech and Slovak university students: Does ignorance determine subjective attitudes? *Sociologia*, 43(6), 674–696.

Ofsted. (2015). Online. Available at: www.clerktogovernors.co.uk/ofsted/ofsted-grade-descriptors-the-behaviour-and-safety-of-pupils-at-the-school/ (accessed 28 April 2016).

Paolini, S., Harwood, J., & Rubin, M. (2010). Negative intergroup contact makes group memberships salient: Explaining why intergroup conflict endures. *Personality and Social Psychology Bulletin*, 36, 1723–1738. doi: 10.1177/0146167210388667

Parker, W. (Ed.). (2002). *Education for democracy: Contexts, curricula, assessment.* Greenwich, CT: IAP.

Pettigrew, T.F. (1971). *Racially separate or together?* New York: McGrawHill.

Pettigrew, T.F. (1998). Intergroup contact theory. *Annual Review of Psychology*, 49, 65–85.

Pettigrew, T.F. (2008). Intergroup prejudice: Its causes and cures. Online. Available at: http://pepsic.bvsalud.org/scielo.php?pid=S0258–64442008000100006&script=sci_arttext (accessed 28 April 2016).

Pettigrew, T.F., & Tropp, L.R. (2000). Does intergroup contact reduce prejudice? Recent meta-analytic findings. In S. Oskamp (Ed.), *Reducing prejudice and discrimination: Social psychological perspectives* (pp. 93–114). Mahwah, NJ: Erlbaum.

Pettigrew, T.F., & Tropp, L.R. (2006). A meta-analytic test of intergroup contact theory. *Journal of Personality and Social Psychology*, 90(5), 751–783.

Pettigrew, T.F., & Tropp, L.R., (2008). How does intergroup contact reduce prejudice? Meta-analytic tests of three mediators. *European Journal of Social Psychology*, 38, 922–934.

Schiappa, E., Gregg, P.B., & Hewes, D.E. (2005). The parasocial contact hypothesis. *Communication Monographs*, 72(1), 92–115.

Schwartz, L.K., & Simmons, J.P. (2001). Contact quality and attitudes towards the elderly. *Educational Gerontology*, 27(2), 127–137.

Shakespeare, W. (1597). *Romeo and Juliet*. London: John Danter & Edward Allde.

Sherburn High School. (2014). Online. Available at: www.sherburnhigh.co.uk/PDF/Assessment%20Descriptors%202014–15.pdf (accessed 28 April 2016).

Shook, N.J., & Fazio, R.H. (2008). Interracial roommate relationships: An experimental field test of the contact hypothesis. *Psychological Science*, 19(7), 717–723. doi: 10.1111/j.1467-9280.2008.02147.x

Sigelman, L., Bledsoe, T., Welch, S., & Combs, M.W. (1996). Making contact? Black–White social interaction in the urban setting. *American Journal of Sociology*, 101, 1306–1332.

Smiley, P.A., & Dweck, C.S. (1994). Individual differences in achievement goals among young children. *Child Development*, 65, 1723–1743.

Souvignier, E., & Kronenberger, J. (2007). Cooperative learning in third graders' jigsaw groups for mathematics and science with and without questioning training. *British Journal of Educational Psychology*, 77, 755–771. doi: 10.1348/000709906X173297

Stephan, W.G. (1985). Intergroup relations. In G. Lindzey and E. Aronson (Eds), *Handbook of social psychology* (3rd edn), vol 2 (pp. 599–658). New York, NY: Random House.

Stephan, W.G. (1987). The contact hypothesis in intergroup relations. In C. Hendrick (Ed.), *Review of personality and social psychology: Group processes and intergroup relations*, vol 9 (pp. 13–40). Newbury Park, CA: Sage.

Stouffer, S.A., Schuman, E.A., DeVinney, L.C., Star, S.A., & Williams, R.M., Jr. (1949). *The American soldier: Adjustment during arms life*, vol 1. Princeton, NJ: Princeton University Press.

The Elton School. (2016). Online. Available at: www.eltonhigh.bury.sch.uk/pupils/reporting-to-parents (accessed 28 April 2016).

The Ferrers School. (2016). Online. Available at: www.theferrers.org/page/?title=Attitude+to+Learning&pid=125 (accessed 28 April 2016).

United Nations (1948). *The universal declaration of human rights*. Online. Available at: www.un.org/en/universal-declaration-human-rights/ (accessed 18 April 2016).

Vygotsky, L.S. (1978). *Mind in society*. Cambridge, MA: Harvard University Press.

Walter, I., & Crogan, M. (1998). Academic performance, prejudice and the jigsaw classroom: New pieces to the puzzle. *Journal of Community and Applied Social Psychology*, 8, 381–393.

Waseley High School. (2016). Online. Available at: www.waseleyhills.worcs.sch.uk (accessed 28 April 2016).

Williams, R.M. Jr. (1947). *The reduction of intergroup tensions*. New York, NY: Social Science Research Council.

Wright, S.C., Aron, A., McLaughlin-Volpe, T., & Ropp, S.A. (1997). The extended contact effect: Knowledge of cross-group friendships and prejudice. *Journal of Personality and Social Psychology*, 73, 73–90. doi: 10.1037/0022-3514.73.1.73

7

LEARNING TO LIVE TOGETHER THROUGH THE PRINCIPLES OF INTERNATIONAL EDUCATION

Introduction

Educational expectations and practices vary from country to country, and by type of school. It is not possible to discuss them all, so one widely known instance, the International School and its International Baccalaureate (IB), will be used to illustrate what an educational system might offer prejudice reduction.

In particular, the International School and IB offers:

  (i) an approach to curriculum design and teaching practices that can be found in diverse countries and contexts; furthermore,
 (ii) the curriculum, its expectations and typical practices are likely to be meaningful to educators in a wide range of systems of education; and
(iii) they should be able to relate their own practices to it and, if they choose, adapt those practices described to their own contexts and, hopefully, use them productively.

(In effect, this makes the International School and the IB an exemplar of good practice.)

This chapter runs through the elements of international education that are particularly powerful as strategies to reduce prejudice. While these strategies can and should be used by many different types of school, it is useful to situate them within the historical and philosophical context of international education specifically as this adds depth to an understanding of their purpose and dynamism.

International: intercultural or multicultural?

Since one of the most commonly recognised domains of prejudice is that of culture, more specifically ethnic identity, a number of responses can be found in multiculturalism, interculturality and internationalism. This chapter explores education within these areas and how it can reduce prejudicial thinking. The construct that operationalises all three domains is international education, a movement that I look at historically and structurally with particular emphasis on the International Baccalaureate.

Multicultural education

The UNESCO Guidelines on Intercultural Education (2006) use multicultural to describe the 'culturally diverse nature of human society' (p. 17). The twenty-first century, with its globalised economy, increased global travel and migratory patterns, is a far more multicultural society than the world has seen in the past. The OECD reported 200 million migrants in the world in 2005, more than double the figure in 1970 (ECOWAS, 2006) whereas the UN reported in 2013 that '232 million people, or 3.2 per cent of the world's population, live abroad worldwide, compared with 175 million in 2000 and 154 million in 1990' (United Nations, 2013).

In countries where immigration is high (France, Germany, Spain, Malaysia, Singapore, Thailand and the United Arab Emirates (IOM, 2013)), multicultural classrooms are a norm. However, this does not mean in and of itself that classroom programmes will grapple with the multiplicity of cultures in any organised or intended manner and does not guarantee that any special effort will be made to investigate or reduce prejudice.

However, when exactly a school becomes multicultural and who decides what this means is not clear. There are no schools that patent themselves as 'multicultural' schools even if the term might transpire as part of their mission statements or general identity. If anything, multicultural is most often used to describe state schools in the United Kingdom, France, Germany and the USA because of strong immigrant populations and/or ethnically diverse populations rather than an intended desire to create multicultural learning environments. It remains a somewhat loaded term that does not necessarily carry any positive currency and is often used in anti-immigration political rhetoric.

As we see in Chapter 6 on Allport's (1954) contact hypothesis, a diverse classroom is not necessarily a tolerant one: it is not by placing people of different backgrounds together that prejudice will be reduced. In fact, if nothing is done about it and clear ground-rules based on equality are not articulated and endorsed, a multicultural classroom can become extremely prejudiced. Therefore, we could say that a multicultural classroom has the potential to lead to the reductions of cultural prejudice but only if activated the right way.

Nieto and Bode (2008) have suggested that constructive multicultural educational programmes should emphasise 'tolerance [. . .], acceptance [. . .], respect [. . .], affirmation, solidarity and critique (pp. 426–427). An emphasis on tolerance is problematic since 'If all we expect of students is tolerance, can we ever hope that they will reach the point where they understand, respect, and affirm differences?'

(Nieto, 2002, p. 257) Indeed, this leads to another problem with multicultural education, namely that as it retains an emphasis on difference, identity and respect, it tends to exacerbate and perhaps create entrenched, even antagonistic, positions from which relationships are formed and is less likely to see integrated group work in the name of a higher force and risks anchoring students in separatist ethnic, cultural or gender-related identity.

Some see in the term 'multicultural' an educational mission: the UNESCO guidelines, for instance, state that 'multicultural education uses learning about other cultures in order to produce acceptance, or at least *tolerance*, of these cultures' (2006, p. 18) whereas Camicia takes it a step further to declare that 'multicultural education enables students to critically examine traditional mainstream and hegemonic narratives across subject areas. In doing so, students develop the critical faculties necessary to challenge the hierarchies that serve as tools for prejudice construction and social injustice' (Camicia, 2007, p. 225).

Critical multicultural theory has been propounded, amongst others, by Sleeter and Bernal (2004), Gorski (2006) and Vavrus (2010), particularly in higher education in the United States. It has its basis in critical race theory and critical pedagogy with, as aim, the re-equilibration of educational master narratives so that 'historically marginalized children and youth and their families and communities are placed in the center of higher education' (Vavrus, 2010, p. 29). Vavrus's suggestion is that the 'center' (sic) is dominated by an ethos of traditional Eurocentric DWEM (Dead White European Males) and should be replaced with more diversity, a position that hinges on positive discrimination, restorative or compensatory bias, which could, of course, be called unwarranted discrimination in the other direction.

Academics referring to multicultural theory tend to discuss critical issues of social justice, representation in master narratives, race and power using frameworks of post-structuralist thinkers such as Foucault, Levinas, Derrida, Bourdieu, Apple and Giroux.

Essential but equally problematic and polemical components of a multicultural education are questions of history, power and justice. If students are to appreciate fully the dynamics of race relations, for instance, they should have some grounding in the history of trans-Atlantic slavery and colonialism and the economic repercussions for countries such as Spain, Portugal, France, the United Kingdom and the United States. Such a focus on history, while necessary for a critical appreciation of the importance of the construct of race in modern economic superstructures, tends to be divisive as it erodes into quarrels about modern day immigration into Europe, Northern-Southern hemisphere inequities, European nation state wealth and the stranglehold many Western multinationals have on African resources.

Few schools would openly embrace this type of Marxist critical pedagogy as it has the potential to scare parents away and excite revolutionary mindsets. Politicised agendas tend to be the remit of universities and, therefore, multicultural education theory is more commonly found in certain liberal arts faculties.

Intercultural education

If the multicultural classroom focusses on dialogue between cultures and common pursuits, it might evolve into an intercultural classroom.

Intercultural 'refers to evolving relations between cultural groups', 'interculturality presupposes multiculturalism' (UNESCO, 2006, p. 17). Different typologies and models of intercultural awareness have been developed by Haywood (2007) and Deardorff (2009), and surveyed by Spitzberg and Changnon (2009). They tend to bring out qualities such as respect, openness and curiosity (Deardorff, 2009); linguistic competence and critical cultural awareness (Byram, 1997) with emphasis placed on interaction, evolving states of awareness and communication skills.

The construct of intercultural education is well researched but features more in the realm of policy statements and competence models than in actual institutions: schools tend not to call themselves 'intercultural' but at the same time there are numerous guidelines on intercultural awareness that can be applied to different educational models.

The conviction that intercultural education has a core role to play in reducing prejudice has been argued in various forms by numerous researchers (Haegel, 1999; Jasinska-Kania, 1999; Peri, 1999; Byran & Vavrus, 2005; Byram, 1997; IB, 2013; UNESCO, 2006). The theoretical foundations of these positions rest on the common thesis that affective, critical, intercultural awareness is needed to combat prejudice and that these qualities can be found in intercultural education.

UNESCO's guidelines on intercultural education state that 'intercultural education aims to go beyond passive coexistence, to achieve a developing and sustainable way of living together in multicultural societies through the creation of *understanding* of, *respect* for and *dialogue* between the different cultural groups' (2006, p. 18). Education should be 'non-discriminatory' and 'aim at eliminating prejudices about culturally distinct population groups within a country', (p. 35) whereas teacher training and curricula should develop 'a critical awareness of the role education ought to play in the struggle against racism and discrimination' (p. 36).

Intercultural education is an aspirational, philosophical statement about how education can bring people together under constructive, humane goals. One area of education where interculturality is operationalised is international education.

International education

Ironically, although the appellation 'international school' is well known and institutionalised, 'international education' as a term has not been universally defined (Simandiraki, 2006). There is 'no single coherent picture of "internationalism" within the individual that . . . international education aims to develop' (Gunesch, 2004, p. 252), while schools 'do not have to meet any criteria to call themselves an international school' (MacDonald, 2006, p. 193).

In this chapter, by 'international education' I will be referring to the same construct as 'intercultural education' for the simple reason that, when it comes to reducing prejudice through education, both concepts are premised on the same fundaments of respect, tolerance and diversity. It would be unhelpfully pedantic to separate the terms here but to read more on the nuances between them see Gunesch (2004) and Hughes (2009).

A definition of international education that can be used in this chapter is of a system where

> emphasis should be laid in a basic attitude of respect for all human beings as persons, understanding of those things which unite us and an appreciation of the positive values of those things which may seem to divide us, with the objective of thinking free from fear or prejudice.
>
> *(Hill, 2012, p. 11)*

International organisations and education to reduce prejudice

The philosophical bases of international education are made clear in statements issued by international organisations such as the International Labour Office, United Nations and UNESCO, which all state clearly the role education has to reduce prejudice.

Article 26.2 of the Universal Declaration of Human Rights (1948) states that education 'shall promote understanding, tolerance and friendship among all nations, racial or religious groups, and shall further the activities of the United Nations for the maintenance of peace'. The International Labour Organization's (1989) convention no. 169, *Indigenous and Tribal Peoples in Independent Countries*, states in Article 31 that classroom materials, particularly history textbooks, should present indigenous and so-called tribal peoples in a fair and accurate manner so as to reduce the prejudice against them that might be harboured by the wider national community.

Article 5.2 of UNESCO's *Declaration on Race and Racial Prejudice* (UNESCO, 1978) asserts that 'states . . . as well as all other competent authorities and the entire teaching profession, have a responsibility to see that the educational resources . . . are used to combat racism' while UNESCO's *Declaration of the Principles of International Cultural Cooperation* (UNESCO, 1966) aims to 'develop peaceful relations and friendship among the peoples and bring about a better understanding of each other's way of life'.

Principle III of the *UN Declaration on the Promotion among Youth of the Ideals of Peace, Mutual Respect and Understanding between Peoples* (United Nations, 1965) stresses the importance for education to develop 'the knowledge (among young people) of the dignity and equality of all men, without distinction as to race, colour, ethnic origins or beliefs' whereas UNESCO's (1992) *International Conference on Education* (43rd Session – published in 1993) on 'The Contribution of Education to Cultural Development' emphasised: 'open-mindedness and an ability to interest the student in learning about and understanding others' (UNESCO, 1993, §100).

Hence the role of education, as seen by these international organisations, should clearly be devoted to reducing cultural prejudice and discrimination. The ontological premise for these discourses is, overwhelmingly, the mission of the United Nations, which is premised on humanism. Byran and Vavrus explain that 'the existence of numerous international organisations devoted to analysing and overcoming intolerance in education and/or promoting tolerance through education is testament both to the promise and peril that education represents' (Byran & Vavrus, 2005, p. 195). This statement can be read two ways: as a testimony to the power of education to shape attitudes and change the world ('education is the most powerful weapon which you can use to change the world' (Mandela, 2003)) or as a reflection on the fact that intercultural education, unlike multicultural education, could lead to quietism in an age where, arguably, the planet is threatened by a wholly unsustainable socioeconomic model.

The question is, how these humanist goals can be successfully elaborated, tracked and assessed and the extent to which international education does this.

International schools

International schooling – in the broadest sense of students joining an institution from all over the world – can be located as far back as the famous Sassanid Jondi Shapour school, which brought together scholars from India, Persia, Greece and Rome in the 2nd century AD. There is minor debate over whether Spring Grove School, the International School for Peace in Boston, the International Folk High School in Elsinore or the Santiniketan school should be considered the first international schools in the more modern sense (Sylvester, 2002, p. 13) but it is generally accepted that the first international school in the world – at least, certainly the oldest continuously operating international school – was the International School of Geneva. This was an experiment in K–12 education that started in 1924 with a clear objective to reduce nationalistic prejudice (Hughes, 2012; Walker, 2009). The school was founded as 'The League School' to offer an education to the children of functionaries working for the League of Nations and the International Labour Office. After the horrors of the First World War, the vision for an international education meant an education for world peace between nations in the vein of the League of Nations. The school was based on tolerance and open-mindedness (Hughes, 2012).

Marie-Thérèse Maurette, the charismatic first director of the school, in a 1948 pamphlet published by UNESCO, laid out the following conditions for an 'education for peace':

- Minimising national sentiments (Maurette, 1948, p. 7). Maurette once told her students, 'furious as you are, you must never use nationality or race as a term of abuse. That, in this school, is the crime of crimes' (Walker, 2009, p. 79).
- Teaching young people about the horrors of war (Maurette, 1948, p. 7).
- The study of world geography and world history (pp. 8–15).
- Bilingualism (pp. 15–17).

- Global affairs/world news (pp. 17–18).
- World citizenship (p. 19).

She added to this a spirit of camaraderie and fair play within a diverse international setting. To a large extent, Maurette's conditions for an international education are still relevant today. The idea in Maurette's model is that of the world citizen, a type of decategorisation (Ensari & Miller, 2001) of social identity and rebaptism under new auspices that transcend national or cultural differences, the earliest models of this coined by Sophists in some of Plato's dialogues (*Protagoras*, 337c7–d3 (Plato, 2009); Apology, 23b4–6 (Plato, 2003)) and most famously by Diogenes the Cynic who described himself not as a citizen of Sinope but as a *kosmopolites* or citizen of the world (Diogenes Laertius, VI 63, 1989). Models of cosmopolitanism ranging from those of supranational governance to moral and economic cosmopolitanism are discussed and problematised by Appiah (2006), Bohman (2004), Habermas (2001) and Nussbaum (2006).

There is a debate in the field of international education between a transnational, world citizen position that sees international mindedness as transcending national identity (Hughes, 2009) – in other words interculturality; and an international model where cultural and national identities should be maintained in a dialogue across and between nations (Tate, 2012) – a debate that resonates with the interculturality/multiculturalism dichotomy. Both positions see the thrust of international education as rising above prejudice but in different ways.

Haywood suggests that 'international mindedness' is a better term to consider than 'international education' because it focusses on outcomes rather than processes. He lists a number of non-prejudicial mindsets as signs of international mindedness, such as:

> open attitudes towards other ways of life and a predisposition to tolerance as regards other cultures and their belief systems, [. . .] recognition of the interconnectedness of human affairs (in place and time) as part of the holistic experience of life, human values that combine respect for other ways of life with care and concern for the welfare and well-being of people in general.
>
> *(Haywood, 2007, pp. 86–87)*

Since the opening of the International School of Geneva, international education has become a widespread phenomenon, spreading through organs such as the International Baccalaureate (Peterson, 1987; Hughes, 2009; Cambridge, 2012), the Council of International Schools and the United World Colleges Movement (Peterson, 1987). The International Schools Consultancy Group estimated more than 7,000 international schools in the world in 2014. The philosophy of most international schools is close to the Universal Declaration of Human Rights and the values articulated by UNESCO (2006): 'openness to cultural exchange' (p. 13), 'mutual respect' (p. 17) and 'dignity, equality, friendship, understanding, and peaceful relations' (p. 25).

The International Baccalaureate

Many of these schools are involved in explicitly international educational pro-grammes, most notably the International Baccalaureate (IB), a programme for chil-dren from 3 to 19 years of age, designed in 1962 whose educational philosophy is 'to develop internationally minded people who, recognizing their common humanity and shared guardianship of the planet, help to create a better and more peaceful world' (IB, 2006). The IB has been described as 'an education for international-mindedness; an education designed to break down the barriers of race, religion and class; an education [that extols] the benefits of cultural diversity; above all else, an education for peace' (Walker, 2011, p. 19).

The IB places 'a strong emphasis on encouraging students to develop inter-cultural understanding, open-mindedness, and the attitudes necessary for them to respect and evaluate a range of points of view' (IB, 2015, p. 2). The mission state-ment of the organisation encourages 'students across the world to become active, compassionate and lifelong learners who understand that other people, with their differences, can also be right' (p. 4). One sees in this statement an example of indi-viduation (Bettencourt et al., 1992) whereby people's qualities are sought outside and beyond social categorisation.

The IB's values are synthesised in the Learner Profile, a set of qualities that are valued and developed in groups and individuals. IB learners should strive to be 'inquirers, knowledgeable, thinkers, communicators, principled, open-minded, caring, risk-takers, balanced and reflective' (IB, 2013). All of these qualities suggest prejudice reduction in different ways.

IB and International School vision statements are clearly directed towards form-ing attitudes of open-mindedness and tolerance. Some discuss prejudice explicitly, for example the Swiss National Coalition Building Institute (NCBI, 2015), which has developed training modules that aim to have 'participants develop their ability to shift prejudicial attitudes'.

Wright (2014) conducted interviews with '23 women and men aged from 20 to 63' (p. 2) who had completed IB programmes between the 1960s and early 2010s and found that participants believed that the IB had provided them with critical thought, 'a broader view of the world' (p. 1) and, to a lesser extent, attitudes influ-encing ongoing commitment to community service.

Skrzypiec et al. (2014) conducted a study on students studying the middle years IB Programme and found that qualities of empathy and self-reflection were being built in IB schools. In a 2010 IB Position Paper, Hare describes holistic learning in the IB as students 'examining their own values and prejudices' (Hare, 2010, p. 7). These findings suggest but do not prove low levels of prejudiced thinking in IB graduates.

Investigating the curriculum of the IB

The IB is a broad-based curriculum that allows for potential prejudice reduction through the study of a number of core elements. Each of these facets of the IB philosophy has the potential to allow students to open their minds to other cultures, people and places. It is worth investigating each of these to discuss the extent to which they have the potential to reduce prejudice, bearing in mind that most of them are common elements to be found in most curricula around the world:

- Service learning.
- The learning of an additional language.
- World literature.
- The humanities.
- Inquiry.
- Reflection.
- Concepts-focused learning.
- Theory of Knowledge.

Service learning

Service learning is central in all of the IB's programmes and is core to the idea of 'learning to live together' (Delors et al., 1996). It is defined by the IB as the 'development and application of knowledge and skills towards meeting an identified community need' (IB, 2015, p. 20). UNESCO's International Bureau of Education and the International School of Geneva state that

> the fundamental goal of service learning is to empower students to take an active part in an education that develops a profound sense of humanity. This implies values such as humility, empathy and open-mindedness, and personal conduct such as commitment and initiative that are mediated by critical, creative, alert and reflective thinking.
>
> *(UNESCO-IBE et al., 2014, p. 29)*

Service learning can be related to Dewey's (1938) theory of experiential learning (see Giles & Eyler, 1994). In this way, service learning has the potential to break down prejudices because it involves concrete experience, contact between people, research and action that allow stereotypes to be nuanced or abandoned. Erickson and O'Connor (2000), referring to Delve, Mintz and Stewart (1990), see service learning as effective in 'changing negative social attitudes towards outgroups' (Erickson & O'Connor, 2000, p. 60) whereas studies by Kendall (1990) have shown that students report a decrease in their own stereotypic depictions of other people when they are involved with them in service programmes that ensure and celebrate diversity.

Rhoads (1998) describes a project he conducted whereby over 200 students from Pennsylvania State University, the University of South Carolina and Michigan State University were observed over a 6-year period as they engaged in community service projects; 108 students were interviewed and 66 completed open-ended surveys as part of a qualitative research design. Similar to Kendall's findings, students reported that the a priori generalisations they had of other people were diminished considerably when they came into contact with members of those groups through community service projects, this being the case in particular for poor people (Rhoads, 1998, p. 288).

Service learning in and of itself will not necessarily reduce prejudicial thinking, especially if it is done the wrong way. Erickson, referring to Erickson and O'Connor (2000), Hollis (2004), Jones (2002) and Kendall (1990), points out that 'researchers have cautioned about the potential for unintended consequences of service-learning – the potential for increased prejudice, stereotyping, and victim blaming in service-learning participants' (Erickson, 2011, p. 1).

As such, the *Guiding Principles for Learning in the 21st Century*, published by the International School of Geneva, and UNESCO's International Bureau of Education state in their principles for service learning that students should not be brought to believe that they are messiahs come to save the less fortunate than themselves but more people who are offering their help if it is needed as learners in a transaction (UNESCO-IBE, 2014, p. 30). Indeed, schools need to be wary of sending out the wrong messages to everybody involved in community service projects as they can easily turn into self-gratifying exercises in patronising charity.

Another important precursor for service learning, if it is to reduce rather than exacerbate prejudice, is to ensure that it is not short-term but sufficiently extended for profound, reflective transaction to take place. Erickson (2011) suggests two-term projects as minimal.

One could add to this the importance of participants taking a positive, anxiety-free attitude to service learning (p. 11).

Service learning programmes outside of the IB are numerous, including the Duke of Edinburgh International Award (Duke of Edinburgh, 2016), an extracurricular learning experience that involves student-designed projects with different aspects to holistic development including action and community service, and the United World Colleges movement (Peterson, 1987), which places particular emphasis on service learning.

The learning of an additional language

Learning an additional language is by no means exclusive to the IB and can be found in most schools. This much said, language learning is central to the programme and can be looked at as an interesting model for schools that do not place a huge importance on second language learning, bilingualism or plurilingualism. It is also interesting to look at the IB as a model because the emphasis is on the intercultural competence and, to a certain extent, prejudice reduction that language acquisition develops.

All of the IB programmes make clear the importance of learning an additional language for greater intercultural understanding. The IB Middle Years Programme (students aged 12 to 16) Language Acquisition Guide opens with the following citation from Savignon (1983): 'learning to speak another's language means taking one's place in the human community. It means reaching out to others across cultural and linguistic boundaries' (IB, 2014, p. 4). The guide goes on to point out that the study of additional languages can 'develop insights into the features, processes and craft of language and the concept of culture, and to realize that there are diverse ways of living, behaving and viewing the world' and 'is valued as central to developing critical thinking, and is considered essential for the cultivation of intercultural awareness and the development of internationally minded and responsible members of local, national and global communities'. Language learning 'equips students with the necessary multiliteracy skills and attitudes, enabling them to communicate successfully in various global contexts and build intercultural understanding' (IB, 2014, p. 4).

The idea that learning an additional language stimulates intercultural awareness and, therefore, has the potential to reduce cultural prejudice has been explored comprehensively by Byram (2011), who argues that it is an important part of global citizenship education and should be situated within a framework of intercultural competence. Kramsch (2009, p. 118) explains that language learning is a subtle manner of penetrating identity, allowing for mature reflection on the construct of culture. He posits that schools need to go much further than teaching grammar to eke out the relationship between language, symbol and identity.

It is perhaps at this deep level of language learning that one is able to move far beyond stereotypes and prejudice into knowledge and understanding of another person's symbolic identity and culture and also, through empathy and shared idiom, to transcend notions of selfhood. In a remarkable passage, the literary critic Stavans expresses the idea of identity being created by language, therefore implying that multilingualism leads to multiple identities and, most fundamentally, a loss of any essentialised, primary identity, which is in itself a fundamental building block of prejudice:

> A language is a set of spectacles through which the universe is seen afresh: Yiddish is warm, delectable, onomatopoeic; Spanish is romantic, perhaps a bit loose; Hebrew is rough, guttural; English is precise, almost mathematical – the tongue I prefer today, the one I feel happiest in. . . . No, perhaps spectacles are the wrong metaphor. . . . Changing languages is like imposing another role on oneself, like being someone else temporarily. My English-language persona is the one that superimposes itself on all previous others. In it are the seeds of Yiddish and Hebrew, but mostly Spanish. . . . But is the person really the same? . . . You know, sometimes I have the feeling I'm not one but two, three, four people. Is there an original person? An essence? I'm not altogether sure, for without language I am nobody. Language makes us able to fit into a context. And what is there to be found in the interstices between contexts?
>
> *(Stavans, 2001, p. 251)*

Language in general has been shown to elicit social essentialism because of its embedded grammatical categorisation (Rhodes, Leslie & Tworeck, 2012; Kite &

Whitley, 2012). By learning another language, learners are able to better relativise the value of symbolic meaning since they can compare it with other linguistic systems. Lindholm (1994) has suggested that bilingual instruction moves towards a more constructive, less-prejudiced learning environment while Genesee (1987), Cummins (1989, 1994) and Lambert and Cazabon (1994) have discussed how bilingual instruction can raise the profile of a minority language to allow for a more equitable climate.

Learning a second language can reduce prejudice according to Tomlinson and Masuhara (2004) through 'suspension of judgement' when communicating with another person (p. 7). Byram, Gribkova and Starkey (2002) suggest that additional language learning should involve critical discourse analysis so that students are brought to investigate text for discourse. They state that 'learners can acquire the skills of critical analysis of stereotypes and prejudice in texts and images they read or see' (p. 28). Wright and Bougie's research has shown bilingual programmes in the USA, particularly heritage-language programmes, can have a positive effect on social identity and have the potential to reduce 'prejudice among members of the dominant group' (2007, p. 157).

It should be noted, of course, that many schools and national curricula are bilingual with numerous examples in the United States, Europe and the Middle East, some taking second language learning to another level by integrating it with the learning of a subject in what is known as content and language integrated learning (CLIL) (Baker, 2006). With an effort to strengthen the effect second language learning has on students' views of culture and identity, thousands of schools across the globe have the potential to reduce prejudicial thinking.

World literature

When it comes to the study of a first language, literature itself can provide students with a mind-opening opportunity to problematise social categories, discover cultures and empathise with other people. Furthermore, some of the famous works of fiction that treat prejudice directly can be used to raise awareness amongst students, something that can happen in any classroom and not only an international school. Some of the commonly cited texts and/or authors that do this include:

Secondary

- *To Kill a Mockingbird* (Harper Lee, 1960) as a general study of prejudice against a backdrop of white on black racism in the USA;
- *I Know why the Caged Bird Sings* (Maya Angelou, 1969), *The Bluest Eye* (1970) and *Beloved* (1987) by Toni Morrison, *Invisible Man* (Ralph Ellison, 1952) and Alex Hayley's *Roots: The Saga of an American Family* (1976) – as studies of black on white racism and/or slavery in the USA;
- *Poppie* (Elsa Joubert, 1978), *A Dry White Season* (André Brink, 1980), *July's People* (Nadine Gordimer, 1981) and the early plays of Athol Fugard on Apartheid;

- The novels of Charles Dickens, the collection of works known as *La Comédie Humaine* by Victor Hugo (1851), the 20 novels collected as *Les Rougons-Macquart* by Emile Zola, *Silas Marner* (George Eliot, 1861) and *Pride and Prejudice* (Jane Austen, 1813) – on class-related prejudice;
- *The Handmaid's Tale* (Margaret Atwood, 1985) and *I am Malala* (Malala Yousafzai, 2013) on sexism;
- *The Crucible* (Arthur Miller, 1953) on the Salem witch trials and more broadly on ideological prejudice;
- *Midnight's Children* (Salman Rushdie, 1981) and *Burmese Days* (George Orwell, 1934) on colonialism;
- *The God of Small Things* (Arundhati Roy, 1997) on Indian identity and the caste system;
- *Othello* (Shakespeare, 1622), *Nervous Conditions* (Tsitsi Dangarembga, 1988), *Wide Sargasso Sea* (Jean Rhys, 1966) and *Americanah* by Chimamanda Ngozi Adichie (2013) on Otherness.

Primary

- *The Sneetches* (Dr Seuss, 1961) – on discrimination and anti-Semitism;
- *Wonder* (R.J. Palacio, 2012) – on prejudice in general;
- *Anne Frank: Diary of a Young Girl* (Frank, 1952), *Number the Stars* (Lois Lowry, 1989) and *The Boy in the Striped Pyjamas* (John Boyne, 2006) – on the Holocaust;
- *The Rabbits* (John Marsden & Shaun Tan, 1998) – on the colonisation of Australia;
- *The Lemonade Club* (Patricia Polacco, 2007) – on children suffering from diseases.

Works of non-fiction that discuss prejudice and can be studied at a secondary level include:

- *Long Walk to Freedom* (Nelson Mandela, 1995);
- *The Wretched of the Earth* (Franz Fanon, 1963);
- *I Write What I Like* (Steve Biko, 1978);
- *Orientalism* (Edward Said, 1978).

On the other hand, books where strong stereotyping is apparent can be read, problematised and discussed. Classic examples include: *Heart of Darkness* (Joseph Conrad, 1899); *Huckleberry Finn* (Mark Twain, 1884); *Robinson Crusoe* (Daniel Defoe, 1719); *Voyage au Bout de la Nuit* (Louis Ferdinand Céline, 1932); *Stupeur et Tremblements* (Amélie Nothomb, 1999); *L'Etranger* (Albert Camus, 1942) or *The Merchant of Venice* (Shakespeare, 1600) and *The Tempest* (Shakespeare, 1623). For younger readers these might include *Tintin in the Congo* (Hergé, 1931); *The Adventures of Tom Sawyer* (Mark Twain, 1876); *The Sign of the Four* (Arthur Conan Doyle, 1890); *The Secret Garden* (Frances Hodgson Burnett, 1911); *Gone With the Wind* (Margaret

Mitchell, 1936) or the *Doctor Dolittle* series by Hugh Lofting, ranging from 1920 to 1952 (Lofting, 2014).

One might also consider works that play out some of the fundamental properties of prejudice formation, hereby allowing students opportunities to investigate the nature of prejudice in subtle guises that lie beneath the more easily detectable domains of racism, sexism and class prejudice. Some works that can be used towards these ends include *Lord of the Flies* (William Golding, 1954); *Nineteen Eighty-Four* (George Orwell, 1949), *Waiting for the Barbarians* (JM Coetzee, 1980) or *The Grass is Singing* (Doris Lessing, 1950).

The IB states that

> the study of literature in translation from other cultures is especially important to IB Diploma Programme students because it contributes to a global perspective, thereby promoting an insight into, and understanding of, the different ways in which cultures influence and shape the experiences of life common to all humanity.
>
> *(IB, 2011, p. 5)*

Teachers are given a literature in translation list from which to choose works that cover a wide variety of cultural expression beyond European and American classics: this is another way that the study of literature can loosen students' minds of cultural prejudice. I would argue that if schools are serious about using literature to drive intercultural competence and prejudice-reduction, whether they are part of the IB or not, they should insist on some degree of intercultural diversity in their literature departments' booklists.

There is some academic work to suggest that the reading of literature can reduce prejudice. A review by Djikic and Oatley (2014) suggests that literature creates more empathy in readers and a study by Sabine and Sabine (1983) whereby 1,382 readers around the USA were interviewed on the power of literature to transform personality showed some self-reported gains. Ross's study (Ross, 1999) showed that 60 per cent of a sample of 194 readers reported that reading had changed their personalities. Johnson (2013) found significant levels of empathy growth and prejudice reduction towards Arab-Muslim women in two studies involving participants reading counter-stereotypical fiction about that outgroup.

The humanities

Students following the IB Diploma programme must study the humanities. Schools choose from a number of options within this area which subjects to offer.

> The DP history course is designed in such a way as to explicitly reinforce the emphasis on the development of international-mindedness. For example, one

of the key concepts that weaves throughout the course is perspectives, and, more specifically, an emphasis on encouraging students to appreciate multiple perspectives.

(IB, 2015b, p. 7)

A salient example of a subject that students can follow is global politics, a course that activates critical thinking, metacognition and understanding beyond the Other by 'developing students' international mindedness and awareness of multiple partial perspectives and approaches' (IB, 2014b, p. 8). The course encourages debate and dialogue around political positions so that students are able to better understand the political climate around them and, of course, make their own decisions about political phenomena. The guide emphasises that 'nurturing students' capacity to listen to themselves and to others in order to understand where each is coming from is important for interpreting competing and contestable claims' (IB, 2014b, p. 8).

Suggested case studies (as part of culture and identity topic) include:

- Gendered violence in anti-Muslim riots in Gujarat in 2002
- Violence between protestors and gay pride march participants in Belgrade in 2010
- Ethnic violence in Bosnia and Herzegovina (1992–1995)
- Ethnicity and genocide in Rwanda in 1994
- Hamas' seizure of power in the Gaza strip in 2007
- The Zapatista Rebellion and the quest for autonomy in Chiapas, Mexico.

(IB, 2014b, p. 35)

Clearly these topics have the potential to engage students in the study of areas that are rife with prejudice, discrimination and/or ethnic violence. Again, the angle that teachers decide to take in covering these issues will be of paramount importance since it is here where the extent of the learning experience reducing prejudice (or, indeed, loading on them) will be defined.

Another humanities option that students can engage with is psychology. The part of the course devoted to socio-cultural cognition investigates prejudice directly, allowing students to grapple with the phenomenon in an in-depth manner. The learning objectives for this part of the course include explaining of human behaviour, investigating cognitive biases (such as 'fundamental attribution error, illusory correlation [and] self-serving bias' (IB, 2009, p. 19), exploring social identity theory and studying stereotypes.

Other learning opportunities related directly to prejudice as a construct that IB students are afforded include philosophy, social and cultural anthropology and world religions.

The position from which the humanities should be studied to reduce prejudicial thinking is articulated by Martha Nussbaum (1997, 2006, 2010). Nussbaum investigates classical figures such as Socrates, Diogenes the Cynic and Marcus Aurelius to remind the reader that

> It is up to us as educators, to show our students the beauty and interest of a life that is open to the whole world, to show them that there is after all more joy in the kind of citizenship that questions than in the kind that simply applauds, more fascination in the study of human beings in all their real variety and complexity than in the zealous pursuit of superficial stereotypes.
> *(Nussbaum, 1997, p. 84)*

However, George Steiner's famous lines remind us of the failure of Western humanistic education to produce the idealised citizen Nussbaum imagines: 'We know that a man can read Goethe or Rilke in the evening, that he can play Bach and Schubert, and go to his day's work at Auschwitz in the morning' (Steiner, 1967, p. 15). Hence the challenge of teaching the humanities for prejudice reduction depends on numerous factors and cannot be expected to shift prejudicial thinking of its own accord.

Research on the study of history to reduce prejudice in Europe (in non-International Schools) conducted by Peuker and Reiter (2007) shows that Holocaust education is instituted to a fairly high degree in European countries but that there is nonetheless a tendency to avoid the topic out of fear that it might lead to some form of confrontation between Muslim and Jewish students. They also point out, worryingly, that some teachers 'seem to deem the topic not to be crucial' (p. 11). They emphasise the importance of visits to concentration camps to allow a more emotional connection with the Holocaust as this is seen as a more effective educational experience than a purely cognitive approach (p. 12). Peuker and Reiter also discuss minority groups and immigration as historical themes and urge history teachers to treat these subjects more systematically by implementing them into schemes of work. In discussing these points, they argue that teachers should not only be sufficiently knowledgeable about migration history to teach it effectively but should also be knowledgeable about varying perspectives on migration, including controversial views. If this is not done, the authors argue, the effects can be that 'topics in history are brought up in a simplistic and unproblematic way, leading to routine and superficial learning and uninterested students' (p. 13).

Schools do not have to be international or IB to teach international humanities, particularly if they have the means to choose or design the subjects they offer. Yucai High School (2016), for instance, teaches 'The Analysis and Deconstruction of the Other' as part of their humanities syllabus while the C.K. McClatchy High School (2013) runs a selective Humanities and International Studies Programme. Teaching the humanities in an international manner is as much about the perspectives and frames of references that are used to discuss issues as the degree of internationalism in the actual syllabus content. Schools teaching the humanities for less prejudice can use the IB models and others from around the world as examples of how this might be designed.

Inquiry

International education models, particularly the IB, contain a major element of inquiry-based learning, a notion whereby the psychodynamics of learning are seen as fundamental and the voyage of discovery involved in learning is promoted.

The active education movement in the early twentieth century, influenced by the writings of Rousseau, Pestalozzi and Froebel, expressed itself in the educational models developed by Dewey, Piaget, Vygotsky and Montessori. The founders of the International School of Geneva were versed in this education theory and the notion that learning is about inquiry has remained a cornerstone of international education.

The IB promotes inquiry-based learning most notably in its Primary Years Programme, articulated around 'units of inquiry' where the emphasis is on project-based understanding through authentic, hands-on discovery. Students engage in research projects throughout their learning in the IB programmes with exhibitions, personal projects and extended essays based on themes or subjects of their choice.

Inquiry-based learning is anchored within social constructivism, a model of learning whereby knowledge is a socially produced phenomenon that must be built up iteratively through dialogue and group experience. This can be opposed to *Deus ex Machina* models where knowledge exists in an outer realm of truth and is to be absorbed and appropriated by individuals. Importantly, constructivism holds the premise that in learning humans build on prior knowledge. As Prince and Felder put it, 'New information is filtered through mental structures (*schemata*) that incorporate the student's prior knowledge, beliefs, preconceptions and misconceptions, prejudices, and fears' (2015, p. 3).

The implications for prejudice reduction in this vision of learning are considerable because the rigid construct of identity that is erected and withheld in the prejudiced mindset is reviewed as an unstable site of interaction and subjectivity – not so much a thing-in-itself to be discovered but a contingent area of potential meaning. Indeed, inquiry-based learning is not just about discovering the world, it is about viewing oneself as a lifelong learner in a voyage to better know other people and oneself.

Inquiry learning is learning by experimenting; it involves students moving away from pure theory to practice. The main idea behind this vision of education is that we learn best through direct experience. The figure who has popularised inquiry learning the most is David Kolb. His experiential learning model is made up of four steps that form a cycle: concrete experience (1) should be observed and reflected upon (2), abstract, transferable concepts should be drawn from that reflection (3), and these concepts should then be tested (4) in the form of new concrete actions (Kolb, Rubin & McIntyre, 1974).

Inquiry-based learning is therefore based on the premise that we learn best when we are actively engaged in our learning, reflecting upon it critically and developing conceptual understanding from real-life experience. In many ways, inquiry-based learning has the potential to dispel or prevent prejudicial thinking because there is necessary ownership and personalisation of learning through action and experience that should, if conducted in the right way and under the right circumstances, challenge a priori sentiments and stereotypes. To give an example, if a child does a project on a group of people (an ethnic group for example) and meets members of the outgroup as part of fieldwork related to the project, (s)he is likely to have a far more grounded, human and personal understanding than the student who is shown pictures in class and takes notes that are dictated by a teacher on the characteristics of the group being studied.

Ainsworth sees inquiry-based learning as part of the larger project of multiculturalism where teachers help 'students to reduce prejudice to groups different from their own' (2013, p. 490). Indeed, inquiry-based learning implies moving out of the classroom into new, real-life settings, be they natural, social or professional. It is an opportunity for the teacher to make the learning of the child come alive so that (s)he can make connections and internalise authentic examples.

Houghton (2010), concluding on action research on stereotypes conducted with 36 Japanese university students who not only learned about stereotypes but took action by designing questionnaires and interviewing foreign students so as to develop a more authentic representation of the concept, states that 'experiential learning seems to be one way in which meta-cognitive awareness and control may be developed in relation to stereotypes' (p. 195). For more detail on this research, see Chapter 4.

R.S. Peters expresses the importance of volition and personal experience in child-centred education:

> The development from within of potentialities rather than 'moulding' from without, that the curriculum should arise from the needs and interests of the child rather than from the demands of the teacher, that self-expression is more important than the discipline of 'subject-matter', that children should not be coerced or punished, that children should be allowed to 'learn from experience' rather than be told things.
>
> *(Curren, 2007, p. 58)*

However, exactly what constitutes a child's experience needs to be analysed as it should not be assumed that experience is a holy grail or is necessarily substantial enough to create strong learning. Allport pointed out that a prejudiced mindset might well use few experiences as a warrant for an over-generalisation (Allport, 1954, p. 6).

For this reason, to build knowledge empirically, many experiences are needed rather than an overgeneralised few. Furthermore, inquiry must be consummated with reflection if it is to be of a higher order and if we are to move beyond mere gut reaction. Experience should be conjugated by the necessary habits of thought for it to be a subtle intellectual process and not mere recollection of experiences.

Inquiry-based learning is by no means the exclusive property of international or IB schools and numerous examples of this type of education can be found in other school systems, notably the Montessori School philosophy that places an emphasis on student choice and discovery learning or Sugata Mitra's Self Organised Learning Environment (SOLE) pedagogical design whereby students engage in research with very little intervention from the teacher in groups of four using a computer (Mitra, 2013). Whichever form of inquiry-based learning used, educators should keep in mind the potential this classroom strategy has to reduce prejudicial thinking.

Reflection

Another element of learning that is emphasised in the IB – one that can be seen as part of the inquiry cycle – is reflection. Students are expected to reflect on their learning to better ensure encoding of information and meaningful afterthought in the relevance and implications of their learning.

The IB's Creativity, Activity, Service programme (CAS) places considerable emphasis on reflection by ensuring that students log their thoughts and experiences in a reflection portfolio. The point of reflection in CAS is to ensure that students are not only 'doing' but drawing conclusions from their actions and reflecting on the consequences of their choices (IB, 2015, p. 7). 'Reflection informs students' learning and growth by allowing students to explore ideas, skills, strengths, limitations and areas for further development and consider how they may use prior learning in new contexts' (p. 9).

Using King and Kitchener's Reflective Judgement Model (1994), research conducted by Devine (1989) suggests that reflective thinkers 'are unsure how to deal with the inherent ambiguity of ill-structured problems. They are more likely to recognize that a stereotype is an inappropriate criterion upon which to base a judgment' (Guthrie, King & Palmer, 2011).

The idea of reflection being a superior level of thought comes to us from John Dewey who saw the process in two movements: 'a state of perplexity, hesitation, doubt; and (b) an act of search or investigation directed toward bringing to light further facts which serve to corroborate or to nullify the suggested belief' (Dewey, 1910, p. 3). In this way, reflection is synonymous with critical thinking in that it involves suspension of belief and justification, a clear cognitive response to prejudice. This is something I develop in detail in Chapter 3.

Concepts-focused learning

Central to learning in all age groups in the IB is the idea of learning through concepts rather than topics. The Primary Years Programme (for students from 3 to 12) bases its curriculum on a conceptual framework centred on the following concepts that are reiterated throughout learning: form, function, causation, change, connection, perspective, responsibility, reflection (IB, 2007, p. 16).

Learning through concepts allows for transfer: 'it is by understanding the key abstract features of a concept that students will be able to recognize them in different circumstances and therefore transfer them to their learning' (UNESCO-IBE et al., p. 22). Concepts-focused learning is a necessary element of deep learning for understanding: Erickson (2013) argues that learners need to synthesise information at a higher level of abstraction than ever before because of the information-saturated world that we live in. Concepts, she states, are useful ways of creating mental schemata for information patterning (including information storage and retrieval) while enabling transfer. Indeed, it is via concepts that lessons learnt, patterns gleaned and strategies attempted can be put to new practice.

The IB Middle Years Programme (for 12- to 16-year-olds) places a similar focus on concepts with the following key concepts used throughout the curriculum: aesthetics, change, communication, communities, connections, creativity, culture, development, form, global interactions, identity, logic, perspective, relationships, systems, time, place and space (IB, 2015c). The idea is that students learn subject matter through these concepts so as to gain a deeper, transferable understanding of their properties across different domains.

Where concepts-focused learning can reduce prejudice is in the cognitive domain through a higher-order moment of understanding that allows for a more subtle appreciation of another person or group. This goes beyond immediate sensory perception or unjustified belief into a realm of abstract thinking.

Allport (1954) explains how a prejudiced person will no doubt have erected simplified concepts that are held on to despite disconfirmation. In order to accommodate inconsistent information, subcategories or exceptions to the rule will be created. This leads to fallacious categories and conceptually weak structures of thought that, in the long term, will cause confusion, cognitive dissonance and a degree of bias that will be difficult to sustain without running into contradictory thoughts.

Therefore, in order to overcome prejudice, individuals need to engage in deep conceptual understanding of themselves and those around them. Understanding prejudice itself is an intense learning experience that is deeply conceptual and could be described as a 'threshold concept':

> a threshold concept represents a transformed way of understanding, or interpreting, or viewing something without which the learner cannot progress. As a consequence of comprehending a threshold concept there may thus be a transformed internal view of subject matter, subject landscape, or even world view, and the student can move on.
>
> *(Land et al., 2005, p. 53)*

To give an example, a woman might have developed a prejudice against men along the lines of 'men do not know how to listen'. When she meets a man who disconfirms this rule by listening, she will usually discard that instance as an exception to the rule or ignore the experience so as not to disturb the stereotype erected in her mind. In order to change the statement 'men do not know how to listen' to 'some men do not know how to listen', the woman will have to revisit her premise, deconstruct it and reshape it. This inner voyage is essentially one whereby a concept is dismantled and replaced or modified. Powerful, transformative learning experiences will restructure prior knowledge and iron out faulty bases in order for 'good' or correct knowledge to be better anchored in understanding. For a prejudiced conclusion to be abandoned, the learner has to go back to the premise that leads to the conclusion and correct it in order to hold onto a coherent sequence of thought. Such an experience is both cognitively difficult as it is emotionally destabilising, a type of reconversion that entails reviewing a number of associated beliefs and assumptions. In this sense, using Land's definition of the threshold concept, the woman will have to 'transform' her 'internal view [. . .] or even world view'.

Indeed, prejudice itself needs to be viewed and understood conceptually for learners to recognise their own prejudices and it is only once the concept of prejudice itself can be named, understood, recognised and opened to discussion that learners will be able to identify it within themselves and work towards reducing it.

Theory of Knowledge

Students enrolled in the IB Diploma Programme follow a 100-hour course in epistemology called Theory of Knowledge. In many ways, this learning experience could be considered the IB's strongest response to prejudicial thinking as the course focusses on how we construct knowledge in different areas and continually reminds students to ask themselves the question 'how do I know?' or 'how do we know?'.

Theory of Knowledge asks students to investigate knowledge through eight ways of knowing (language, sense perception, emotion, reason, imagination, faith, intuition and memory) and eight areas of knowledge (mathematics, natural sciences, human sciences, history, the arts, ethics, religious knowledge systems and indigenous knowledge systems). The course aims all relate to prejudice reduction:

> 1. make connections between a critical approach to the construction of knowledge, the academic disciplines and the wider world; 2. develop an awareness of how individuals and communities construct knowledge and how this is critically examined; 3. develop an interest in the diversity and richness of cultural perspectives and an awareness of personal and ideological assumptions; 4. critically reflect on their own beliefs and assumptions, leading to more thoughtful, responsible and purposeful lives; 5. understand that knowledge brings responsibility which leads to commitment and action.
>
> *(IB, 2013b, p. 14)*

The Theory of Knowledge guide unravels many of the stereotype-inducing facets of thought and feeling that lead to prejudice. However, prejudice is not discussed explicitly at any point in the guide with the emphasis being more on the relationship between areas of knowledge and ways of knowing.

In the Theory of Knowledge course, teachers have a tool that can be used to problematize emotion, perception, logic and knowledge systems to investigate social, cognitive and behavioural enterprises of meaning making and, hence, prejudice.

Conclusion

Education clearly has the potential to reduce prejudicial thinking. International education, which has its roots in The International School of Geneva's vision for an education for peace at the outset of World War I, is an expression of an approach to learning that is premised on value of respectful and humane collaboration. There is much theoretical research on the benefits of models of intercultural competence for prejudice reduction but fewer reliable studies on the effects of international school projects on prejudice reduction.

Although it is difficult to establish a coherent definition of international education, when looking at school education, the best known and most clearly articulated vision of international education is the International Baccalaureate, a curriculum framework for students from 3 to 19 years of age with a focus on international mindedness and humanitarian values articulated in a learner profile.

There is some evidence that prejudice can be reduced through service learning, the learning of an additional language, world literature and the humanities. These elements are all developed in the IB Diploma Programme (for 16- to 19-year-olds) with service learning and the learning of an additional language common to all of the IB's programmes. However, these educational experiences are not the exclusive remit of the IB or international education and can be found and should be developed in all schools.

Educational and psychological theory points to inquiry-based learning, reflection and concepts-focused learning as areas with strong potential to reduce prejudicial thinking. These are developed at all age levels of the IB's programmes and are strongly characteristic of the IB but, again, are developed in numerous other educational models and should be considered by all educational institutions.

Theory of Knowledge, a course developed in the Diploma Programme, has many of the constituents necessary to discuss and problematize prejudice although the guide does not explicitly ask teachers to use the learning experience to this end.

Therefore, international education as expressed in the IB contains these central research-informed strategies that are aimed at increasing empathy, understanding, cognitive flexibility and metacognition – and therefore reducing prejudice. However, crucially, this may or may not be the case depending on the level of critical engagement that the teacher and/or school wishes to dedicate to them.

In earlier articles I have suggested that the IB offers opportunities to reduce prejudice but that these must be activated thoughtfully in international schools for any profound change to take place and that if they are not, a type of fanfare of nationalities that encourage stereotype enforcement might be the result: celebrating diversity also means encouraging diversity and this can become forced if students are reluctant to take on the essentialising national and ethnic identities that are required for international days, evenings or fairs to take place (Hughes, 2009, 2014). This is particularly the case in the twenty-first century where many students have multiple identities and might not want to become ambassadors for only one. For a rich discussion on the difficulty of living out multiple identities see Maalouf (1998).

In sum, a prejudice-reducing experience of international education is something that may or may not be done by the school or teacher depending on the open-mindedness and degree of nuance stakeholders are willing to tolerate and to what extent they are able to see beyond the limiting and sometimes unhelpful notion of cultural identity.

The questions of application and praxis remain the burning issues in international education: it is the extent to which the mission of international education is operationalised that will determine the extent to which it is used to effectively combat prejudice.

For schools that are not international schools or do not run IB programmes, this chapter has suggested elements of international education that can be used across all systems to reduce prejudice. The worldwide exemplar of international education with focus on the IB illustrates the potential for good and effective practice and could be readily relatable to practices elsewhere. Taking all together, no practice, including that associated with the IB, is necessarily perfect. This much said, all might benefit from more attention to the fundamental tenets of international education.

References

Ainsworth, J. (Ed.), (2013). *Sociology of education. An A to Z guide*. Thousand Oaks, CA: Sage.

Allport, G. (1954). *The nature of prejudice*. Cambridge, MA: Addison-Wesley.

Angelou, M. (1969). *I know why the caged bird sings*. New York, NY: Random Books.

Appiah, Kwame A. (2006). *Cosmopolitanism: Ethics in a world of strangers*, New York, NY: W.W. Norton.

Atwood, M. (1985). *The handmaid's tale*. Toronto: McClelland and Stewart.

Austen, J. (1813). *Pride and prejudice*. Whitehall: T. Egerton.

Baker, C. (2006). Foundations of bilingual education and bilingualism (4th edn). Clevedon: Multilingual Matters.

Balzac, H. (1851). *La comédie humaine*. Paris: Béchet, Gosselin, Mame, Charpentier, Dubochet Furne et Hetzel.

Bettencourt, B., Brewer, M.B., Croak, M.R., & Miller, N. (1992). Cooperation and the reduction of intergroup bias: The role of reward structure and social orientation. *Journal of Experimental Social Psychology*, 28(4), 301–319.

Biko, S. (1978). *I Write What I Like*. Heinemann: Berkshire.

Bohman, J. (2004). *Democracy across borders: From Dêmos to Dêmoi*. Cambridge, MA: MIT Press.

Boyne, J. (2004). *The boy in the striped pyjamas*. London: David Fickling.

Brink, A. (1980). *A dry white season*. New York, NY: William Morrow and Co.

Byram, M. (1997). *Teaching and assessing intercultural communicative competence*. Clevedon: Multilingual Matters.

Byram, M. (2011). From foreign language education to education for intercultural citizenship. *Intercultural Communication Review*, 9, 17–36.

Byram, M., Gribkova, B., & Starkey, H. (2002). *Developing the intercultural dimension in language teaching. A practical guidebook for teachers*. Strasbourg: Council of Europe.

Byran, A., & Vavrus, F. (2005). The promise and peril of education: The teaching of in/tolerance in an era of globalisation. *Globalisation, Societies and Education*, 3(2), 183–202.

Cambridge, J. (2012). International education research and the sociology of knowledge. *Journal of Research in International Education*, 11(3), 230–244.

Camicia, S.P. (2007). Prejudice reduction through multicultural education: Connecting multiple literatures. *Social Studies Research and Practice*, 2(2), 219–227.

Camus, A. (1942). *L'Etranger*. Paris: Gallimard.

Céline, L.F. (1932). *Voyage au bout de la nuit*. Paris: Denoel & Steele.

Coetzee, JM. (1980). *Waiting for the Barbarians*. London: Secker & Warburg.

Conan Doyle, A. (1890). *The sign of the four*. London: Spencer Blackett.

Conrad, J. (1899). *Heart of darkness*. London: Blackwood's Magazine.

Cummins, J. (1989). *Empowering minority students*. Sacramento, CA: California Association for Bilingualism Education.

Cummins, J. (1994). Knowledge, power, and identity in teaching English as a second language. In F. Genesee (Ed.), *Educating second language children: The whole child, the whole curriculum, the whole community* (pp. 33–58). Cambridge: Cambridge University Press.

Curren, R. (Ed). (2007). *Philosophy of education*. Oxford: Blackwell.

Dangarembga, T. (1988). *Nervous conditions*. London: The Women's Press.

Deardorff, D. (2009). Synthesizing conceptualizations of intercultural competence: A summary and emerging themes. In D. Deardorff (Ed.), *The Sage handbook of intercultural competence* (pp. 264–270). Thousand Oaks, CA: Sage.

Defoe, D. (1719). *Robinson Crusoe*. London: W. Taylor.

Delors, J. et al. (1996). *Learning: The treasure within*. Paris: UNESCO.

Delve, C.I., Mintz, S.D., & Stewart G,. M. (1990). Community service as values education. *New Directions for Student Services*, 50. San Francisco, CA: Jossey-Bass.

Devine, P.G. (1989). Stereotypes and prejudice: Their automatic and controlled components. *Journal of Personality and Social Psychology*, 56(1), 5–18.

Dewey, J. (1910). 'What is thought?' Chapter 1 in *How we think*. Lexington, MA: D.C. Heath, 1–13.

Diogenes Laertius. (1989). *Lives of the eminent philosophers: vol 2 (books 6 to 10)*. (Trans R.D. Hicks). New York: Loeb.

Djikic, M., & Oatley, K. (2014). The art in fiction: From indirect communication to changes of the self. *Psychology Of Aesthetics, Creativity, And The Arts*, 8(4), 498–505. doi: 10.1037/a0037999

ECOWAS-SWAC/OECD (2006). Online. Available at: www.oecd.org/migration/38409521.pdf (accessed 28 April 2016).

Eliot, G. (1861). *Silas Marner*. London: William Blackwood & Sons.

Ellison, R. (1952). *Invisible man*. New York: Random House.

Ensari, N., & Miller, N. (2001). Decategorization and the reduction of bias in the crossed categorization paradigm. *European Journal of Social Psychology*, 31(2), 193–216.

Erickson, J.A. (2011). Service-learning's impact on attitudes and behavior: A review and update. Online. Available at: http://web.augsburg.edu/~erickson/MCC2012/Erickson_2011.pdf (accessed 28 April 2016).

Erickson, J.A., & O'Connor, S.E. (2000). Service learning: Does it promote or reduce prejudice? In C. O'Grady (Ed.), *Integrating service learning and multicultural education in colleges and universities*. New York, NY: Lawrence Erlbaum.

Erickson, L. (2013). *Concept-based curriculum and instruction: Engaging the child's mind*. [Presentation at the ninth Annual Education Conference at the International School of Geneva, 2014.]

Fanon, F. (1963). *The wretched of the Earth*. (C. Farrington, Trans.). New York, NY: Grove Press.

Frank, A. (1952). *Anne Frank: The diary of a young girl* (B.M. Mooyaart, Trans.). New York, NY: Doubleday.

Genesee, F. (1987). *Learning through two languages: Studies of immersion and bilingual education*. Cambridge, MA: Newbury House.

Giles, D.E., Jr. & Eyler, J. (1994). The impact of a college community service laboratory on students' personal, social, and cognitive outcomes. *Journal of Adolescence*, 17, 327–339.

Golding, W. (1954). *Lord of the flies*. London: Faber & Faber.

Gordimer, N. (1981). *July's people*. London: Jonathan Cape.

Gorski, P. (2006). The unintentional undermining of multicultural education: Educators at the equity crossroads. In J. Landsman and C.W. Lewis (Eds), *White teachers/diverse classrooms: A guide to building inclusive schools, promoting high expectations, and eliminating racism* (pp. 61–78). Sterling, VA: Stylus Publishing.

Gunesch, K. (2004). Education for cosmopolitanism? Cosmopolitanism as a personal cultural identity model for and within international education. *Journal of Research in International Education*, 3(3), 251–275.

Guthrie, V.L., King, P.M., & Palmer, C.J. (2011). Higher education and reducing prejudice: Research on cognitive capabilities underlying tolerance. Online. Available at: www.diversityweb.org/digest/sp.sm00/tolerance.html (accessed 28 April 2016).

Habermas, J. (2001). *The postnational constellation: Political essays* (M. Pensky, Trans. and Ed.). Cambridge, MA: MIT Press.

Haegel, F. (1999). The effect of education on the expression of negative views towards immigrants in France: The influence of the republican model put to the test. In L. Hagendoorn & S. Nekuee (Eds), *Education and racism: A cross national inventory of positive effects of education on ethnic tolerance*. Aldershot: Ashgate.

Hare, J. (2010). *Holistic education: An interpretation for teachers in the IB programmes*. Cardiff: IBO.

Hayley, A. (1976). *Roots: The saga of an American family*. New York. Doubleday.

Haywood, T. (2007). A simple typology of international-mindedness and its implications for education. In M. Hayden, J. Thompson and J. Levy (Eds), *The Sage handbook of international education* (pp. 79–90). London: Sage.

Hergé. (1931). *Tintin au Congo*. Paris: Casterman.

Hill, I. (2012). An international model of world-class education: The International Baccalaureate. *Prospects*, 42(3), 341–359. doi:10.1007/s11125-012-9243-9.

Hodgson Burnett, F. (1911). *The secret garden*. London: Heinemann.

Hollis, S. (2004). Blaming me, blaming you: Assessing service learning and participants' tendency to blame the victim. *Sociological Spectrum*, 24, 575–600.

Houghton, S. (2010). Managing stereotypes through experiential learning. *Intercultural Communication Studies*, XIX(1), 182–198.

Hughes, C. (2009). International education and the International Baccalaureate Diploma Programme: A view from the perspective of postcolonial thought. *Journal of Research in International Education*, 8(2), 123–141.

Hughes, C. (2012). Child-centred pedagogy, internationalism and bilingualism at the International School of Geneva. *International Schools Journal*, 32, 1.

Hughes, C. (2014). Theory of Knowledge aims, objectives and assessment criteria: An analysis of critical thinking descriptors. *Journal of Research in International Education*, 13(1), 30–45.

IB. (2006). *IB Learner Profile booklet*. Cardiff: IB.

IB. (2007). *Making the PYP happen*. Cardiff: IB.

IB. (2009). *Psychology guide*. Cardiff: IB.

IB. (2011). *Language A: language and literature guide*. Cardiff: IB.

IB. (2013). *IB Learner Profile booklet*. Cardiff: IB.

IB. (2013b). *Theory of knowledge guide*. Cardiff: IB.

IB. (2014). *Middle Years programme Language Acquisition guide*. Cardiff: IB.

IB. (2014b). *Global politics guide*. Cardiff: IB.

IB. (2015). *Diploma Programme: Creativity, activity, service guide*: Geneva: IB.

IB. (2015b). *History guide*. Cardiff: IB.

IB. (2015c). *MYP: From principles into practice*. Online. Available at: https://ibpublishing.ibo. org/server2/rest/app/tsm.xql?doc=m_0_mypxx_guu_1409_1_e&part=6&chapter=2 (accessed 28 April 2016).

International Labour Organization. (1989). Indigenous and tribal peoples convention, 1989 (no. 169). Online. Available at: www.ilo.org/dyn/normlex/en/f?p=NORMLEXPUB: 12100:0::NO::p12100_instrument_id:312314 (accessed 19 April 2016).

IOM. (2013). *World migration report 2013*. Geneva: International Organization for Migration.

Jasinska-Kania, A. (1999). The impact of education on racism in Poland compared with other European countries. In L. Hagendoorn and S. Nekuee (Eds), *Education and racism: A cross-national inventory of positive effects of education on ethnic tolerance* (pp. 75–92). Aldershot: Ashgate.

Johnson, D. (2013). Transportation into literary fiction reduces prejudice against and increases empathy for Arab-Muslims. *Scientific Study of Literature*, 3(1), 77–92.

Jones, S. (2002). The underside of service learning. *About Campus*, 7(4), 10–15.

Joubert, E. (1978). *Die swerfjare van Poppie Nongena (The long journey of Poppie Nongena)*. Cape Town: Tafelberg.

Kendall, J.C. (Ed.). (1990). *Combining service and learning: A resource book for community and public service*, vol 1. Raleigh, NC: National Society for Experiential Education.

King, P.M., & Kitchener, K.S. (1994). *Developing reflective judgment: Understanding and promoting intellectual growth and critical thinking in adolescents and adults*. San Francisco, CA: Jossey-Bass.

Kite, M.E., Whitley, B.E. (2012). Ethnic and nationality stereotypes in everyday language. *Teaching of Psychology*, 39(1), 54–56. doi: 10.1177/0098628311430314

Kolb, D.A., Rubin, I.M., & McIntyre, J.M. (1974). *Organizational psychology: A book of readings* (2nd edn). Englewood Cliffs, NJ: Prentice-Hall.

Kramsch, C. (2009). *The multilingual subject*. Oxford: Oxford University Press.

Lambert, W.E., & Cazabon, M. (1994). Students' views of the Amigos program (Research Report No. 11). Santa Cruz: University of California, National Center for Research on Cultural Diversity and Second Language Learning.

Land, R. et al. (2005). Threshold concepts and troublesome knowledge (3)*: Implications for course design and evaluation. In C. Rust (Ed.), *Improving student learning diversity and inclusivity*. Oxford, UK: Oxford Centre for Staff and Learning Development.

Lee, H. (1960). *To kill a mockingbird*. New York, NY: Grand Central Publishing.

Lessing, D. (1950). *The grass is singing*. London: Michael Joseph.

Lindholm, K.J. (1994). Promoting positive cross-cultural attitudes and perceived competence in culturally and linguistically diverse classrooms. In R.A. Devillar, C.J. Faltis and J.P. Cummins (Eds), *Cultural diversity in schools: From rhetoric to practice* (pp. 189–206). Albany, NY: State University of New York Press.

Lofting, H. (2014). *The voyages of Doctor Dolittle*. United States: Createspace.

Lowry, L. (1989). *Number the Stars*. New York, NY: Houghton Mifflin Harcourt.

Maalouf, A. (1998). *In the name of identity: Violence and the need to belong (les identities meurtrières*, B. Bray, Trans.). New York, NY: Arcade.

MacDonald, J. (2006). The international school industry: Examining international schools through an economic lens. *Journal of Research in International Education*, 5(2), 191–213.

Mandela, N. (1995). *Long walk to freedom*. New York, NY: Little Brown & Co.

Mandela, N. (2003). Lighting your way to a better future. Online. Available at: http:// db.nelsonmandela.org/speeches/pub_view.asp?pg=item&ItemID=NMS909 (accessed 28 April 2016).

Marsden, J., & Tan, S. (1998). *The rabbits*. Vancouver: Simply Read.

Maurette, M.T. (1948). Techniques d'éducation pour la paix, existent-elles? UNESCO. Online. Available at: http://alumni.ecolint.net/authors/maurette/ (accessed 28 April 2016).

Miller, A. (1953). *The crucible*. New York, NY: Penguin.

Mitchell, M. (1936). *Gone with the wind*. New York, NY: Warner Books

Mitra, S. (2013). SOLE: How to bring Self-Organized Learning Environments to your community. Online. Available at: www.ted.com/pages/835 (accessed 28 April 2016).

Morrison, T. (1970). *The bluest eye*. New York, NY: Holt, Rinehart and Winston.

Morrison, T. (1987). *Beloved*. New York, NY: Knopf Doubleday.

National Coalition Building Institute. NCBI. (2015). Online. Available at: www.ncbi.ch/de/international-schools/ (accessed 28 April 2016).

Ngozi Adichie, C. (2013). *Americanah*. New York, NY: Alfred A. Knopf.

Nieto, S. (2002). *Language, culture, and teaching: Critical perspectives for a new century*. Mahweh, NJ: Lawrence Erlbaum.

Nieto, S., & Bode, P. (2008). *Affirming diversity: The sociopolitical context of multicultural education*. Boston, MA: Pearson.

Nothomb, A. (1999). *Stupeur et tremblements*. Paris: Albin Michel.

Nussbaum, M.C. (1997). *Cultivating humanity: A classic defense of reform in liberal education*. Cambridge, MA: Harvard University Press.

Nussbaum, M.C. (2006). *Frontiers of justice: Disability, nationality, species membership*, Cambridge: Belknap Press.

Nussbaum, M. (2010). *Not for profit: Why democracy needs the humanities*. Princeton, NJ: Princeton University Press.

Ofsted. (2015). Online. Available at: www.clerktogovernors.co.uk/ofsted/ofsted-grade-descriptors-the-behaviour-and-safety-of-pupils-at-the-school/ (accessed 28 April 2016).

Orwell, G. (1934). *Burmese days*. New York, NY: Harper & Brothers.

Orwell, G. (1949). *Nineteen eighty-four*. London: Secker & Warburg.

Palacio, R.J. (2012). *Wonder*. New York, NY: Alfred A. Knopf.

Peri, P. (1999). Education and prejudice against immigrants. In L. Hagendoorn and S. Nekuee (Eds), *Education and racism: A cross national inventory of positive effects of education on ethnic tolerance* (pp. 21–32). Aldershot: Ashgate.

Peterson, A. (1987). *Schools across frontiers*. La Salle, Illinois: Open Court.

Peuker, M., & Reiter, S. (2007). Educational tools, resources and informal learning frameworks that help to reduce prejudice mapping study on behalf of the Rothschild Foundation Europe. European forum for migration studies, Institute at the University of Bamberg. Online. Available at: www.efms.uni-bamberg.de/pdf/Summary_Mapping_Study.pdf (accessed 28 April 2016).

Plato. (2003). *The last days of Socrates*. London: Penguin Classics.

Plato. (2009). *Protagoras*. Oxford. Oxford University Press.

Polacco, P. (2007). *The lemonade club*. New York, NY: Philomel Books.

Prince, M. J & Felder, R.M. (2015). Inductive teaching and learning methods: Definitions, comparisons and research bases. Online. Available at: www4.ncsu.edu/unity/lockers/users/f/felder/public/Papers/InductiveTeaching.pdf (accessed 28 April 2016).

Rhoads, R.A. (1998). In the service of citizenship: A study of student involvement in community service. *The Journal of Higher Education*, 69(3), 277–297.

Rhodes, M., Leslie, S.J., & Tworeck, C.M. (2012). Cultural transmission of social essentialism. *PNAS*, 109(34), 13526–13531; published ahead of print August 6, 2012, doi: 10.1073/pnas.1208951109. Online. Available at: www.pnas.org/content/109/34/13526.full.pdf (accessed 28 April 2016).

Rhys, J. (1966). *Wide sargasso sea*. New York: Norton.

Ross, C.S. (1999). Finding without seeking: The information encounter in the context of reading for pleasure. *Information Processing and Management*, 35, 783–799.

Roy, A. (1997). *The god of small things*. New York, NY: Random House.

Rushdie, S. (1981). *Midnight's children*. London: Jonathan Cape.

Sabine, G., & Sabine, P. (1983). *Books that made the difference*. Hamden, CN: Library Professional Publications.

Said, E. (1978). *Orientalism*. New York, NY:Vintage Books.

Seuss,T. (1961). *The Sneetches and other stories*. New York, NY: Random House.

Shakespeare,W. (1600). *The Merchant of Venice*. London:Thomas Heyes.

Shakespeare,W. (1622). *The Tragedy of Othello, the Moor of Venice*. London: Nicholas Okes.

Shakespeare,W. (1623). *The Tempest*. London: Blount & Jaggard.

Simandiraki, A. (2006). International education and cultural heritage: Alliance or antagonism? *Journal of Research in International Education*, 5(1), 35–56.

Skrzypiec, G., Askell-Williams, H., Slee, P., & Rudzinski, A. (2014). *International Baccalaureate Middle Years Programme: Student social-emotional well-being and school success practices*. Bethesda, MD, USA. International Baccalaureate Organization.

Sleeter, C.E., & Bernal, D.D. (2004). Critical pedagogy, critical race theory, and antiracist education: Implications for multicultural education. In J.A. Banks and C.A. McGee Banks (Eds), *Handbook of research on multicultural education* (2nd edn, pp. 240–258). San Francisco, CA: Jossey-Bass.

Spitzberg, B.H., & Changnon, G. (2009). Conceptualizing intercultural competence. In D. Deardorff (Ed.), *The Sage handbook of intercultural competence* (pp. 2–52). Thousand Oaks, CA: Sage.

Stavans, I. (2001). *On borrowed words. A memoir of language*. New York, NY: Penguin.

Steiner, G. (1967). *Language and silence: Essays 1958−1966*. London: Faber.

Sylvester, R. (2002). The first international school: The story of the London College of the International Education Society (1866–1889). Paper presented at the University of Bath/International Baccalaureate conference Interpreting International Education − Dimensions of Theory and Practice Geneva, 11–13 September.

Tate, N. (2012). Challenges and pitfalls facing international education in a post-international world. *Journal of Research in International Education*, 11(3), 205–217.

Tomlinson, B., & Masuhara, H. (2004). Developing cultural awareness. *Modern English Teacher*, 13(1), 5–11.

Twain, M. (1876). *The adventures of Tom Sawyer*. London: Chatto & Windus.

Twain, M. (1884). *Adventures of Huckleberry Finn*. London: Chatto & Windus.

UNESCO. (1951). Statement on race. Online. Available at: http://unesdoc.unesco.org/images/0017/001789/178908eb.pdf (accessed 28 April 2016).

UNESCO. (1966). Declaration of the principles of International cultural cooperation. Online. Available at: http://portal.unesco.org/en/ev.php-URL_ID=13147&URL_DO=DO_TOPIC&URL_SECTION=201.html (accessed 28 April 2016).

UNESCO. (1978). Declaration on race and racial prejudice. Online. Available at: www.unesco.org/webworld/peace_library/UNESCO/HRIGHTS/107–116.HTM (accessed 28 April 2016).

UNESCO. (1993). International conference on education (43rd session) on The Contribution of Education to Cultural Development. Paris: UNESCO International Bureau of Education. Online. Available at: www.unesco.org/education/pdf/31_42.pdf (accessed 28 April 2016).

UNESCO (2006). UNESCO guidelines on intercultural education. Paris: UNESCO. Online. Available at: http://unesdoc.unesco.org/images/0014/001478/147878e.pdf (accessed 28 April 2016).

UNESCO-IBE & Ecole International de Genève. (2014). Guiding principles for learning in the 21st century. Geneva: UNESCO-IBE.

United Nations. (1948). The Universal Declaration of Human Rights. Online. Available at: www.un.org/en/universal-declaration-human-rights/ (accessed 18 April 2016).

United Nations. (1965). UN Declaration on the promotion among youth of the ideals of peace, mutual respect and understanding between peoples. Online. Available at: www.un-documents.net/a20r2037.htm (accessed 28 April 2016).

United Nations. (2013). Department of Economic and Social Affairs. Online. Available at: www.un.org/en/development/desa/news/population/number-of-international-migrants-rises.html (accessed 28 April 2016).

Vavrus, M. (2010). Critical multiculturalism and higher education: Resistance and possibilities within teacher education. In S. May and C.E. Sleeter (Eds), *Critical multiculturalism: Theory and praxis* (pp. 19–31). New York, NY: Routledge.

Walker, G. (2009) *Marie-Thérèse Maurette: Pioneer of International Education*. Geneva: Ecolint.

Walker, G., (ed.). (2011). *The Changing Face of International Education: Challenges for the IB*. Cardiff, Wales. International Baccalaureate Organization.

Wright, K. (2014). International Baccalaureate programmes: Longer term outcomes. Melbourne Graduate School of Education, The University of Melbourne.

Wright, S.C., & Bougie, E. (2007). Intergroup contact and minority-language education reducing language-based discrimination and its negative impact. *Journal of Language and Social Psychology*, 26(2), 157–181. Online. Available at: http://isites.harvard.edu/fs/docs/icb.topic472736.files/Wright-Bougie-Intergroup.pdf (accessed 28 April 2016).

Yousafzai, M. (2013). *I am Malala*. New York: Little, Brown & Company.

PART III
A framework for schools

8

A PREJUDICE REDUCTION
FRAMEWORK FOR SCHOOLS

Introduction

The purpose of this framework is to provide schools and educators with a resource that can be adapted to educational settings so that prejudice reduction can be operationalised in schools. The framework covers the domains explored in this book and offers comprehensive suggestions for implementation.

Framework design

When designing frameworks, questions of detail and scale need to be addressed. Frameworks should be:

1 Complete → no major elements missing
2 Compact → actionable and deployable
3 Uncorrelated → no duplication and confusion
4 At the appropriate layer of abstraction → for robustness and clarity – sensical [sic]
5 Globally relevant → for broad acceptability.

(Bialik et al., 2015, p. 4)

The framework developed in this chapter aims to respect criteria 2, 4 and 5 mentioned above by being directly deployable and applicable in a broad variety of circumstances. The main purpose of the framework is for different schools around the world to be able to apply it as a tool relatively easily and quickly. Each area that is described represents a synthesis of the chapter's findings – therefore being 'compact' – but should be used alongside a more detailed reading of the chapter in question (for example, the assessment criteria and tasks suggested for 'understanding beyond the Other' should be considered in relation to Chapter 2. This is to ensure that there is some background exposure to and understanding of the domain in question when considering the area of focus. Without this, knowing how to adopt and adapt the framework would run the risk of becoming a superficial exercise.

As for criteria 1 and 2 ('complete' and 'uncorrelated'), the framework respects these notions less cohesively since 'completeness' for an area such as prejudice reduction is not altogether realistic given its far reaching, context-specific nature. Nor is each area of the framework entirely exclusive with no risk of duplication. This is because the constituents of prejudice and prejudice reduction are naturally intertwined (perception, culture, behaviour, belief, fear, experience, reason, emotion and reflection). It is true that some of the tasks in the framework and the assessment criteria involve similar competences and attitudes. This should not be viewed as a weakness but a necessary reinforcement with varying degrees of focus and slightly different perspectives for each (for example, tasks exploring diversity and multiplicity feature at baseline levels in both critical thinking and 'understanding beyond the Other' but will be experienced differently in each area since the focus will be more cognitive in thrust in the former and more affective in thrust in the latter.

Selection of frameworks

I have only chosen those strategies with some researched evidence indicating educational impact. Mixed methods were considered in judging the research index of a given strategy, ranging from effect size derived from meta-analyses (mainly the case for the contact hypothesis) to statistically significant findings for associated studies (such indices can be ascertained for strategies such as the reading of literature and certain empathy programmes). Qualitative data were considered too, ranging from well-developed theoretical positions to case studies, narratives, different types of interviews, surveys, focus groups as well as reports on practice in schools. For some domains, where there is enough research granularity for this to be done, the research index is by level (for example, understanding beyond the Other) whereas for others general research for all levels of the domain is referenced, as is the case for critical thinking, which comprises a natural continuum.

Assessing social phenomena can be done either through experimental methods with a positivistic world view whereby researchers seek to eliminate subjectivity, control variables and produce clearly operationalised data through statistical modelling or, on the other hand, through naturalistic methods whereby the researcher engages purposefully and consciously with the social phenomenon in question and embraces interaction, subjectivity, human impressions and thoughts. At the core of the former method is an emphasis on reliability, pure science method and a belief that truth can be extracted through experiment. At the core of the latter method is an emphasis on validity by allowing freedom of the subject's expression and efforts not to create contrived inauthentic settings; it is predicated on a belief that truth is constructed and reconstructed through interaction and experiences (Kvale, 2007; Hammersley & Atkinson, 2007).

This much said, qualitative or quasi experimental methods can be considered to be at an epistemological disadvantage 'since they lack quantitative gauges such as regression results or observations across multiple studies, they may be unable to assess which are the most important relationships and which are simply idiosyncratic to a particular case' (Eisenhardt, 1989, p. 547).

Given the nature of prejudice reduction, its context-bound, highly localised meaning-making structures, screening studies by methodological rigour, while academically valid as a method, would lose many areas of research and create a too narrow framework. Therefore, the research index has not been organised hierarchically or scaled in any manner since this would give the illusion of one approach being better than another when in reality various methods should be considered with relevance to the specifics of their specific research span.

What this means is that strategies should be considered as examples of methods that have worked in certain contexts and will not automatically transfer into new contexts. They have to be socialised and contextualised appropriately to the environment in question.

Criteria, tasks and integration into different curricular structures

Criterion referenced assessment

Glaser (1963) introduced the idea of criterion referenced assessment as a method whereby students would be evaluated against standards rather than against one another (norm referencing): 'measures which assess student achievement in terms of a criterion standard provide information as to the degree of competence attained by a particular student which is independent of reference to the performance of others' (p. 519).

This assessment method takes into account the notion of progress within cognitive architecture and represents a more dynamic, developmental spectrum of competence development, allowing learners and teachers to situate learning as a process on a continuum. Glaser wrote in 1997:

> The assessment of achievement is now being integrally tied to the nature of learning. The relevant learning theory can be conceived of as a developmental psychology of performance changes – the changes that occur as knowledge and complex cognitive strategies are acquired. Achievement measurement should be designed to assess these performance changes and identify attainment at various levels of acquisition, emphasizing not only content considerations but also structural and process considerations that are involved in sources of difficulty and in facilitators of the growth of competence.

> *(Glaser, 1997, p. 7)*

This approach is particularly appropriate for a construct like prejudice reduction since the amelioration of thinking, interacting and responding cannot realistically be assessed alongside the perceived performance of peers and should be conceived as work in progress on a spectrum. Furthermore, criterion-based assessment allows for pertinent self-assessment as the learner can reflect on his/her development with regard to established standards whereas this cannot be done in a norm-referenced system.

A disadvantage with criterion referenced assessment descriptors is that there is a high level of subjectivity that is involved in determining levels. What exactly does 'high' or 'low' mean to different learners or practitioners in various settings? Professional judgement is needed here to determine what the thresholds should entail for a judgement to be made as to whether the learner is at one level or the other. These can be operationalised and made clear with more granular metrics so as to give standardised descriptors of behaviours that would represent universally accepted levels, but I think that this would defeat the purpose since the scales suggested are meant to produce reflection and self-reflection rather than performance. Furthermore, typical behaviours or exhaustive typological descriptions would encourage mimicry and performance as opposed to internalisation and personalised goal-setting. Indeed, the focus should be on each individual or group to consider what these levels will mean in their context. Schools are encouraged to discuss what 'low' or 'high' might mean to them within their frame of reference as this discussion alone would be a constructive exercise leading to thought and meditation on the subject of prejudice.

As concerns scale design, I have deliberately avoided a Likert-type scale allowing for middle descriptors since a five-point scale would encourage regression to the mean and the least interesting outcome from use of the framework would be one whereby users describe their efforts as 'satisfactory'. By using an even-numbered scale, the mid-point is a pivot that enforces users to be either inadequately or somewhat engaged in the prejudice-reducing process.

The framework gives the reader generic assessment criteria that contain descriptors that can be adapted to different learning environments. The criterion descriptors move from low to high levels. These core, generic assessment criteria can be extended into specific subject domains in two ways: either by modifying them to suit the domain in question or by extending them by adding descriptors to develop the competence in question within a specific domain. This is something that educational institutions would consider based on the pressures of context.

Learning experiences

The learning experiences suggested in this framework are not exhaustive but represent particularly salient examples of learning experiences that can nurture prejudice-reducing thinking and behaviour. More detailed examples are given in each of the book's chapters. To integrate the suggested learning experiences into a school's context, they can be expressed as lessons, projects, entire units or simple assessed tasks. In order for them to be taken seriously by learners, they should be assessed using criteria explicitly devoted to the construct in question, as suggested in the framework. However, this might not always be possible or necessary, particularly for lower levels of prejudice-reduction.

An integrated approach

It is important for schools to view the different components listed here as necessarily working together and not in isolation: critical thinking and metacognition should run through learning beyond the Other and developing empathy. Similarly, learning about social categories and how to make sound judgements (in critical thinking) should be conjugated by empathy and sensitivity about otherness. If schools are serious about reducing prejudice in learners, the domains should all be nurtured and assessed so that students' experience of prejudice reduction are holistic.

Student learning (tables 8.1–8.4)

The framework addresses individual and group levels of prejudice reduction in the areas of understanding beyond the Other, critical thinking, metacognition and empathy.

Levels

The framework for student learning (tables 8.1–8.4) is designed using three levels. These should be read as levels of sophistication, moving from basic to intermediary to complex. Although the levels can be applied to age-appropriate levels, roughly covering Piaget's four stages of cognitive development in three phases (sensorimotor to pre-operational: 0–5; pre- to concrete operational: 5–11; and abstract thinking: 11+), it is more helpful to view them as areas of successively demanding cognitive and affective positioning. For the areas of critical thinking and empathy there are four levels; the last level representing an extension where learners can stretch to an extremely high level that transcends the taxonomy entirely (for critical thinking, being able to get beyond generalising to theorising and for empathy, being able to transcend the subject–object relational dichotomy to an appreciation of pluralistic commonality).

Schools can use these phases to differentiate learning in a single age group, to design programmes that contain vertically articulated learning objectives or to generate age-appropriate learning experiences.

Institutional support (tables 8.5 and 8.6)

The framework here offers suggestions for institutional strategies or environments that can be created to ensure a climate of prejudice reduction. Descriptors should not be used to evaluate individuals or people but institutions.

TABLE 8.1 Understanding beyond the Other

Level	Learning experiences	Assessment criteria	Research index
1 (Appreciating difference): working closely with people who are different in a learning environment that does not make difference a handicap (playground arrangements, diverse programmes, assessments encouraging the appreciation of difference).	**Diversity rules** Care taken to offer a physical educational programme that does not polarise groups and play on gender stereotypes (skipping and tic tac toe for girls, football and basketball for boys) but allows for single-sex learning environments (swimming, gymnastics, martial arts) or intercultural sports (Kabbadi) and different voices of expression. **Respecting differences** In-class presentations on where we come from.	1 The learner shows **little** interest in other people's backgrounds. 2 The learner shows **some** interest in other people's backgrounds. 3 The learner shows **considerable** interest in other people's backgrounds. 4 The learner shows **high** interest in other people's backgrounds.	Thorne, 1992; Connell, 1996; Danforth, 1995; Gardner, 2004.
2 (Diversity): knowing more about other cultures and histories in relation to one's own culture and history (international history courses, discovery of different cultures).	**International history courses** - An internationally oriented, pluralistic History course. - Visits to cultural and/or religious centres. - Films/books/case studies from different parts of the world. **Intercultural competence training** - Baseline exposure to major religious texts (The Bible, The Quran, Ramayana & Mahabarta, Upanishads, Tao Te Ching). - Baseline exposure to major defining customs across different cultural systems (marriage, burial, family, hierarchy, notions of hospitality and respect, greetings, mourning, eating, etc).	1 The learner demonstrates **poor, limited** knowledge of his/her own culture and the history and culture of at least one other group. 2 The learner demonstrates **baseline** knowledge of his/her own culture and the history and culture of at least one other group. 3 The learner demonstrates **good, reasonably in-depth** knowledge of his/her own culture and the history and culture of at least one other group. 4 The learner demonstrates **sound, in-depth** knowledge of his/her own culture and the history and culture of at least one other group.	Levi-Strauss, 1979; Malinowski, 1922; Hamerz, 1990, 1992; Kumashiro, 2004; Motha, 2006; UNESCO, 2006.

Releasing individuals from labels	Training in social psychology, politics, critical pedagogy	Rubric	References
3 Releasing individuals from labels, deconstructing sites of identity and understanding the role of power, politics and ideology in the shaping of identity (study of psychology, ethnology, critical pedagogy, gender studies; debates and artistic representations).	**Training in social psychology, politics, critical pedagogy** - Exposure to notions of peer pressure, conformity, in- and out-grouping, prejudice, stereotyping, the role of the media in representing different political and social phenomena. - Exposure to notions of femininity and masculinity, hetero-, bi- and trans-sexuality, women's and gay rights. - Study of core literary texts dealing with some of the fundaments of identity (authors include A. Roy, S. Rushdie, C. Achebe, J. Rhys, T. Morrison, Chimamanda Ngozi-Adichie, JM Coetzee, etc). - Printemps de la Jupe (2014): an example of gender awareness practised in schools.	1 The learner shows **little** understanding of the complexity underlying identity (allegiances, beliefs, experiences) and articulates a **simplistic, homogeneous** representation of other people based on **single facets** such as race, nationality, gender, class or profession. 2 The learner shows **some** understanding of the complexity underlying identity (allegiances, beliefs, experiences) and articulates a **reasonably nuanced** representation of other people based on **more than one facet** such as race, nationality, gender, class or profession. 3 The learner shows **good** understanding of the complexity underlying identity (allegiances, beliefs, experiences) and articulates a **nuanced, heterogeneous** representation of other people based on **more than one facet** such as race, nationality, gender, class or profession. 4 The learner shows **deep** understanding of the complexity underlying identity (allegiances, beliefs, experiences) and articulates a **sophisticated, heterogeneous** representation of other people based on **multiple facets** such as race, nationality, gender, class or profession.	Said, 1993; Berger & Luckmann, 1966; Bhabha, 1990; Hall, 1997; Koedt; Levine & Rapone, 1973; Connell, 1996; Diamond, 2005.

TABLE 8.2 Critical thinking

Level	Learning experiences	Assessment criteria	Research index
1 Low levels of differentiation, nuance or weighed up criteria for categorisation.	**Set theory** – Basic work on set theory using Venn diagrams. – Exploring the categorical syllogism ('all men are mortal, Socrates is a man, therefore Socrates is mortal') with multiple examples, drawing out connections with the real world.	1 The learner shows **little** critical appreciation of criteria for categorisation. 2 The learner shows **some** critical appreciation of criteria for categorisation. 3 The learner shows **good** critical appreciation of criteria for categorisation and **is able to differentiate elements using rules and principles.** 4 The learner shows strong, **reflective** critical appreciation of criteria for categorisation and is **able to differentiate elements clearly using rules and principles and can explain the rationale for categorisation clearly.**	Paul, 1990, 1992, 2011; Halpern, 1997, 1999, 2002, 2014; Lipman, 1991, 2003; Siegel, 1985, 1988; Ennis, 1986; Perkins & Ritchhart, 2004; Dweck, 2006, 2012.
2 Awareness of societal labels erected by media, family, culture and language. Generalisations are less crude and tend to be based on empirical evidence that is still, however, often overgeneralised.	**Syllogisms** – Discussion groups that explore core identifying features and accidental or non-essential elements, differentiating so as to guide learners towards conclusions that are less systematically 'all Xs are Ys' to postulates such as 'some Xs are Ys'. – Exposure to different types of syllogism (disjunctive and hypothetical) exploring notions of non-reversibility with real-world applications.	1 The learner shows **limited** understanding of the role of convention in determining social categories and exceptions to the rule. 2 The learner shows **some** understanding of the role of convention in determining social categories and exceptions to the rule. 3 The learner shows **good** understanding of the role of convention in determining social categories and **can offer basic arguments** for exceptions to the rule. 4 The learner shows **deep** understanding of the role of convention in determining social categories and **can offer reflective, discerning arguments** for exceptions to the rule.	

3 A more considered set of social categories begins, learners are guided from literal level of social categorisation towards a more abstract approach to making knowledge claims.

Personal testimonies related to identity and culture
Structured discussion groups allowing students to share their personal, socially related experiences and draw conclusions from them. Teachers should be careful to scaffold these discussions subtly so as to allow for gentle disagreement and reconsideration.

Stereotype analysis in the humanities
Analysis of social categories, reflection on potential stereotype formation in humanities textbooks (overgeneralisations about groups, oversimplification of historical phenomena, bias and propaganda).

Media study
Media analysis with a strong emphasis on audience manipulation, persuasion by argument, statistics and image, vested interests, emotive language and iconography and loading on stereotypes.

Critical appreciation of axioms and scientific rules
Analysis of mathematical axioms and scientific rules with a view to understanding their relative function and instability.

1 The learner shows **little** level of abstract thinking in generalising postulates that categorise social groups or individuals. Observations of categories are **critical but literal**.

2 The learner shows **some** level of abstract thinking in generalising postulates that categorise social groups or individuals. Observations of categories are **critical, mostly literal but also theoretical**.

3 The learner shows a **good** level of abstract thinking in generalising postulates that categorise social groups or individuals. Observations of categories are **critical and theoretical**.

4 The learner shows a **deep** level of abstract thinking in generalising postulates that categorise social groups or individuals. Observations of categories are **highly critical and theoretical, allowing for transfer from one domain to the next.**

(Continued)

TABLE 8.2 (Continued)

Level	Learning experiences	Assessment criteria	Research index
4 An abstract or theoretical level of critical thinking that allows students to make valid generalisations, temper hasty judgements, evaluate various criteria for or against categorisation, and to do so in the absence of immediate empirical data but rather on principle and through deductive critical thinking. Evidence of application of theory in real-life situations. Evidence of a disposition to critical thinking.	**Study of cognitive bias** Lessons in psychology on the nature of generalisations and how they are erected cognitively and socially, therefore an understanding of the mind's predisposition to prejudice but at a high level of analysis. **Debates on current affairs** Drawn-out, challenging debates/discussions/ conferences on the construct of social identity; politics and global affairs with opportunities for interaction and sharing of ideas, opinions and positions. **Reflective Community and Service** Critically minded Community Service projects that allow for action and deep reflection through documented portfolio work. **Pure logic** Truth tables. **Interdisciplinary projects in the humanities** Interdisciplinary and comparative studies that allow for synthesis and analysis across historical movements and social phenomena.	1 **Low** levels of deductive reasoning and **little** ability to identify errors in thinking or to generate well-reasoned mental products. 2 **Reasonable** levels of deductive reasoning and **some** ability to identify errors in thinking or to generate well-reasoned mental products. 3 **Good** levels of deductive reasoning and a **good** ability to identify errors in thinking **and** to generate well-reasoned mental products. **Some** disposal to critical thinking. 4 **High** levels of deductive reasoning and a **strong** ability to identify errors in thinking, to generate well-reasoned mental products **and to generate theories on human behaviour using strongly argued critical thinking. Strong** disposal to critical thinking.	

TABLE 8.3 Metacognition

Level	Learning experiences	Assessment criteria	Research index
1 Novice metacognition and basic self-awareness.	**Discussion about feeling** Discussion-based activities and/or self-evaluations where participants 'open up' the way they feel about members of different groups. **Transpositions of feeling** Transposition exercises that allow participants to put into symbols: artistic productions, skits, song, movement or some other form a representation of the way they feel about members of different groups. Philosophy for Children at a basic level.	1 **Little** self-awareness and/or awareness of one's own level of prejudiced thinking. 2 **Some** self-awareness and/or awareness of one's own level of prejudiced thinking. 3 **Good** self-awareness and/or awareness of one's own level of prejudiced thinking. 4 **Deep** self-awareness and/or awareness of one's own level of prejudiced thinking.	Lacan, 1977; Flavell, 1976; Pellegrino, Chudowsky & Glaser, 2001; Lipman, 1991, 2003; Pintrich, 2000.
2 Intermediary metacognition and self-awareness, elements of self-regulation.	**Discussion about prejudice** Discussion-based activities and/or self-evaluations where participants admit their prejudices. **Transposition of prejudice** Transposition exercises that allow participants to give precise form and expression (artistic, non-verbal or other) to their prejudice with some explanation of what might explain them. **Self-regulation to dampen prejudice** Self-selected strategies to dampen prejudice such as admitting alternative viewpoints, listening and considering counter-arguments and/or bracketing one's convictions. Philosophy for Children at an intermediary level.	1 **Little** ability to accept alternative viewpoints, positions and arguments to the extent of being able to change one's own mind. 2 **Some** ability to accept alternative viewpoints, positions and arguments to the extent of being able to change one's own mind. 3 **Good** ability to accept alternative viewpoints, positions and arguments to the extent of being able to change one's own mind; **demonstrates the capacity** to reduce prejudice using self-selected strategies. 4 **Strong** ability to accept alternative viewpoints, positions and arguments to the extent of being able to change one's own mind; **demonstrates a clear, systematic capacity** to reduce prejudice **significantly** using self-selected strategies.	

(Continued)

TABLE 8.3 (Continued)

Level	Learning experiences	Assessment criteria	Research index
3 Expert metacognition and deep self-awareness with frequent self-regulation.	**Discussion about prejudice reduction** Discussion based activities and/or self-evaluations where participants compare and contrast their prejudiced sentiments and seek ways of reducing them. **Extended transposition of prejudice** Detailed descriptions of one's own thinking with an emphasis on the origin, development and closing of prejudiced thinking. This could be done through portfolios, extended pieces of writing, documentaries or projects. **Self-regulation to significantly reduce prejudice** Self-selected strategies to significantly reduce prejudice such as admitting alternative viewpoints, listening actively, considering counter-arguments, bracketing one's convictions and transforming one's viewpoint. Philosophy for Children at an advanced level.	1 The learner is **able to describe** his/her thinking processes when concerned with other social groups; **positions taken are somewhat relativised** and tentative with an overarching sensitivity to diversity. 2 The learner is **able to describe** his/her thinking processes **fluently** when concerned with other social groups; positions taken are **frequently relativised** and tentative with an overarching sensitivity to diversity. 3 The learner is **able to describe** his/her thinking processes **fluently and critically** when concerned with other social groups; positions taken are **systematically relativised** and tentative with an overarching sensitivity to diversity; **multiple strategies** to explain thought processes related to social phenomena are **explored carefully.** 4 The learner is **able to describe** his/her thinking processes **fluently, critically and elegantly** when concerned with other social groups; positions taken are **systematically relativised, using discerning arguments,** and tentative with an overarching sensitivity to diversity; **multiple strategies** to explain thought processes related to social phenomena are **explored thoroughly.**	

TABLE 8.4 Empathy

Level	Tasks	Assessment criteria	Research index
1 Empathy through imagination and production.	**Literature** – Hot seating; – Writing from a character's perspective; – Role play. **Theatre** – Choice of plays allowing for empathy across historical, cultural or social lines. **Art** – Focus on subjects in a painting; – Focus on expression of human experience through an art work; – Artistic production from a designated person or group's perspective.	1 The learner shows **little or no** empathy for the target person or group. 2 The learner shows **a low level** of empathy for the target person or group. 3 The learner shows a **reasonable level** of empathy for the target person or group. 4 The learner shows a **high level** of empathy for the target person or group.	Finlay & Stephan, 2000; Galinsky & Moscowitz, 2000.
2 Empathy through contact and communication.	Model United Nations; Student League of Nations; Dots/non-dots exercise; blue eyes/brown eyes experiment; 'Roots of Empathy'; Amnesty International letter writing; pen pals; pairing up with other classes or schools through the Internet.	1 The learner **does not** take on the perspective of another person or group or relate personally to the experience in question. 2 The learner takes on the perspective of another person or group **to some extent** and **only somewhat** relates personally to the experience in question. 3 The learner takes on the perspective of another person or group **to a considerable extent** and relates personally to the experience in question **to a reasonably high degree.** 4 The learner takes on the perspective of another person or group **to a high extent** and relates personally to the experience in question **to a high degree.**	Byrnes & Kiger, 1990; Schonert-Reichl et al., 2012; Santos et al., 2011; Rolheiser & Wallace, 2005; Jaramillo, Buote & Schonert-Reichl, 2008; 'Roots of Empathy', MacDonald et al., 2013.

(Continued)

TABLE 8.4 (Continued)

Level	Tasks	Assessment criteria	Research index
3 Empathy through direct experience of conditions.	Narrative 4 (2016); Medair's Relief and Recovery Orientation Course (Medair, 2016); recreation activities and in small classes; fieldtrips and outdoor education; science projects involving fieldtrips and direct analysis of living conditions (traffic, air and water quality); learning experiences where students have to work in conditions affecting the elderly or handicapped (*Moi Personne Agée* (Croix Rouge, 2016); sports programmes where students have to be in wheelchairs, blindfolded, wearing weights to slow them down etc; scaffolded exchange programmes.	1 The learner **does not engage** with the situation as an insider, taking into account the local context and culture and **remains separated** from phenomena as an outsider or onlooker. 2 The learner **shows some signs of engaging** with the situation as an insider, taking into account the local context and culture and **makes some effort not to remain separated** from phenomena as an outsider or onlooker. 3 The learner **shows clear signs of engaging** with the situation as an insider, taking into account the local context and culture and **makes considerable efforts not to remain separated** from phenomena as an outsider or onlooker. 4 The learner **engages with the situation as an insider**, taking into account the local context and culture and **does not remain separated** from phenomena as an outsider or onlooker.	Lovell, 2014; Schoenfeld et al., 2014.
4 Collective approaches.	**Group work** – Working together on practical work (project-based learning where students are expected to work in groups and are assessed collectively as a group). Examples include The Duke of Edinburgh Award (2016) and Outward Bound (2016). – Group work on millennium goals and the environment. **Community-based conflict resolution** – Interpeace (2016) – Friends of Roots (2016)	1 The learner **remains locked** in a me/you or us/them approach to the situation. 2 The learner **is able to relativise** a me/you or us/them approach to the situation and **shows signs of a collective approach.** 3 The learner **is able to transcend** a me/you or us/them approach to the situation and **mostly engages in a collective approach.** 4 The learner **relativises and transcends** a me/you or us/them approach to the situation and **seamlessly engages in a collective approach with an inclusive plural vocabulary.**	Lamm & Silani, 2014; Muller, Pfarrer & Little, 2014; Ayoob, 2002.

TABLE 8.5 Contact

Mediators	Environments or strategies	Descriptors	Research index
Equality of different groups.	Mission statements, policies, recruitment and admissions protocols.	1 Mission statements, policies, recruitment and admissions protocols give **little or no** importance to the notion of equality. 2 Mission statements, policies, recruitment and admissions protocols give **some** importance to the notion of equality. 3 Mission statements, policies, recruitment and admissions protocols give **quasi-systematic** importance to the notion of equality. 4 Mission statements, policies, recruitment and admissions protocols give **extensive and systematic** importance to the notion of equality.	Allport, 1954; Stephan, 1985; Aronson, 2000; Dixon, Durrheim & Tredoux, 2005; Pettigrew, 2008; Pettigrew & Tropp, 2000, 2006; Connolly, 2000.
Cooperation in the pursuit of common goals.	Ground rules for project work, awarding team work.	1 Team work is **not** recognised or celebrated by school leadership. 2 Team work is **somewhat** recognised or celebrated by school leadership. 3 Team work is **often** recognised or celebrated by school leadership. 4 Team work is **systematically** recognised or celebrated by school leadership.	
Social norms supporting contact.	Ensuring diversity in class composition, school trips, exchange programmes, student council, staff committees and decision-making bodies.	1 Criteria for diversity are **not** established. 2 Criteria for diversity are established but **only somewhat** respected. 3 Criteria for diversity are established and **mostly** respected. 4 Criteria for diversity are established and **consistently** respected.	
Anxiety reduction.	Ensuring an atmosphere of open dialogue, creating outlets for student or staff fear/frustration or stress (counsellors, mentors, psychologists, human resource partners, student life leadership); ensuring that ongoing student debates take place in an atmosphere of mutual respect and confidence.	1 There is **little** attention given to ensure an atmosphere where individuals feel confident to speak their mind, interact with others openly and confidently. 2 There is **some** attention given to ensure an atmosphere where individuals feel confident to speak their mind, interact with others openly and confidently. 3 There is **reasonable** attention given to ensure an atmosphere where individuals feel confident to speak their mind, interact with others openly and confidently. 4 There is **high** attention given to ensure an atmosphere where individuals feel confident to speak their mind, interact with others openly and confidently.	

(Continued)

TABLE 8.5 (Continued)

Mediators	Environments or strategies	Descriptors	Research index
Empathy and perspective-taking.	**Symbolic gestures to show empathy** - Observing a minute of silence in the wake of major humanitarian disasters. - Collective statements by the school on world problems. - Commemorative assemblies that create empathy for given human stories. - Guest speakers allowing students to empathise with a person or group.	1 Symbolic gestures by the community in the form of statements, gatherings or assemblies are **essentially non-existent.** 2 Symbolic gestures by the community in the form of statements, gatherings or assemblies are **few and far between without any discernible impact.** 3 Symbolic gestures by the community in the form of statements, gatherings or assemblies are **few and far between but when they take place, make an impact.** 4 Symbolic gestures by the community in the form of statements, gatherings or assemblies are **frequent and clearly make an impact.**	

TABLE 8.6 International education strategies

Mediators	Environments or strategies	Descriptors	Research index
Service Learning.	Ensuring that there is a Service Learning Coordinator; articulating clear expectations and principles on Service Learning with a focus on learning rather than charity; ensuring that Service Learning activities have some long-term resonance and are not only one-offs; ensuring that students are brought to problematize their own prejudices and assumptions through Service Learning; care is taken for Service Learning not to anchor students in patronising, essentialising positions.	1 There is **no** Service Learning at the school. 2 Service Learning is **mainly one-way charity work** with **no or very little** student reflection. 3 Service Learning is a **recognised learning process** within the school that **goes beyond charity** with a **reasonable degree** of student reflection. 4 Service Learning is a **central learning experience** within the school involving **reciprocal relationships** between those receiving and **giving service** and **frequent, careful and structured** reflection by students.	Delve, Mintz & Stewart, 1990; Kendall, 1990; Rhoads, 1998; UNESCO-IBE, 2014; Erickson, 2011.
The learning of an additional language.	Ensuring that the curriculum allows for the learning of at least two languages; aiming for the presence of at least one non-Western language in the offering; ensuring an atmosphere of respect for linguistic diversity.	1 Students **only learn one language** at school. 2 Students **learn more than one language** at school. 3 Students learn **more than one language and are offered explicit opportunities to explore and discover different cultures** through language learning. 4 Students learn two or three languages, are **offered explicit opportunities to explore cultures deeply through language learning and are able to learn a non-Western language** in the curriculum.	Wright & Bougie, 2007; Byram, Gribkova & Starkey, 2002; Tomlinson & Masuhara, 2004; Stavans, 2001; Rhodes, Leslie & Tworeck, 2012; Kite & Whitley, 2012; Lindholm, 1994; Genesee, 1987; Cummins, 1989, 1994; Lambert & Cazabon, 1994; Byram, 2011; Savignon, 1983.

(Continued)

TABLE 8.6 (Continued)

Mediators	Environments or strategies	Descriptors	Research index
World literature.	Ensuring that the literature syllabus of any given year contains authors from at least three different parts of the world; ensuring that the literature syllabus contains works addressing problems of identity, prejudice and/or discrimination; ensuring that the literature syllabus is reviewed and revised frequently whenever possible.	1 The literature syllabus is **mainly monocultural** with **no real attention paid to texts that problematise cultural identity.** 2 The literature syllabus **explores more than one part of the world** with no real attention paid to texts that problematise cultural identity. 3 The literature syllabus **explores more than two different parts of the world** and contains **some texts that problematise cultural identity.** 4 The literature syllabus **explores more than three different parts of the world** and contains **many texts that problematise cultural identity.**	Djikic & Oatley, 2014; Sabine & Sabine, 1983; Johnson, 2013.
International Humanities.	Ensuring that the study of the humanities (economics, geography, history and in some cases philosophy, anthropology, economics) allows for the exploration of various cultural world views; ensuring that at least three continents feature in students' history syllabus; ensuring that the humanities address fundamental historical events related to prejudice (such as the Transatlantic Slave Trade, colonialism, decolonisation, the Holocaust, Civil Rights movement, Muslim and Western interactions); ensuring that students discuss prejudice through their humanities syllabus.	1 The humanities syllabus is **largely monocultural with no, little or superficial** treatment of fundamental historical events related to prejudice. 2 The humanities syllabus **explores two or three cultural views and continents with some** treatment of fundamental historical events related to prejudice. 3 The humanities syllabus is **diverse, explores three or more cultural views and continents with detailed** treatment of fundamental historical events related to prejudice. 4 The humanities syllabus is **extremely diverse, explores three or more cultural views and continents with detailed treatment of** fundamental historical events related to prejudice. The syllabus **allows opportunities for students to discuss their humanities learning explicitly through the lens of prejudice.**	Nussbaum, 1997; Peuker & Reiter, 2007.

| Inquiry. | Inquiry-based learning should feature in the curriculum and should allow for discovery of identity and culture; inquiry-based learning should be scaffolded by teachers and not be left to happen of its own accord; inquiry should be followed by reflection; inquiry should involve active learning, real-life scenarios and opportunities for students to come into contact with other groups and reflect on those encounters; students should be brought to inquire into their own prejudices. | 1 There is **no** inquiry-based learning in the curriculum.
2 Inquiry-based learning is **infrequent** in the curriculum with **low levels** of teacher scaffolding.
3 Inquiry-based learning is **frequent** in the curriculum with **reasonable levels** of teacher scaffolding. It **allows students to come into contact with other groups.**
4 Inquiry-based learning is **frequent** in the curriculum with **high levels** of teacher scaffolding. It **allows students to come into contact with other groups and to reflect on those encounters as well as their own prejudices.** | Kolb, Rubin & McIntyre, 1974. |
| Reflection. | The curriculum allows opportunities for students to reflect on themselves as learners and on what they have learnt; reflection should be extended to the social domain so that students reflect carefully on assumptions, relationships, conflicts, friendships and fears of others; reflection should be carefully guided by instructors who bring students to overarching conceptual understanding through the reflective process; students should reflect on their prejudices. | 1 There is **little or no** opportunity for guided reflection in the curriculum.
2 There is **some** opportunity for guided reflection in the curriculum with **some instances** of it being extended to the social domain.
3 There is **extensive** opportunity for guided reflection in the curriculum with **many instances** of it being extended to the social domain.
4 There is **extensive** opportunity for **rich** guided reflection of a conceptual nature in the curriculum with **many instances** of it being extended to the social domain. **There are instances of reflection that focus explicitly on prejudice.** | King & Kitchener, 1994; Dewey, 1910. |

(Continued)

TABLE 8.6 (Continued)

Mediators	Environments or strategies	Descriptors	Research index
Concepts–focused learning.	The curriculum allows students to go from topic-based learning to conceptual understanding and, if possible, theory generation; the curriculum allows for students to learn about other people and groups within a conceptual framework, covering concepts of culture, perception, belief and social interaction; students discuss prejudice as a concept.	1 Learning is topic-based with **little or no** conceptual focus. 2 **Some** learning goes beyond topics into overarching concepts. 3 **Much** learning is conceptual, **covering concepts of culture, perception, belief and social interaction.** 4 **Most** learning is conceptual, covering concepts of **culture, perception, belief and social interaction. Students discuss prejudice as a concept.**	Erickson, 2013; International Baccalaureate (IB, 2007; IB, 2015); Land et al., 2005.
Theory of knowledge.	The curriculum allows students opportunities to break down knowledge into its various components (truth, belief, justification, language, experience and memory); students go beyond face-value approaches to knowledge and problematize it as a construct; prejudice is analysed as a problem of knowledge.	1 Learning objectives focus on subject specific **knowledge only without allowing** for opportunities to learn about knowledge itself. 2 Learning objectives **push students to go beyond subject specific knowledge.** The curriculum **creates opportunities** for students to learn about knowledge itself. 3 Learning objectives **push students to go beyond** subject specific knowledge. The curriculum **creates opportunities** for students to learn about knowledge itself and to **problematise it in detail.** 4 Learning objectives **push students to go well beyond** subject specific knowledge. The curriculum **creates ample opportunities** for students to learn about knowledge itself and to **problematise it in detail with connections made to prejudice.**	International Baccalaureate (IB, 2013); Hughes, 2014.

Education and examination boards are encouraged to take these guidelines into account when selecting texts and themes for study whereas schools working off a prescribed curriculum should look for ways to integrate elements of international education into their provision wherever possible. As is explained in Chapter 7, many principles of international education can be adapted to multiple settings and should not be considered inaccessible to non-international schools. The institutional support framework does not use levels but mediators.

Conclusion

The frameworks offered in this chapter can be used in a plethora of different ways: to evaluate the extent to which a school is employing researched strategies against prejudice, for classroom teachers as a checklist to ensure that strategies to dampen prejudicial thinking are interwoven into course design, by students to self or peer assess levels of prejudice and as stimuli or models for schools to develop their own detailed, specific or contextualised frameworks to reduce prejudice.

The advantage of employing the frameworks used in this chapter is that they are cohesive, research based and linked to established theory in the fields of social psychology, cognitive psychology, critical thinking, research on empathy and cultural studies. Above all, the frameworks use practices that have been shown to work in the battle against prejudice.

References

Allport, G. (1954). *The nature of prejudice.* Cambridge, MA: Addison-Wesley.

Aronson, E. (2000). The jigsaw strategy: Reducing prejudice in the classroom. *Psychology Review,* 7(2), 2–5.

Ayoob, M. (2002). Inequality and theorising in international relations: The case for subaltern realism. *International Studies Review,* 4(3), 27–48.

Bhabha, H.K. (1990). The third space: Interview with Homi Bhabha. In J. Rutherford (Ed.), *Identity, community, culture, difference* (pp. 207–221). London: Lawrence and Wishart.

Berger, P., & Luckmann, T. (1966). The social construction of reality. Harmondsworth: Penguin.

Bialik, M., Bogan, M., Fadel, C., & Horthavotha, M. (2015). *Character education for the 21st century: What should students learn?* Centre for curriculum redesign. Online. Available at: http://curriculumredesign.org/wp-content/uploads/CCR-CharacterEducation_FINAL_27Feb2015.pdf (accessed 28 April 2016).

Byram, M. (2011). From foreign language education to education for intercultural citizenship. *Intercultural Communication Review,* 9, 17–36.

Byram, M., Gribkova, B., & Starkey, H. (2002). *Developing the intercultural dimension in language teaching. A practical guidebook for teachers.* Strasbourg: Council of Europe.

Byrnes, D.A., & Kiger, G. (1990). The effect of a prejudice-reduction simulation on attitude change 1. *Journal of Applied Social Psychology,* 20(4), 1559–1816. doi:10.1111/j.1559-1816.1990.tb00415.x

Connell, R.W. (1996). Teaching the boys: New research and gender strategies for schools. *Teachers College Record,* 98(2), 206–235.

Connolly, P. (2000). What now for the contact hypothesis? Towards a new research agenda. *Race, Ethnicity and Education,* 3, 169–193.

Croix Rouge. (2016). Moi, personne agée! Online. Available at: http://www.croix-rouge-ge. ch/index.php?page=moi-personne-agee (accessed 28 April 2016).

Cummins, J. (1989). *Empowering minority students.* Sacramento, CA: California Association for Bilingualism Education.

Cummins, J. (1994). Knowledge, power, and identity in teaching English as a second language. In F. Genesee (Ed.), *Educating second language children: The whole child, the whole curriculum, the whole community* (pp. 33–58). Cambridge: Cambridge University Press.

Danforth, S. (1995). Toward a critical theory approach to lives considered emotionally disturbed, *Behavioral Disorders*, 20, 136–143.

Delve, C.I., Mintz, S.D., & Stewart G.M. (1990). Community service as values education. *New Directions for Student Services*, 50. San Francisco, CA: Jossey-Bass.

Dewey, J. (1910). 'What is thought?' Chapter 1 in *How we think.* Lexington, MA: D.C. Heath, 1–13.

Diamond, M. (2005). Sex and gender: same or different? In D. Inglis, J. Bone and R. Wilke (Eds), *Critical concepts in the social sciences.* Oxford: Routledge.

Dixon, J.A., Durrheim, K., & Tredoux, C. (2005). Beyond the optimal strategy: A 'reality check' for the contact hypothesis. *American Psychologist*, 60, 697–711.

Djikic, M., & Oatley, K. (2014). The art in fiction: From indirect communication to changes of the self. *Psychology of Aesthetics, Creativity, And The Arts*, 8(4), 498–505. doi: 10.1037/a0037999

Dweck, C.S. (2006). *Mindset: The new psychology of success.* New York, NY: Random House.

Dweck, C.S. (2012). *Mindset: How you can fulfill your potential.* London: Constable & Robinson Limited.

Eisenhardt, K.M. (1989). Building theories from case study research. *Academy of Management Review*, 14, 532–550.

Ennis, R.H. (1986). A taxonomy of critical thinking dispositions and abilities. In J.B. Baron & R.S. Sternberg (Eds), *Teaching thinking skills: Theory and practice* (pp. 9–26). New York, NY: Freeman.

Erickson, J.A. (2011). Service-learning's impact on attitudes and behavior: A review and update. Online. Available at: http://web.augsburg.edu/~erickson/MCC2012/Erickson_2011.pdf (accessed 28 April 2016).

Erickson, L. (2013). *Concept-based curriculum and instruction: Engaging the child's mind.* [Presentation at the ninth Annual Education Conference at the International School of Geneva, 2014.]

Finlay, K.A., & Stephan, W.G. (2000). Improving intergroup relations: The effects of empathy on racial attitudes. *Journal of Applied Social Psychology*, 30, 1720–1737.

Flavell, J. (1976). Metacognitive aspects of problem solving. In L. Resnick (Ed.), *The Nature of Intelligence* (pp. 231–236), Hillsdale, NJ: Lawrence Erlbaum Associates.

Friends of Roots. (2016). Online. Available at: http://www.friendsofroots.net/about-roots. html (accessed 28 April 2016).

Galinsky, A.D., & Moskowitz, G.B. (2000). Perspective-taking: Decreasing stereotype expression, stereotype accessibility, and in-group favoritism. *Journal of Personality and Social Psychology*, 78(4), 708–724.

Gardner, H. (2004). *Frames of mind: The theory of multiple intelligences*, Twentieth Anniversary Ed. New York: Basic Books.

Genesee, F. (1987). *Learning through two languages: Studies of immersion and bilingual education.* Cambridge, MA: Newbury House.

Glaser, R. (1963). Instructional technology and the measurement of learning outcomes: Some questions. *American Psychologist*, 18(8), 519–521. Online. Available at: http://dx.doi. org/10.1037/h0049294 (accessed 28 April 2016).

Glaser, R. (1997). Assessment and education: Access and achievement. CSE Technical Report 435. Online. Available at: https://www.cse.ucla.edu/products/reports/TECH435.pdf (accessed 28 April 2016).

Hall, S. (1997). The local and the global: Globalization and ethnicity. In Anthony D. King (Ed.), *Culture, globalization and the world-system: Contemporary conditions for the representation of identity* (pp. 20–39). Minneapolis, MN: University of Minnesota Press.

Halpern, D. (1997). *Critical thinking across the curriculum: A brief edition of thought and knowledge*. Mahwah, NJ: Lawrence Erlbaum Associates, Inc.

Halpern, D. (1999). Teaching for critical thinking: Helping college students develop the skills and dispositions of a critical thinker. *New Directions for Teaching and Learning*, 80 (Winter), 69–74.

Halpern, D. (2002). *Thinking critically about critical thinking*. Mahwah, NJ: Lawrence Erlbaum Associates.

Halpern, D. (2014). *Thought and knowledge: An introduction to critical thinking* (5th edn). New York, NY: Psychology Press.

Hammersley, M., & Atkinson, P. (2007). *Ethnography: Principles in practice* (3rd edn). London: Routledge.

Hannerz, U. (1990). Cosmopolitans and locals in world culture. In M. Featherstone (Ed.), *Global culture: Nationalism, globalisation and modernity* (pp. 237–251). London: Sage.

Hannerz, U. (1992). *Cultural complexity: Studies in the social organisation of meaning*. New York: Columbia University Press.

Hughes, C. (2014). Theory of Knowledge aims, objectives and assessment criteria: An analysis of critical thinking descriptors. *Journal of Research in International Education*, 13(1), 30–45.

Interpeace. (2016). Online. Available at: http://www.interpeace.org/ (accessed 28 April 2016).

International Baccalaureate (IB). (2007). *Making the PYP happen*. Cardiff: IB.

International Baccalaureate (IB). (2013). *Theory of Knowledge guide*. Cardiff: IB.

International Baccalaureate (IB). (2015). *MYP: From principles into practice*. Online. Available at: https://ibpublishing.ibo.org/server2/rest/app/tsm.xql?doc=m_0_mypxx_guu_1409_1_e&part=6&chapter=2 (accessed 28 April 2016).

Jaramillo, A., Buote, D., & Schonert-Reichl, K.A. (2008). *An evaluation of the implementation of the Seeds of Empathy program*. Report prepared for Roots of Empathy. University of British Columbia.

Johnson, D. (2013). Transportation into literary fiction reduces prejudice against and increases empathy for Arab-Muslims. *Scientific Study of Literature*, 3(1), 77–92.

Kendall, J.C. (Ed.). (1990). *Combining service and learning: A resource book for community and public service*, vol. 1. Raleigh, NC: National Society for Experiential Education.

King, P.M., & Kitchener, K.S. (1994). *Developing reflective judgment: Understanding and promoting intellectual growth and critical thinking in adolescents and adults*. San Francisco, CA: Jossey-Bass.

Kite, M.E., & Whitley, B.E. (2012). Ethnic and nationality stereotypes in everyday language. *Teaching of Psychology*, 39(1), 54–56. doi: 10.1177/0098628311430314

Koedt, A., Levine, E., & Rapone, A. (Eds). (1973). *Radical feminism*. New York, NY: Quadrangle Books.

Kolb, D.A., Rubin, I.M., & McIntyre, J.M. (1974). *Organizational psychology: A book of readings* (2nd edn). Englewood Cliffs, NJ: Prentice-Hall.

Kumashiro, K.K. (2004). *Against common sense: Teaching and learning toward social justice*. New York, NY: Routledge Falmer.

Kvale, S. (2007). *Doing interviews*. London: Sage.

Lacan, J. (1977). *Ecrits: A selection* (A. Sheridan, Trans.). London: Tavistock.

Lambert, W.E., & Cazabon, M. (1994). Students' views of the Amigos program (Research Report No. 11). Santa Cruz: University of California, National Center for Research on Cultural Diversity and Second Language Learning.

Lamm, C., & Silani, G. (2014). The neural underpinnings of empathy and their relevance for collective emotions. In C. Scheve and M. Salmella (Eds), *Collective emotions*. Oxford: Oxford University Press.

Land, R. et al. (2005). Threshold concepts and troublesome knowledge (3)★: Implications for course design and evaluation. In C. Rust (Ed.), *Improving student learning diversity and inclusivity*. Oxford: Oxford Centre for Staff and Learning Development.

Levi-Strauss, C. (1979). *Myth and meaning*. New York, NY: Schocken.

Lindholm, K.J. (1994). Promoting positive cross-cultural attitudes and perceived competence in culturally and linguistically diverse classrooms. In R.A. Devillar, C.J. Faltis and J.P. Cummins (Eds), *Cultural diversity in schools: From rhetoric to practice* (pp. 189–206). Albany, NY: State University of New York Press.

Lipman, M. (1991). *Thinking in education* (1st edn). Cambridge: Cambridge University Press.

Lipman, M. (2003). *Thinking in education* (2nd edn). Cambridge: Cambridge University Press.

Lovell, J. (2014). The tale of two schools. *The New York Times Magazine*. Online. Available at: www.nytimes.com/interactive/2014/05/04/magazine/tale-of-two-schools.html?_r=0 (accessed 28 April 2016).

MacDonald, A., Bell, P., McLafferty, M., McCorkell, L., Walker, I., Smith, V., Balfour, A., & Murphy, P. (2013). Evaluation of the Roots of Empathy Programme by North Lanarkshire Psychological Service. *North Lanarkshire Psychological Service Research* (unpublished).

Malinowski, B. (1922). *Argonauts of the Western Pacific*. New York, NY: E.P. Dutton.

Medair. (2016). Online. Available at: http://relief.medair.org/en/jobs/field-selection-and-orientation/ (accessed 28 April 2016).

Motha, S. (2006). Out of the safety zone. In A. Curtis & M. Romney (Eds), *Color, race, and English language teaching: Shades of meaning* (pp. 161–172). Mahwah, NJ: Lawrence Erlbaum Associates.

Muller, A., Pfarrer, M.D., & Little, L.M. (2014). A theory of collective empathy in corporate philanthropy decisions. *Academy of Management Review*, 39(1), 1–21. Online. Available at: http://ssrn.com/abstract=2229122 (accessed 28 April 2016).

Nussbaum, M.C. (1997). *Cultivating humanity: A classic defense of reform in liberal education*. Cambridge, MA: Harvard University Press.

Paul, R. (1990). *Critical thinking: What every person needs to survive in a rapidly changing world*. Santa Rosa, CA: Foundation for Critical Thinking.

Paul, R. (1992). Critical thinking: What, why and how? *New Directions for Community Colleges*, 20(1), 3–24.

Paul, R. (2011). Reflections on the nature of critical thinking, its history, politics, and barriers and on its status across the college/university curriculum: Part I. *Inquiry: Critical Thinking Across the Disciplines*, 26(3), 5–24.

Pellegrino, J.W., Chudowsky, N., & Glaser, R. (2001). *Knowing what students know: The science and design of educational assessment*. Washington, DC: National Academy Press.

Perkins, D.N., & Ritchhart, R. (2004). When is good thinking? In D.Y. Dai and R.J. Sternberg (Eds), *Motivation, emotion, and cognition: Integrative perspectives on intellectual functioning and development* (pp. 351–384). Mahwah, NJ: Erlbaum.

Pettigrew, T.F. (2008). Intergroup prejudice: its causes and cures. Online. Available at: http://pepsic.bvsalud.org/scielo.php?pid=S0258–64442008000100006&script=sci_arttext (accessed 28 April 2016).

Pettigrew, T.F., & Tropp, L.R. (2000). Does intergroup contact reduce prejudice? Recent meta-analytic findings. In S. Oskamp (Ed.), *Reducing prejudice and discrimination: Social psychological perspectives* (pp. 93–114). Mahwah, NJ: Erlbaum.

Pettigrew, T.F., & Tropp, L.R. (2006). A meta-analytic test of intergroup contact theory. *Journal of Personality and Social Psychology*, 90(5), 751–783.

Peuker, M., & Reiter, S. (2007). Educational tools, resources and informal learning frameworks that help to reduce prejudice mapping study on behalf of the Rothschild Foundation Europe. European forum for migration studies, Institute at the University of Bamberg. Online. Available at: www.efms.uni-bamberg.de/pdf/Summary_Mapping_Study.pdf (accessed 28 April 2016).

Pintrich, P.R. (2000). The role of goal orientation in self-regulated learning. In M. Boekaerts, P.R. Pintrich and M. Zeidner (Eds), *Handbook of self-regulation* (pp. 451–502). San Diego, CA: Academic Press.

Rhoads, R.A. (1998). In the service of citizenship: A study of student involvement in community service. *The Journal of Higher Education*, 69(3), 277–297.

Rhodes, M., Leslie, S.J., & Tworeck, C.M. (2012). Cultural transmission of social essentialism. *PNAS*, 109(34), 13526–13531; published ahead of print August 6, 2012, doi: 10.1073/pnas.1208951109. Online. Available at: www.pnas.org/content/109/34/13526.full.pdf (accessed 28 April 2016).

Rolheiser, C., & Wallace, D. (2005). *The Roots of Empathy Program as a strategy for increasing social and emotional learning. Report prepared for Roots of Empathy.* Ontario Institute for Studies in Education, University of Toronto.

Sabine, G., & Sabine, P. (1983). *Books that made the difference.* Hamden, CN: Library Professional Publications.

Said, E. (1993). *Culture and Imperialism.* New York, NY: Vintage Books.

Santos, R.G., Chartier, M.J., Whalen, J.C., Chateau, D., & Boyd, L. (2011). Effectiveness of school-based violence prevention for children and youth: Cluster randomized field trial of the Roots of Empathy program with replication and three-year follow-up. *Healthcare Quarterly*, 14, 80–91.

Savignon, S. (1983). *Communicative competence: Theory and classroom practice.* Reading, MA. Addison Wesley.

Schoenfeld, S., Zohar, A., Alleson, I., Suleiman, O., & Sipos-Randor, G. (2014). A place of empathy in a fragile, contentious landscape: Environmental peacebuilding in the eastern Mediterranean. In N. Megoran, F. McConnell & P. Williams (Eds), *The geographies of peace: New approaches to boundaries, diplomacy and conflict* (pp. 171–193). I.B.: Taurus.

Schonert-Reichl, K.A., Smith, V., Zaidman-Zait, A., & Hertzman, C. (2012). Promoting children's prosocial behaviours in school: Impact of the 'Roots of Empathy' program on the social and emotional competence of school-aged children. *School Mental Health*, 4(1), 1–12.

Siegel, H. (1985). Educating reason: Critical thinking, informal logic, and the philosophy of education. Part two: Philosophical questions underlying education for critical thinking. *Informal Logic*, 7, 2–3.

Siegel, H. (1988). *Educating reason.* New York, NY: Routledge.

Stavans, I. (2001). *On borrowed words. A memoir of language.* New York, NY: Penguin.

Stephan, W.G. (1985). Intergroup relations. In G. Lindzey and E. Aronson (Eds), *Handbook of social psychology* (3rd edn), vol 2 (pp. 599–658). New York, NY: Random House.

Thorne, B. (1992). Girls and boys together . . . but mostly apart: Gender arrangements in elementary schools. In J. Wrigley (Ed.), *Education and gender equality* (pp. 117–132). London: Falmer Press.

Tomlinson, B., & Masuhara, H. (2004). Developing cultural awareness. *Modern English Teacher*, 13(1), 5–11.

UNESCO (2006). *UNESCO guidelines on intercultural education.* Paris: UNESCO. Online. Available at: http://unesdoc.unesco.org/images/0014/001478/147878e.pdf (accessed 29 April 2016).

UNESCO-IBE & Ecole International de Genève. (2014). *Guiding principles for learning in the 21st century*. Geneva: UNESCO-IBE.

Wright, S.C., & Bougie, E. (2007). Intergroup contact and minority-language education reducing language-based discrimination and its negative impact. *Journal of Language and Social Psychology*, 26(2), 157–181. Online. Available at: http://isites.harvard.edu/fs/docs/icb.topic472736.files/Wright–Bougie-Intergroup.pdf (accessed 29 April 2016).

9

CONCLUSION

Twenty-first-century challenges to education and prejudice

Introduction

While research-informed practice suggests the ways that education can reduce prejudice in individuals and institutions, the world in the early part of the twenty-first century is by no means a static stage for policy application: it presents itself to schools as an ever-morphing arena of VUCA (Volatility, Uncertainty, Complexity and Ambiguity). Knowing which strategies will work best for individuals or groups is highly contingent on context and future contexts. The scaffolds within which human society shall operate are not only unknown to us now but stand every chance of being radically different from the present. This is because of the exponential nature of the rate of much environmental, social and demographic change (Fadel, 2015).

Indeed, we are living in an age that poses a number of worldwide threats to human security such as terrorism and mass migration and it looks very much as if, in the future, these threats will increase in magnitude and velocity. Following Realistic Conflict Theory (Sherif, 1966; Vivian, Brown & Hewstone, 1995), it stands to reason that this mounting pressure could exacerbate prejudice and would therefore mean that a more concerted effort would be needed by educators to draw learners out of the vortex of self-defence and the paralysis of fear that can so easily translate into prejudice, discrimination and, ultimately, violence.

At another level, the information age has brought with it an historically unprecedented communication ethos that challenges the conversation dynamics one might associate with freedom of speech. Social media have allowed for highly prejudiced opinions to enjoy a currency that would be difficult to imagine before the advent of the Internet. An ethically ambiguous state of affairs comes with the fact that social networkers often operate behind pseudonyms and therefore benefit from the rights but are exempted of the responsibilities that come with freedom of speech.

Linked to the explosion in information is the phenomenon of globalisation that has swept over the planet, meaning that humans are more interconnected than ever before and are able to form opinions and make generalisations (albeit superficially) about other groups with more confidence than ever before. The age of tourism means that rapid and frequent communication between different cultures will affect intergroup perception and interaction in complex ways ranging from commercial encounters bathed in ersatz depictions of folklore to well-intended but often disastrously paternalistic efforts at aid.

Running through these strata of change and instability are discourses that range from political correctness to xenophobia and racism. With the normalising of xenophobic discourses in many areas and the increasingly popular idea that efforts to reduce prejudice should be discredited as institutional, politically correct attempts to stop people from saying what they really think, the enterprise to educate against prejudice faces an insidious, powerful ideological force.

These forces (security threats, complex open communications systems, globalisation and ideological discourse) need to be problematised in detail to suggest how the educational strategies developed in this book can be adapted to them.

Terrorism, immigration and environmental challenges as accelerators of prejudice

Terrorism

Maslow's hierarchy of needs (Maslow, 1943) has shown how human beings need to consolidate baseline levels of physical security if they are to grow morally and spiritually. When, at the baseline of the hierarchy of needs, we feel threatened, we close our thinking down, dedicate our energy to coping and defence mechanisms and view the world with caution. This process heightens anxiety and exacerbates prejudice (Brown, 1995).

Terrorism in the second decade of the twenty-first century is proving to be an extremely widespread phenomenon: according to the statistics portal, between 2006 and 2013 approximately 130,000 people were killed in terrorist attacks (Statista, 2016) with over 32,000 in 2014 (*The Economist*, 2015). The effect that this has had on intergroup perception has been negative with extremist depictions of Muslims being propagated in many Western countries and hardened generalisations about Westerners made more prevalent on Fundamentalist websites. The fear and uncertainty created by terrorism is clearly an accelerator to prejudice and has led to the normalisation of strong anti-Muslim discourses. For example, US presidential candidate Donald Trump promised to stop foreign Muslims entering the US were he elected (Allen, 2015) while Czech president Miloš Zeman has been accused by the United Nations of making Islamophobic speeches and legislating prejudicial policies against Muslim asylum seekers (*The Guardian*, 2015).

Educational responses to terrorism need to be manifold, ensuring that students feel physically secure enough to think clearly and creatively, providing a forum for discussion so that fears and emotions can be communicated and mediated whilst ensuring that extremist discourses do not proliferate without being intercepted by common sense. Indeed, the mediatised responses to the more recent spate of terrorist attacks in Western Europe, West and North Africa and the Middle East have tended to use divisive language with a strong currency of the words 'barbarian', 'barbarity', 'savagery' and 'horror'. While it is understandable that emotive language is used in the aftermath of terrorist attacks, educational institutions have a role to play in de-escalating polarised and extreme positions by using language that is measured and constructive, so that students are taught to respond to extreme situations not with aggressive, blanket terms but with cautious reflections. The challenge in teaching for less prejudice in an era of terrorism is for students not to conflate separate acts with an entire ethnic or religious group: the desire to over-generalise is strong when one feels threatened and it takes a concerted effort to understand that each phenomenon, no matter how violent, has its own localised parameters and explanations.

Prejudice reduction frameworks discussed in this book that would be particularly important to activate as a response to terrorism would be critical thinking and metacognition at an individual level and contact (with an emphasis on anxiety reduction) and international education (with an emphasis on international humanities) at an institutional level. As concerns contact, ensuring that positive interaction takes place between members who share the identities of the group of victims and perpetrators would be an important step to take.

Immigration

Mass immigration is another phenomenon that has become pronounced in the second decade of the twenty-first century. Never before have such large numbers of people been displaced on such a scale due to war and poverty. The situation is particularly critical in Europe where refugees fleeing conflicts mainly in the Middle East trying to enter the United Kingdom, Greece or Eastern Europe are concentrated in camps, perish in the Mediterranean as they attempt to reach European shores by raft and risk their lives trying to jump on moving trucks and trains. Responses have been strong and mixed, ranging from Germany's response to harbour large numbers of refugees to closed-door approaches such as that of Slovakia's. The wall built along the Mexican–US border is a symbol of the attempt to clamp down on immigration while some populations react to immigration with violence: in South Africa there have been successive waves of xenophobic murder with a particularly sharp spike in a series of attacks throughout the country in 2008 (Landau, 2011). In Switzerland, the right wing Swiss People's Party has repetitively used a particularly aggressive image to depict unwanted foreigners in the form of a poster depicting a black sheep being kicked off a map of Switzerland by a white sheep (Foulkes, 2007).

Educational institutions need to develop understanding and acceptance beyond Otherness more than ever and to dispel some of the myths and fears that circulate about foreigners. Many schools and universities have been involved in aid programmes for refugees while students are put into contact with refugees directly or with people working to assist refugees on the front line. By insisting that human beings are of equal value, drawing parallels between modern and ancient forms of immigration and explaining that human movement always has been and will continue to be a fundamental constituent of humanity, teachers, headmasters, programme coordinators and educational leaders can develop in students respect and empathy for immigrants. These can happen through programmes allowing for regular contact, interventions by specialists in the field or programmes that allow students to help other populations. However, keeping a sense of humility in these interactions is important so that materially privileged students are not brought to patronise others or develop superiority complexes. Furthermore, positions against immigration need not be prejudiced, so educational institutions should encourage students to air their views without ideological pressure or the fear of being branded as prejudiced because of conservative views.

Prejudice reduction frameworks that could be used as a response to immigration would be understanding beyond the Other and empathy at an individual level with contact (emphasising the mediator of empathy and perspective taking) and international education (with an emphasis on service learning) at an institutional level.

Environmental challenges

Although environmental sustainability might not be considered a direct predictor of prejudice, the increased scarcity of natural resources conjugated with overpopulation, pollution, energy consumption and global warming are clearly creating a general sentiment of threat, despair and fatality that must be combatted if students are to free their minds of fearful and potentially closed-minded thoughts that come with knowledge of the extent of the natural world's endangerment. For students to be comfortable and secure enough about global prospects to view other people in a positive manner so as to build a future together, a collective approach should be nurtured rather than a zero-sum game approach to resource scarcity. It is now commonly accepted that humans have overshot the world's biocapacity to the extent that dramatic changes in lifestyle must be carried out for a sustainable future.

A good education today must make learners aware of the problems the world is facing but, at the same time, it should indicate pathways for the future that involve living with less, making informed decisions about what to consume or not, knowing how to share resources and how to respect the environment. By viewing the planet as a shared responsibility that requires a concerted effort on each person's part, students will be encouraged to view the overarching aim of the survival of life on earth as a superordinate goal that federates and unites.

This can be done in numerous ways including use of this book's institutional frameworks for inquiry and concepts-focused learning (as part of international education) to ensure that students work in groups to research the state of the world and seek to solve environmental problems while understanding those problems in a broad, conceptual manner. The idea of cooperation in the pursuit of common goals should also be activated as part of contact theory.

Political correctness

A serious threat to the mission to educate for less prejudice is the notion of political correctness, a fuzzy concept that essentially entails ideological pressure not to offend others in the realms of prejudice and discrimination. The affirmative action policies that swept through American universities during the 1970s and the New Left discourses that accompanied them led to the modern, often ironic and largely pejorative understanding of political correctness, largely discredited today as an ideologically straight-jacketed way of viewing the world that is both tyrannical and inflexible (Bloom, 1987; Hughes, 2010). Political correctness means that one is not 'allowed' to speak out against minority groups, especially if one belongs to a traditionally empowered group such as WASPs (White Anglo-Saxon Protestants). Critics of political correctness range from those representing intellectual freedom to those who use it to trivialise the struggle against prejudice by labelling the plight of minority groups as politically correct hypersensitivity and therefore a type of nonsense or hyperbole.

The reason why the entire concept of political correctness is damaging to an education against prejudice is that it offers an excuse for prejudiced views. More insidious still is the false dichotomy that is created where there is liveliness, truth (for example, the idea that 'this is what people think deep down inside but do not have the courage to say it out loud') and courage on the one hand and a sterile, neutering, institutionally created groupthink made up of disingenuous platitudes and self-righteousness on the other. Political correctness actually encourages prejudice as it gives a rebellious spice to it, positioning the prejudiced individual in a romantic light as a humorous old-fashioned individual fighting against the artificial and constraining ideological injunctions of a Brave New World.

Educational institutions should not allow political correctness as a concept to hijack the struggle to reduce prejudice by over-institutionalising anti-prejudice stances and therefore opening pathways for critics to show themselves as more sincere and human than the soulless 'machine' that is a large organisation. Schools and universities, much like the workplace and other institutionalised social gatherings, can kill off the best of intentions if they overdo things by repeating messages ad nauseam and/or creating an overflow of monomaniac zeal around a single topic. The human spirit wants to rebel and should be brought to do so against the pernicious field of prejudice rather than in its name. While prejudice should be studied in the classroom and debated in the open and while educational programmes should design interactions, learning materials and even physical spaces in such a way that prejudice is reduced, it has to be done in subtle, compelling ways so that there is 'buy in'. If school leadership is made up of unimaginative, poor communicators and generally uninspiring people, then there is a risk that they might push students to create a counter-culture and therefore do more bad than good in tackling prejudice albeit with the best of intentions. Like anything in education, for students to be engaged, incentives have to be meaningful and genuine.

This book's framework for the development of empathy in the individual and that of contact (more specifically social norms supporting contact) as concerns institutional support, should be considered and adapted carefully to contexts when educating against the negative effects of political correctness.

The age of tourism

The late tongue-in-cheek philosopher and social critic Philippe Muray (2007) described the twenty-first century as a post-historical age of tourism where modern man, named 'homo festivus', would fly from one airport and hotel to the next, consuming his way through an ersatz world of entertainment and staged folklore. Muray's critique cannot be taken entirely seriously as it only speaks to a specific societal group but it does point to a challenge facing education and prejudice since, arguably, many cross-cultural exchanges have been cheapened or subsumed by the tourist industry. At the time of Marco Polo and Jacques Cartier, or even Carlos Castaneda, an age when travel literature was a portal into other cultures and ways of living, travel suggested a type of spiritual pilgrimage: it was arduous, long, risky and rare. Most critically, hotels were less frequent and contact with the so-called locals, even in a highly prejudiced setting such as colonisation, was protracted and necessary. In a hyper-connected twenty-first century, travel is far more accessible, happens *en masse* and clearly does not have the same weight or significance that it did in earlier periods of history. This means that sociological encounters from travel that might lead to anthropological reflections are less likely to take place and travel can, in the end, resemble what Muray ironises about in his vision of third culture inanity.

It is in many ways much easier to make hasty generalisations about countries in a globalised age because travel is far more accessible than ever before. Furthermore, there is something of a stamp-collecting mania about the globe-trotter culture that allows tourists to boast that they have 'done China' and so on, as if entire countries had somehow been appropriated or vanquished when in reality very little of the country and customs will have been seen. With English as a world language, Western tourists do not have to move out of their comfort zone or make any effort to learn the local language. It is quite possible for the modern tourist to spend a fortnight in a foreign country but to remain in a hotel for the entirety of the stay, interacting with locals uniquely through that context. Knowing and understanding the Other becomes troublesome if it only takes place through the highly constrained trappings of the tourist industry.

This means that an education for less prejudice should teach students the virtues of a genuine voyage as opposed to a mere holiday; how to take some interest in the history, geography and language of a place before and after visiting it and why it is so important to view the experience as a cultural exchange and not just an act of consumerism. A simple approach is to have students read an historical work about a country before travelling to it, be it Nelson Mandela's *Long Walk to Freedom* (1995) before visiting South Africa, Salman Rushdie's *Midnight's Children* (1981) before a trip to India or Gabriel Garcia Márquez's *Cien años de soledad* (1967) before visiting Colombia. Educational exchange programmes and school trips should be designed in such a way that students are not merely moving though places and people to get to a landmark, museum or famous site (and to take 'selfies in front of them') but are made to interact with the local population and learn something about where they are. Stays in foreign countries should be sufficiently lengthy, challenging, project-based and reciprocal for them to dampen stereotypes and prejudices. This book's framework on understanding beyond the Other (as an individual trait) with particular focus on diversity and inquiry and service learning (as part of the international education framework for institutional support) can help educators reflect on how best to develop meaningful voyages for students that reduce stereotypes and prejudice.

The freedom of prejudiced speech: rights without responsibilities in an age of social media

Another challenge that faces educating for less prejudice is how to teach students to use social media in responsible ways. The Internet has brought with it a host of ethical problems connected to communication: people can post their ideas on the world wide web using fake identities and may use platforms such as Facebook to express insalubrious ideas without any fear of direct confrontation or reprisal. As opposed to more traditional forms of communication such as face-to-face debate or epistolary exchange, where two clearly identified parties engage in an explicit, overt exchange of words, the Internet has blurred some of the boundaries of conversation to allow for greater degrees of anonymity, mass mailing and postings to an invisible and essentially unquantifiable number of views. I would argue that Internet users do not feel as inhibited to express prejudiced ideas as they might were they visible and therefore directly accountable for their statements. Any website user who reads through the thread of comments at the foot of YouTube videos of speeches by Martin Luther King will very quickly come across racist slurs and calamitous hate speech. In fact, prejudiced comments on the web are so rife that many comment functions on YouTube posted speeches by Martin Luther King have been disabled altogether.

Sociology has taught us that human beings are disinhibited when they feel anonymous, even when they are only partly anonymous, in large groups for instance, which would explain the extreme levels of racism that plague football fans who, when absorbed in a large enough group, will resort to Nazi salutes, spitting on players and monkey chants. These acts of deindividuation are similar in the form they take on Internet postings as there is a cumulative effect created by inflammatory statements that provoke a response and lead very quickly to a snowball effect: Internet users like football fans can become swept up in an accumulation of infectious negative energy, forgetting their habitual social contract and letting extremely prejudiced views and actions take control.

Social media does not only involve postings but easy access to videos, pamphlets, websites and a host of communications that can vehicle extremely prejudiced views. Because Internet consumers are anonymous, or at least believe they are anonymous, a further level of disinhibition occurs and the temptation to consult illicit, racist, sexist, fundamentalist, homophobic and anti-Semitic platforms is great. Educational institutions in the twenty-first century are faced with a perennial counter-discourse that lurks on the Internet and can be consulted at any time.

The educational response to this state of affairs must be to develop in students the ability to self-monitor efficiently and frequently. Since decisions around social media use will mostly take place during individuals' free time, an internal moral compass and sense of decency has to be strong enough for poor decisions to be avoided without explicit guidance. Posting an angry response is something that is understandable but can and should be avoided through restraint. Students need to be reminded of the dangers of Internet use and encouraged to use the Internet with a strong sense of digital citizenship. This book's framework on metacognition at an individual level can be used to this effect. If Internet users are to surf the web conscientiously, they will need to operate at the expert level of metacognition (deep self-awareness with frequent self-regulation). At the same time, this book's framework for critical thinking can help students sift through the information they stumble across with a healthy degree of scepticism.

Guiding students to a better future

It is easy to be fatalistic about prejudice. There are many who see it is a neurobiological constituent of human beings, something that can never be eradicated and, therefore, something that we have to accept and live with. I would argue that this feeling is particularly strong in the workplace, perhaps understandably: Dobbin, Kalev and Kelly surveyed 829 American companies, covering more than 16,000 data points (2007, p. 23) and came to the conclusion that:

> On average, programs designed to reduce bias among managers responsible for hiring and promotion have not worked. Neither diversity training to extinguish stereotypes, nor diversity performance evaluations to provide feedback and oversight to people making hiring and promotion decisions, have accomplished much. This is not surprising in the light of research showing that stereotypes are difficult to extinguish.
>
> *(Dobbin et al., 2007, p. 26)*

However, while it may be true that stereotypes and prejudice are not extinguishable, young people going through schools and university should not believe that we cannot reduce them or that it is not worth the time and effort to attempt to lessen them, even in the most modest of cases. At the end of every prejudiced action, there is bound to be some level of injustice, and just one case where such a phenomenon can be overturned is worth considerable effort.

In the final analysis, the mission to reduce prejudice through education is no simple affair and requires a host of skills, attitudes, knowledge and contexts that need to be activated continually over an extended period of time. Schools, universities and training programmes can only do so much in this voyage, plant the seeds as it were, for the real test is in the world outside of education, where the mettle of the individual will be tested in pressurised, coercive environments.

Beyond formal education, communication skills, group work, knowing how to listen and how to take tough decisions will all be coloured by the degree of prejudice that the person at the nexus of these processes harbours. By teaching students to reduce prejudice, they will become more empathetic communicators, more knowledgeable and curious group-workers, more self-reflective listeners and critically minded, ethical decision-makers: reducing prejudice is a skill for life.

Guidance departments should encourage students to see themselves as contributors to the world rather than merely individualistic consumers of available high-status positions: tomorrow's jobs will have to be focused on finding solutions, sharing selflessly, mediating conflicts and having the courage to take steps in one of many fundamentally different and opposing directions with social ramifications. Educating for less prejudice is educating for more productive and humane social capital, more happiness and sustainability.

Conclusion

This book has argued for four lines of individual prejudice-reducing development: understanding beyond the Other, critical thinking, metacognition and empathy, while advocating two fundamental institutional approaches (the contact hypothesis and using some of the principles of international education).

The four lines of individual development have the potential to forge a powerful educational experience that can lift young people from the all-to-easy temptations of lazy thinking and uncritical group identity based on unjustified hostile feelings towards an outgroup. These temptations are, sadly and in many cases, not the exception but the rule. Let us make no mistake, to be a critical thinker, a metacognitive and empathetic person, and to seek to understand other people beyond stereotypes is arduous and requires ongoing conviction and resilience.

The two institutional approaches are necessary to prevent schools or other social organisations from becoming moral vacuums where questions of respecting one another, being kind and empathetic or even-handed in decision-making, are not seen as important or are aped superficially as one goes through the motions cynically and disingenuously.

It takes courage to stand up against prejudice as one appears sentimental, romantic, perhaps tiresome and predictable, but if one does not, the forces that will prevail might be far more insidious and pernicious.

As young people become adults and educators bring out of them the mental, spiritual and physical forces not to make the world a place of ignorance, ugliness and evil but of truth, beauty and goodness, these lines can help raise each individual, and therefore entire groups of people, from the dark but comforting doldrums of prejudice to the more challenging, lofty and opportunity-opening peaks of open-mindedness.

References

Allen, N. (2015). Trump on Muslims: 'They're not coming to this country if I'm president'. *The Telegraph*. Online. Available at: www.telegraph.co.uk/news/worldnews/republicans/12052760/republican-debate-donald-trump-las-vegas.html (accessed 29 April 2016).

Bloom, A.B. (1987). *The closing of the American mind*. New York, NY: Simon & Schuster.

Brown, R. (1995). *Prejudice: Its social psychology*. Oxford: Blackwell.

Dobbin, F., Kalev, A., & Kelly, E. (2007). Diversity management in corporate America. *Contexts*, 6(4), 21–27. Online. Available at: http://scholar.harvard.edu/dobbin/files/2007_contexts_dobbin_kalev_kelly.pdf (accessed 29 April 2016).

Fadel, C. (2015). Four-dimensional education: The competencies learners need to succeed. Center for curriculum redesign. Online. Available at: http://curriculumredesign.org/our-work/four-dimensional-21st-century-education-learning-competencies-future-2030/ (accessed 29 April 2016).

Foulkes, I. (2007). Swiss row over black sheep poster. BBC News Europe. Online. Available at: http://news.bbc.co.uk/2/hi/europe/6980766.stm (accessed 29 April 2016).

Hughes, G.I. (2010). *Political correctness: A history of semantics and culture*. Oxford: Blackwell-Wiley.

Landau, L.B. (Ed.). (2011). *Exorcising the demons within: Xenophobia, violence and statecraft in contemporary South Africa*. Johannesburg: Wits University Press.

Mandela, N. (1995). *Long walk to freedom*. New York: Little Brown & Co.

Márquez, G.G. (1967). *Cien años de soledad*. New York: Harper & Row.

Maslow, A.H. (1943). A theory of human motivation. *Psychological Review*, 50(4), 370–396.

Muray, P. (2007). *Après l'histoire*. Paris: Gallimard.

Rushdie, S. (1981). *Midnight's children*. London: Jonathan Cape.

Sherif, M. (1966). *Group conflict and co-operation: Their social psychology*. London: Routledge.

Statista. (2016). Online. Available at: www.statista.com/statistics/202871/number-of-fatalities-by-terrorist-attacks-worldwide/ (accessed 29 April 2016).

The Economist. (2015). The plague of global terrorism. Online. Available at: www.economist.com/blogs/graphicdetail/2015/11/daily-chart-12 (accessed 29 April 2016).

The Guardian. (2015). Czech president rejects UN claims of refugee rights violations. Online. Available at: www.theguardian.com/world/2015/oct/22/czech-republic-president-rejects-un-claims-refugees-rights-violations-migration (accessed 29 April 2016).

Vivian, J., Brown, R., & Hewstone, M. (1995). Changing attitudes through intergroup contact: The effects of group membership salience. Unpublished manuscript. Wales: Universities of Kent and Cardiff.

INDEX

Note: Page numbers in **bold** are for figures, those in *italics* are for tables.